D0649864

A QUESTION OF NUMBERS

A QUESTION OF NUMBERS

HIGH MIGRATION, LOW FERTILITY,
AND THE
POLITICS OF NATIONAL IDENTITY

Michael S. Teitelbaum

and

Jay Winter

HILL & WANG
A DIVISION OF FARRAR, STRAUS, GIROUX
NEW YORK

Hill and Wang
A division of Farrar, Straus and Giroux
19 Union Square West, New York 10003

Distributed in Canada by Douglas & McIntyre Ltd.
Printed in the United States of America
Designed by Monika Keano
First edition, 1998

        Library of Congress Cataloging-in-Publication Data
Teitelbaum, Michael S.
    A question of numbers : high migration, low fertility, and the
politics of national identity / Michael S. Teitelbaum and
Jay Winter.
        p.   cm.
    Includes bibliographical references and index.
    ISBN 0-8090-7781-7 (alk. paper)
    1. Emigration and immigration—Political aspects.   2. Demography—
Political aspects.   3. Nationalism.   4. North America—Emigration
and immigration.   5. Demography—North America.   6. Europe—
Emigration and immigration.   7. Demography—Europe.   I. Winter, Jay.
    II. Title.
JV6255.T45   1998
304.6'2'09182109045—dc21
                                                    97-38931

CONTENTS

Foreword and Acknowledgments **vii**

Introduction **3**

PART 1: WESTERN EUROPE **9**

1. Germany: Immigration, Refugees, and Unification **11**
2. "Marianne and the Rabbits": The French Obsession **31**
3. Britain and the "Immigrant Wave" **49**

PART 2: EASTERN EUROPE **63**

4. The Yugoslav Tragedy: Forced Migration and Ethnic Cleansing **65**
5. The End of the Soviet Empire **85**
6. The Politics of the Birthrate in Socialist Romania **109**

PART 3: NORTH AMERICA **125**

7. A Generation of Demographic Debate in the United States **127**
8. American Political Interests and Population Statistics **155**
9. Canada: Civil Fissures **173**

PART 4: TRANSNATIONAL ISSUES **193**

10. Development, Migration, and Fertility **195**
11. Refugees, Asylum Seekers, and Immigrants **209**
12. Islamic Fundamentalism and the West **221**

Conclusion **241**

Bibliography **253**

Notes **263**

Index **281**

FOREWORD AND ACKNOWLEDGMENTS

In recent years, international migration has become the subject of intense public debate. For politicians in many countries, this once-marginal matter is now a major preoccupation and, occasionally, a massive headache. It simply will not go away.

One reason this issue is so problematic is that it touches on other sensitive aspects of contemporary affairs. In North America and in eastern and western Europe, migration is but one of many major demographic changes. Populations are on the move, while family structures and patterns of reproduction are being transformed. Not only family life but fundamental features of political life are changing radically. In the aftermath of the Cold War and with the appearance of new international alliances, a massive debate is under way about the meaning and limits of national identity and national sovereignty. None of these issues is isolated. The intersection of these three subjects—national identity, migration, and fertility—over the past thirty years is the subject of this book.

A word or two is necessary on what this book is *not* about. We limit our discussion to the industrial nations of Europe and North America, though we know that migration and population politics are vital to understanding international affairs in the developing world, the complexities of which require separate and extended treatment. For purposes of our discussion, we have treated migration within the developing world and outside it solely and arbitrarily as an element in the North American and European stories. This Eurocentrism has its costs, and we can justify our decision only as a way to limit the dimensions of a work that has always threatened to resist our efforts to control it.

Other subjects are also treated only tangentially or left for other scholars to take up. Southern Europe has some of the lowest fertility rates in the world today and experiences many of the political controversies explored in this book. An analysis of population politics in Spain, Portugal, Italy, and Greece would be fruitful, as would research on Australia, New Zealand, Japan, and the newly industrialized countries of Asia. We have done what we could to cover a huge terrain; extending analysis to these areas is necessary but beyond the scope of a volume of this kind.

We contend that a host of political, economic, and demographic changes defines the 1960s to the 1990s as a period of fundamental transition in world affairs. We have tried to make the analysis as up-to-date as possible, and, while circumstances undoubtedly will change rapidly in the coming years, the basic elements of the story, we believe, were set in the thirty years following the 1960s and are likely to remain intact in the foreseeable future. How and why those elements emerged are questions at the heart of each chapter of this book.

Many people have generously given their time and advice in helping us to complete this book. Martine Segalen guided us through the French maze; Emmanuel Sivan offered his unparalleled knowledge of Islamic fundamentalism; Jeff Passel provided insights on the U.S. Census. A special word of gratitude is due to Tony Wrigley, who took time off from his busy schedule to comment on the entire manuscript. Ivo Banac offered expert advice on Balkan history and gave permission for the use of material he has had published. We happily acknowledge the help of the staff at the Cambridge University Library and Yale University Library—two islands of peace in the academic world.

In addition, this book could not have been completed without the support of the Rockefeller Foundation and its director of population sciences, Steven W. Sinding, with whose support we enjoyed the graceful hospitality of the Villa Serbelloni in Bellagio, Italy, in 1993. In that peninsula of congenial company and stunning beauty, we convened a conference of demographers, historians, and political scientists, who surveyed with us the themes of this book. We owe these colleagues a debt of thanks, though we exculpate them from responsibility for any errors or misjudgments that we took from these discussions. We hope they understand how much these exchanges meant to us. A month as scholars-in-residence at Bellagio after the conference helped to nurture the book in its early stages. If our prose even remotely suggests the elegance of that environment and the generosity of our hosts and colleagues, then we will be both surprised and gratified.

Michael S. Teitelbaum
Alfred P. Sloan Foundation, New York

Jay Winter
Pembroke College, Cambridge

A QUESTION OF NUMBERS

INTRODUCTION

In the past decade, the fear of population decline—time-honored in Western intellectual and social history—has remained a persistent element in contemporary political conflict. But alongside it has emerged a powerful new cluster of issues that animates debate about population questions. That new set of concerns arises from the overlap of low fertility and international migration and the intersection of both in domestic and international politics.

We wrote a book about the fear of population decline more than ten years ago; now we would like to consider some striking demographic elements in recent political history and some new political elements in demographic debates today. Our field of inquiry is the developed world of Europe and North America. Our study is thus about what students of development refer to as the "North," as opposed to the "South." We are fully aware, though, that the boundaries between the two are porous, and the fact that populations move both within the countries of each and from other parts of the world is central to this book.

The first claim we advance is that the three decades of roughly 1965–95 form what may be termed a generation in demographic and political history, characterized by fundamental shifts in the parameters of political and demographic life that make it distinctive and identifiable. A major break resulted from varied, often unrelated developments. These unfolded in parallel, intensifying the political consequences of demographic issues, and vice versa, more than ever before. We believe that only by understanding this extraordinary mix of politics and demography can our situation today be fully illuminated and understood.

Our second generalization is that the trends we examine mark the experience of every developed nation. The contours of the intersection of fertility, migration, and political conflict differ, however, according to a nation's institutions and traditions, which is why we present national case studies. The way these issues are perceived and configured varies across national boundaries, but the overall story has common features.

Our third argument is that, despite national differences, an observable pattern links demographic change to political change in this period. Since the mid-1960s, basic demographic features—marriage patterns, fertility rates, age structures—have changed rapidly: domestic fertility levels fell to record lows, while substantial and unpredicted inflows of migrants to North America and Europe occurred; the convergence of these apparently unrelated trends provoked many conflicts and tensions. And these conflicts seemed ominous, for they arose when many countries were experiencing fundamental political shifts and transformations. Radical, in some ways unprecedented, demographic movements intersected with highly charged debates about national identity. These convergences led everywhere to friction and in some places to violence—against immigrants, between ethnic groups, or among political insurgents.

Again, we must consider both the general pattern and national particularities. That fertility, migration, and issues of national identity intersect is a truth common to many developed countries; the forms in which that nexus has been elaborated always reflect local histories, attitudes, and interests. That is why we emphasize the distinctive national features of the new forms of population politics today.

The fourth position we advance is more specialized. It concerns the development of the scientific study of population, the discipline of demography. Many of the issues we discuss are specifically demographic, and demographers are professionals trained to help us understand them. Their work is invaluable, but it has not been insulated from the sea changes described here. To the contrary, ideological debates have entered forcefully the domain of demographic science; occasionally, as we shall see, the distinction between the two has almost vanished. The best way forward is to recognize that both ideology and science inform current discussion; both have a place, but neither is likely to supplant the other.

The problem, though, is that, once activated and aired publicly, volatile debates about fertility, international migration, and national identity tend to take on a life of their own. This is no reason to ignore the scientific issues involved. Indeed, the debaters must redouble their efforts to separate population measurement from political advocacy and both from first principles. But the significance, drama, and danger of these issues are due to their capacity to touch fundamental values.

Our hope is that by locating the key elements in the debates we can contribute to dispassionate, knowledgeable discussion of these problems. Understanding problems is no recipe for resolving them, but, in this field, the alternatives to informed debate and understanding are unattractive, even alarming. Not to face the issues of population and politics is to condone the kind of disputatious friction that, left unexamined or uncontained, can burst into flame.

For purposes of our discussion, we group regions into three categories: western Europe, eastern Europe, and North America. Throughout western Europe, debates on public policies turn time and again around the nexus of fertility decline, volatile migratory flows, and national identity. This leitmotif is a signature of the generation that has had to confront the dilemmas associated with the project of European integration initiated by the Treaty of Rome in 1957.

Farther east, the same issues are expressed in different forms and with different emphases. There, the structural change underlying public debate and controversy has been the unraveling and ultimate collapse of the Soviet Union and its satellite system, a turbulent context for demographic issues to come to the fore. As one might expect in a region with deeper sources of political instability and fewer democratic traditions, the ways in which population issues and politics have intersected have been harsher—in the case of Yugoslavia, bloodier—than those in western Europe.

Lest the reader think that these matters are merely a European preoccupation, we find similar themes and worries on the other side of the Atlantic. The zigzags and reversals of American policy on population matters reflect changes in political outlook, but, through it all, population questions have become more prominent, more divisive, and more difficult to handle. International migration of uncertain magnitude and of distinctive ethnic, racial, and national character clouds public debate today in a manner remote from anything known in the 1960s. Again, we are making both particular and general claims here. The American story has special features, but it is part of a wider generational experience in the developed world as a whole. Further documentation of the ubiquity of these issues comes in Canada, a country where in recent years demography has been an element in debates over the very survival of the nation.

A brief explanation about the sequence of chapters might be helpful. Our claim is that nearly every developed nation in the 1990s faces problems arising from specific demographic and political instabilities in the period we discuss, notably the coupling of very low fertility rates with rising levels of volatile international migration. This combination of powerful demographic factors will not go away, nor will its political implications. We discuss these themes in chapters on individual countries where different facets of this new form of population politics have appeared. In Germany, asylum seekers have created dilemmas that are inseparable from certain features of the German past. In France, low fertility and the immigration of many Muslims have created a combustible mix that flared up in—of all places—the sedate corridors of the country's Institut National d' Etudes Démographiques (INED). In Great Britain, immigration in general and Islamic fundamentalism in particular became front-page news when the novelist Salman Rushdie, who lived there, was sentenced to death by Iran for publishing a novel that the Iranian government considered blasphemous. All this happened in the midst of a painful debate about the transformation of British sovereignty in light of European integration.

National traditions and historical experience dominate population politics in eastern Europe, too. In Yugoslavia, forced migration turned into ethnic cleansing, a deliberate use of terror to transform the demographies of states that were created when the federal structure of the old Yugoslavia fell apart. In Russia, violence has attended the collapse of the Soviet empire, where the variation in levels of fertility and mortality is so great that multiple and ominous fault lines exposed by population politics are visible. This darker side of demographics since the mid-1960s also appears in the extreme—indeed at times bizarre—twists and turns of Romanian population policy in the time of Ceausescu.

In North America, democratic traditions have helped to constrain and preclude some of the severe experiments in population politics found in eastern Europe. But one should not be smug or complacent about the capacity of American institutions to contain the tensions arising from immigration, legal or otherwise. We show some of the ways in which demographic issues have become foci of American political argument, first with respect to population policy in general, then in the design of the U.S. Census, and last in the allocation of representation. An even sharper example is provided by Canada. Canada's story is powerful, since it shows the tendency of population issues to spill over into virtually every facet of political and public life.

After discussing these national forms of the debate over fertility, migration, and national identity in the developed West, we turn to some critical cross-national themes. Here we accept completely the argument that the "North" and "South" can never be separated analytically, since what happens in the "South" turns up in the "North" sooner or later—more and more often sooner, given the increasing volume of international migration. That migratory flow is one of the central themes of this book.

The sequence of chapters in this book is arbitrary, but our hope is that we have presented a fair treatment of the variations among national and regional forms as they occur in increasing complexity. Our overall conclusion is that every developed country has a history like the ones we have described in this book. We have tried to support this by isolating and analyzing the fundamental features of recent history. The issues are not new, but their combination is and will be important for generations to come.

This book, in sum, is about countries that have gone through the upheavals of industrialization but that face an uncertain future because their political institutions and demographies are in dramatic flux. No one can predict future fertility in nations currently registering unprecedentedly low fertility rates. No one knows how many people are on the move today, illegally or legally crossing frontiers to seek safety or a new life, but they are there and their number is legion. No one knows how the newcomers will adjust to living with their new neighbors; the family structures of both have been transformed. And no one knows how well political and governmental institutions will respond to the new demographic situations or how population issues will affect broader and deeper patterns of national and regional realignments.

8

Uncertainties abound, but of one thing we may be sure. Every country's public life is vitally affected by demographic issues and the underlying realities they reflect and at times distort. We present evidence on a number of countries in the hope that readers will become more informed and cautious in considering these issues than many politicians are today. It is our future those politicians are dealing with; we have a right to know what is going on.

WESTERN EUROPE

chapter 1

GERMANY:
IMMIGRATION, REFUGEES, AND UNIFICATION

In November 1992, two German youths threw firebombs into a home in the northern German town of Mölln. A Turkish woman, her daughter, and her niece were burned to death.[1] The German press and the world reacted with shock and horror.

The attack was not just an isolated criminal incident. It exposed a disturbing set of problems associated with international migration to Germany since its reunification. Here is an example of how international immigration, in the context of below-replacement fertility,* reveals profound political and moral problems in a democratic country with an undemocratic past. Demographic trends in Germany are only a little different from those of its neighbors, but Germany's past is unique. In the context of that unique German history, we can understand why these issues are so explosive. As soon as the vexed questions are raised as to who has the right to German citizenship or the right to residence in Ger-

---

*Several technical terms are used throughout this book:

Total fertility rate: A composite of age-specific fertility rates in a given year or years for all age groups within the reproductive life span. A period rate (see below).

Period vs. cohort fertility rates: Period fertility rates, the most commonly used form, are calculated for a given time period, typically a calendar year, for women of all ages. The cohort concept calculates fertility rates on the basis of the behavior of generations or age groups over their lifetime.

Replacement fertility: The fertility level at which a population is said to be reproducing itself, given its mortality rate and the human sex ratio at birth. In most industrialized countries discussed in this book, a fertility rate of 2.1 children per woman is considered replacement level.

Natural increase or decrease: The difference between birthrates and death rates, i.e., the rate at which a population grows (or declines) without reference to migration.

many, the terrible shadow of the German past falls across the public debate and is likely to do so indefinitely.

Before turning to the tortured history of German nationality and immigration, it is useful to consider some basic facts about the link between migration and German population growth in recent decades. A major change in the components of German demographic growth took place prior to reunification in 1990. In 1960, West Germany's—the Federal Republic's—population was growing 1.19 percent per year, a growth equally divided between natural increase and net migration. Over the next decade, a decline in fertility changed this: the total fertility rate fell below the notional replacement level of 2.1 in 1970 and reached the unprecedentedly low level of 1.3 in 1984. A subsequent modest rise stabilized the rate at about 1.4 in the early 1990s.

The consequences are clear. In 1970, the population growth rate of 1.07 percent was composed of a natural-increase rate of 0.13 percent and a net-migration rate of 0.95 percent. A decade later, the ratio between these two elements was even more pronounced: natural increase turned negative by 1980 (i.e., there were fewer births than deaths), and all of West Germany's population increase was attributable to migration. This remains true for western Germany.

In East Germany, also in the early 1970s, the total fertility rate fell below the replacement level, and it has been exceptionally low in the 1990s, since the collapse of the German Democratic Republic. But an even larger difference between the two Germanies is the direction of the migratory flows they have experienced. Net emigration is as characteristic of eastern Germany's demography as net immigration is of western Germany's. The population decline in East Germany, a compound of low fertility and emigration, produced in 1990 an annual rate of population *decrease* of 2.47 percent.

It is too soon to tell what the effect of reunification will be on these components of Germany's demographic profile. The only certainties are that intra-regional migration is high and that international migration dominates the nation's population increase.

The ethnic composition of Germany had altered radically during and after World War II. About fifteen million Germans who had once lived farther east came to West Germany in 1945–55—most were forced to do so as part of the postwar settlement—and they eventually constituted about one-quarter of the total population of the Federal Republic in the 1960s. In addition, the *Gastarbeiter*, or "guest worker," program brought millions of non-Germans to West Germany during the 1950s, 1960s, and early 1970s. By now, almost five million of these—workers, their families, and their descendants—live in Germany without German citizenship. Taken together, the inflow of Germans in 1945–55 and of "guest workers" means that about one-third of Germany's population today consists of immigrants or the children of immigrants. Among developed countries, only Israel has so high a proportion of newcomers.[2]

Yet international migration has always been of fundamental importance in the political history of Germany, and population movements helped to make it a dominant actor in world affairs. Even after the debacle of World War II, and after reconstruction and reunification, this is still true. The continuity is in part a simple matter of geography. Germany, by its very location, is and always has been an ethnically mixed state. From the late Middle Ages to the eighteenth and nineteenth centuries, population flows brought Germans, Poles, and other eastern Europeans westward into Prussia and along the Baltic coast to the old Hanseatic ports of Rostock, Lübeck, Hamburg, and Bremen. These and other migratory flows were essential to the economic and cultural development of central Europe. Immanuel Kant wrote *Critique of Pure Reason* in the Prussian city of Königsberg, now Kaliningrad, in Russia. The nineteenth-century kingdom of Prussia stretched from what is now northern Germany across to eastern Poland and the Baltic states.

The character and complexity of this linguistic and ethnic mosaic in central and eastern Europe have created major themes in modern European history. The texture and tensions of this region may be glimpsed in the Polish film *The Promised Land,* directed by Andrzej Wajda, the story of three textile industrialists in late-nineteenth-century Lodz, in what is now Poland. The three capitalists are a Catholic Polish nobleman, a Lutheran German, and a Polish Jew, and their partnership suggests the social, religious, and economic collage on which national and imperial rivalries were superimposed. The firm fails, the Polish nobleman and the German Lutheran withdraw, and the Jew starts over again.

Ethnic Germans lived in eastern Prussia for centuries. They were part of the social landscape, despite a complex and troubled relationship to the Poles among whom they lived. To the west, Polish migrants worked in German coal mines, staffed German factories, and built German cities, where hostility to them took many forms, including the anti-Catholic prejudice endemic among many German Protestants. These migratory movements were a fact of life, but however familiar or useful, they were never without national, racial, and class tensions. The people of Slavic descent who lived throughout Germany in the late nineteenth century never became German in the eyes of many of their German neighbors. And the political fragmentation of Germany before 1871 only further complicated the situation.

The city of Berlin offers a case in point. It grew from a small settlement to a world city of two million by the turn of the twentieth century, when migrants from the east flowed into Berlin as the capital of a new empire, which they helped to build but in which many of them lived as poorly paid aliens squashed into *Mietskasernen*, or tenements. Among the least well integrated were the *Ostjüden*, eastern European Jews with customs and religious beliefs that troubled many of their more assimilated co-religionists who had long been resident in Germany. Other immigrants knew similar hostility, but however unpleasant it was, it did not stem the flow of newcomers from the east.

Given high migration, ethnic diversity, and political disunity, the answer to the question of who was a German emphasized language, culture, and ethnic background. This "ethnocultural" approach to German national identity,[3] reinforced by strains of German romanticism and idealism that were particularly important to the *Bildungsbürgertum* (the cultivated middle classes), dominated the subject before the unification of the German empire in 1871.

In that year, the political fragmentation of Germany was reduced and reconfigured (though never completely eliminated). An empire of federated states, the Kaiserreich, was founded at Versailles in 1871, after the momentous victory of the Prussian army over the French army in the war of 1870–71, with the kingdom of Prussia as its core. It incorporated the ethnically mixed areas of Prussia, Pomerania, Brandenburg, and Silesia, while excluding many German-speaking communities—notably Austria. The constitution of 1871 left a substantial non-German population within Germany and a large German population outside it. The new domestic order was also deeply flawed. The new Germany mixed elements of parliamentary democracy with those of an autocratic monarchy holding absolute authority over the army and the executive.

In short, the settlement of 1871 created a politically unstable but economically dynamic regime. This explosive mixture detonated twice in the twentieth century, in 1914 and 1939. Its repercussions are still felt today.

Any consideration of contemporary German population politics must still confront the question as to what constitutes Germany, which is as much a demographic and cultural matter as a political and economic one. Here the contrast with France is clear-cut, as we shall see. Second-generation immigrants in France are considered French; second-generation immigrants in Germany are not considered German. The divergence arises out of many factors in the history of the two countries, but one feature stands out: France did not have a problem of the magnitude of the German-Slav divide that both marked and distorted the process of state building in Germany; the integration of the Breton and Provençal populations in France was, in comparison, a minor issue. French nation building was difficult, and the people faced profound political instabilities, but in Germany the task was harder still.

Before 1914, there was no unified, overarching German citizenship but, rather, a vertical ordering of loyalties that proceeded from citizenship in a *Land*, or state, to citizenship in the empire. But within each state, there were large groups that were not considered German, and outside them were large groups that, by the same criteria of language and culture, were as German as the kaiser. This ambiguous history is inscribed in the 1913 definition of German citizenship as a community of descent (jus sanguinis), in contrast to the French definition of citizenship as a community of residence (jus soli). It protected the German nation, defined culturally, from being swamped by non-Germans and opened a door to the Germans living beyond the borders. (The origins of this principle were a matter of social administration. Local authorities should not, it was believed, be held responsible for the maintenance of poor immigrants, whose plight imposed financial burdens that the local populations were unprepared to shoulder.) And this German approach to citizenship is with us still. It survived World War I, the Weimar Republic, and the Third Reich to be inscribed in the *Grundgesetz*, the basic law of the Federal Republic of Germany, in 1949 and underlies German population politics today.

The shadows of the German past are evident as well in other features of population politics. The most salient is the legacy of institutionalized racism at the heart of the National Socialist state.

The Nazis did not invent ethnic cleansing, but they took it to a level never before seen. They did so in part because of the cachet widely accorded to pseudoscientific notions of racial characteristics during the early twentieth century, when the word "race" was used interchangeably with the word "nation"; even popular literature and the works of more sophisticated writers disseminated notions of racial difference. To Adolf Hitler and his henchmen, Jews formed a race just as clearly as did Aryans, blond, blue-eyed Nordic Christians. That Hitler himself did not fit the Aryan stereotype was irrelevant.

How did racism become a principle of statecraft? One answer lies in the history of eugenics, a late-nineteenth-century "science of race improvement" that emanated from a selective reading of the new science of genetics. Some advocated limiting the fertility of the mentally ill and the poor. Others promoted higher fertility among the well-to-do and the well educated. Such arguments were rejected by some French Roman Catholics, but eugenics prospered in other Catholic countries, as well as in Protestant states such as Britain, the United States, and Germany and among social engineers of both the left and the right.

By the 1930s, the Nazis had converted eugenics into an instrument of social policy that the scientific founders of eugenics would have found abhorrent. One way in which this shift from eugenics to state-authorized ethnic cleansing took place in Germany was through the efforts of biological and medical scientists to help prevent the proliferation of what were deemed "socially undesirable" groups.[4] And controlling "race pollution" was an idea not restricted to fanatics. Most cultural pessimists flirted with the concept of racial degeneration, and many found a biological explanation for it. Such notions were useful to bureaucratic elites determined to reduce social and economic problems to technical ones. In this spirit, experts in medical science, public health, and demography entered into what one scholar has called an "alliance of convenience" with state authorities.[5] After the Nazis took power in 1933, this alliance gained new forms.

One facet of this social policy, which antedated Hitler, was the treatment of mentally disabled people. There is a vast literature in western European and U.S. eugenics on the idea that all mental illness is congenital. Among the policy lines advocated were physical segregation, sterilization, and (more rarely) euthanasia. In Nazi Germany, euthanasia was carried out first on the mentally disabled, creating a precedent for other kinds of extermination to follow.

There were many reasons why millions of Germans supported the Nazis, and, especially after the world economic crisis of 1929–32, their racial doctrine was only part of their appeal. But it was clear that those who tacitly or actively went along with the Nazis were (at best) fellow travelers in racism. By 1934, the Nazis had made new laws that separated citizens into two categories—Jews and Germans. It was only a matter of time before more than civil liberties were taken away. After the assassination by a Polish Jew of a German diplomat in Paris, mass expulsions of Polish-born Jews living in Germany took place. And after the 1939 carve-up of Poland between Germany and the Soviet Union, millions more Poles—Jews and non-Jews alike—were expelled to the new Government-General that ruled over the rump of Poland.

What followed were events no one had ever seen before. The Nazis' systematic extermination of the Jews was the greatest campaign of ethnic cleansing in history. Gypsies, Communist and non-Communist opponents of the regime, and innocents caught in the Nazi machine were also massacred, but what distinguished the (inaptly termed*) Holocaust from other wartime mass killings was its specifically and obsessively racial character. One million children had to die so that a race (the Jewish people) would become historical memory, recalled only in the collection of artifacts that Hermann Göring hoarded for the planned "museum of the extinct race" in Prague.

There is some evidence that after eradicating the Jews the Nazis

---

*"Holocaust" is a Greek word for ritual sacrifice. There was nothing sacred or ritually meaningful about the Nazis' extermination of the Jews.

planned to eliminate the Poles,[6] and after the Poles, there were millions of Russians and other eastern Europeans to be disposed of. Once more the German-Slav divide appears central, for the Nazis may have contemplated erasing that divide simply by wiping out the Slavs. Whether or not such plans would have been realized is of course a moot point. What matters is that they mirror the original crime, surely the crime of the century.

The staggering loss of life in World War II and the huge population movements the war created were at the heart of another chapter in the history of German migration. This was imposed on millions of Germans by the victorious Allies and the new states created after their defeat in 1945, when millions of people of German descent in central and eastern Europe were forced to pay the price for Nazi ethnic cleansing. They were expelled from their homes, lost their property, and fled west in a gigantic wave.

Estimates vary as to the number of people forced to move west. The first group—the *Reichsdeutsche*, as they were called—came from East Prussia, eastern Pomerania and Brandenburg, and Silesia. Their German population in 1939 had been more than nine million. Six years later, their presence within the newly defined borders of Poland, Russia, and Hungary was proscribed by fiat, and most were pushed westward into occupied Germany. The second group—the *Volksdeutsche*, Germans living as minorities in Czechoslovakia, Poland, Hungary, Yugoslavia, and Romania—numbered another seven million, a so-called fifth column of ethnic Germans who had no future in the successor states of 1945. Between 1945 and 1950, about three million were expelled from Czechoslovakia and nearly two million from other countries. A third group was the Lebensraum colonizers—approximately one million *Volksdeutsche* and *Reichsdeutsche* whom the Nazis had sent to settle parts of Poland, Yugoslavia, and Russia.

Thus, approximately twelve million Germans were forced from their homes. The Lebensraum colonizers had already been evacuated by the German army during their retreat from the east in 1944–45, and the other two groups had been caught by the advance of the Red Army. The Allies agreed to the principle of mass population transfers in 1944, and over the next five years they carried out this policy. The outcome was a new ethnic map of Europe. Whole areas of German culture and civilization were transferred west, root and branch. Mass expropriations of German property and land took place throughout eastern Europe. Perhaps two million people of German descent died in the flights and expulsions, and the survivors have never forgotten the trauma. In 1966, the presence of more than 11 million people in West Germany and 3.5 million in East Germany, about one-quarter of the population of the two Germanies, was a direct result of this mass expulsion.

The postwar history of Germany may be divided into two parts: the reconstruction of West Germany as a democratic state between 1945 and 1950; and the remarkable period of economic growth in the 1950s that turned Germany into the most powerful nation in Europe and a magnet for foreign workers. Between 1970 and 1990, this revived central European power then shifted from being one that recruited migrant workers to one deeply concerned about the presence within its borders of substantial non-German populations. Communist East Germany also drew foreign workers and students from afar, but the inflow was less substantial than in the West.

There were three components in the process of rebuilding Germany that informed population politics in the postwar years: the rebuilding of family life, the expansion of the labor force, and the difficult absorption of guest workers and other newcomers.

The war had torn family life asunder in Germany as everywhere in Europe. And the sex ratio of the population was skewed by military casualties: while women suffered in bombings and in the course of the final defeat, most of the casualties were male; perhaps five million German men died in military service. In addition, the sheer disruption of life made the reunion of families infinitely complicated. In 1945, thousands of women stood on railway platforms with placards asking passersby if they had any knowledge of their missing men. In some cities, the ratio of women to men was higher than 170 to 100. The first postwar census indicated that roughly one-third of all households in Germany were headed by divorced women or widows.[7] This helps to explain why the Basic Law of the Federal Republic, the *Grundgesetz*, guaranteed equal rights for men and women within a framework for the "protection of the family" understood in traditional terms.

In the meantime, the urgent need was to provide financial assistance to increase the coherence of families. Such a focus for social policy had the advantage of shifting attention from the issues of class power that had so disfigured the politics of the Weimar Republic and the subsequent Nazi period. It also appealed to a part of the Roman Catholic community that had worked for generations for an extension of social policy to help alleviate the material burdens of family life. Under Konrad Adenauer, West Germany's first minister for family questions was a Roman Catholic conservative, Franz-Josef Wuermeling, who saw himself as "the protective patron of the family."[8]

What guided these diverse groups was the idea that men founded families and earned wages to support them; family allowances should supplement incomes insufficient to cover child-rearing expenses without a second salary. The clear implication was that women's most important work was to conduct moral education in the home, a service for which the state would pay. Single-parent families were not in this vision; the norm was a nuclear family with a man working outside the home and a woman working in it.

This was one reason family allowances were construed as supplements to be distributed by employers. In 1954, the Christian Democratic coalition government pushed through a law instituting monthly payments to workers (meaning male workers) with three or more children. This measure left unresolved the problems of most couples, who had fewer than three children, let alone those of single women trying to raise families by themselves. The Kindergeld system had an ideological basis. It was directed toward the production of a stable and, if possible, classless society.

Economic growth undercut the ideology of domesticity promulgated in these ways after the war. The expansion of the West German economy proved the dominance of human capital over material capital. No one should minimize the impact of the Marshall Plan in the rebirth of the West German (and through it, the western European) economy, but the real impetus and continuing strength of the West German economy was its people, their skills, and their productivity.

And within the West German labor force, women became increasingly important: in 1950, one in four married women was in paid labor outside the home; ten years later, the ratio was one in three; by 1970, it was more than one in two.

The *Wirtschaftswunder* (economic miracle) was made possible by expanding the labor force and giving it the tools to dominate European and, ultimately, international markets in durable light consumer goods like home appliances as well as heavy engineering and producer goods. The European Economic Community established in 1957 created a stable political environment within which this economic growth could take place. Gross-industrial-output growth rates quadrupled between 1948 and 1963. In roughly the same period, wage rates doubled and foreign trade rose from negligible levels to rank (by the mid-1960s) second behind the United States. The old nemesis, inflation, was nowhere in sight; with a stable currency, high levels of investment, and virtually no defense expenditure, West Germany earned through industry what it had failed to earn by armed force: a predominant position in European affairs and a standard of living higher than that of many other nations on the Continent.

The expanding labor force was only partly domestic. The recovery of the birthrate in West Germany after the war mirrored, though on a much briefer and smaller scale, the baby boom of the United States, Canada, Australia, and New Zealand, but by the late 1950s, a perceived shortage of labor led to the institution of the *Gastarbeiter* system.[9] The *Gastarbeiter* were supposed to be temporary workers coming to Germany in a rotation process according to which a first group would be replaced by a second and then a third. However, employers bridled at the costs of continuous recruiting and training, and temporary stays stretched into years with little publicity.

The large numbers of non-German and non-European resident workers in Germany are, therefore, the outcome of policy choices made in the interests of German economic development. Sections of Berlin such as Kreuzberg are now Turkish neighborhoods because both employers and government officials recruited the Turks to come to West Germany.

When the system began, few realized how high the social costs would be for the recruitment of what became a large, permanent pool of unskilled and semiskilled labor from poorer parts of the world. Among those costs has been the periodic recrudescence of xenophobia and racial violence, phenomena that are not unknown elsewhere in Europe but that take on a nightmarish form when played out against the backdrop of German history.

By the mid-1980s, the West German economic miracle was a thing of the past. When the division between East and West Germany collapsed in 1989, fundamental economic problems in the Federal Republic were multiplied by even more difficult problems in the east. Two fundamental flash points underlie recent German ethnic relations: the first is racial, pitting a visibly non-European population against the indigenous German population experiencing considerable economic stress; the second is social and economic in the form of tensions arising from reunification at a time of chronic economic difficulties. As a result, one can see elements of late-1920s Germany: a society terrified of inflation, only partially unified, and tainted by the language of racial hatred, which is used by marginalized and criminal elements to hurl abuse at those they blame for their plight.

But the similarities between the 1920s and the 1990s should not be exaggerated. The very structure of the European Community—largely French-inspired—protects against the risk that German racial tensions will fester. In addition, the horrific nature of the Nazi experience is a powerful, though partial, immunization against recurrence of its crimes. Yet immigration to Germany and the treatment of immigrants within Germany are critical tests in which both Germans and their neighbors can measure the stability of postwar German democracy. Germany is one of the few states that in this century has had, in the historian Fritz Stern's phrase, a second chance at making liberalism a reality.[10] The tasks and tensions of absorbing, first, non-German workers, second, East Germans, and, third, refugees and asylum seekers tell us in part what Germany now is and how far removed it is from the Nazi years. The comparison is unavoidable; it will continue to be made in the future, and in that questioning of what has been called for generations "the German problem," demographic issues are likely to loom large.

The difference between incomes in Germany and those in the states from which guest workers came was so substantial that it was unlikely the guest workers would think of staying in Germany only temporarily. Labor visas were for one year, but workers, their employers, and, eventually, liberal church groups opposed the rotation of migrant workers; as in other countries, immigrants began to form long-term communities and create ethnic clusters in Germany's major cities.

Many, but by no means all, of these guest workers were Muslim. They built mosques, observed Islamic rituals, and added a colorful, not very troublesome element to Berlin, Hamburg, and Cologne. These cities had hosted immigrants before, and all had managed to contain the ethnic tensions commonly generated by such population movements. But the limits of tolerance are both economic and cultural. Guest workers of many kinds have lived in German cities for centuries. What made their presence difficult in recent years were two familiar features of German insecurity: the perennial worry about economic instability and the perennial puzzle as to what constitutes German national identity.

Germans now in their eighties have a full repertoire of memories of economic crises: the great inflation after World War I, when people lost all they had; the world economic crisis of 1929–32, which had similarly catastrophic results; the Nazi period and the war, after which Germany was in ruins and, once again, everyone had to start over. Start they did, but with lingering doubts as to the permanence of their achievement.

Many commentators argue that by the 1970s the *Gastarbeiter* policy was widely opposed on mostly cultural grounds and that the energy crisis following the 1973 Arab-Israeli war was the shock needed to reassess and ultimately terminate the policy. The days of untroubled growth were over, and while guest workers were in Germany because there was demand for their services, now austerity was in order, though some workers from abroad were still wanted. One very rough estimate was that in the early 1990s the German economy needed 350,000 guest workers (whose wages were lower than those of German workers) in order to maintain the Germans' living standard.[11] Such estimates are sharply disputed by others.

The alien presence thus became the alien problem, through no fault of the aliens themselves. The survival of nativist and xenophobic elements in German political culture ensured that the issue would have profound political repercussions. On the one hand, right-wing parties were indifferent at best, hostile at worst, to guest workers who (as the phrase went) had overstayed their welcome. On the other hand, the trauma of the German past guaranteed that such hostility would be subtle or unexpressed. Deep ethnic and racial prejudices were there, nonetheless, under the surface.

This problem would have been difficult enough for local and national authorities, but additional crises made the situation infinitely harder: notably, the unanticipated collapse of Soviet hegemony in eastern Europe and the subsequent collapse of the East German state. The speed with which German reunification took place was breathtaking. Within fifteen months, East Germany, a feature of the landscape of central Europe for more than four decades, simply vanished. But the costs of this transformation were formidable. In material terms, splicing together the two Germanies was a mammoth undertaking.

Before the Wall came down, anyone going from West Berlin to East Berlin or from any town in West Germany to an Eastern city was used to two simple indicators of the gap between the two states: the ring around a visitor's collar immediately produced by the untreated coal dust that permeated East German air and the dimness of the streetlights. But the condition of the coal industry and of the electrical system in East Germany was only part of it; the cost of linking infrastructures— telephone lines, for instance—was astronomical, as was the slow but steady process of adjusting the gap between wage levels in the two newly merged parts of Germany.

Chancellor Helmut Kohl's government either underestimated the costs of unification or deliberately misled the German people into thinking it could be accomplished without too much economic distress. In either case, the task was much more difficult than most people had thought, and the economic pressures it generated produced a wave of fear about inflation among bankers and economists. Here, Germany's past resurfaced with a vengeance. The tight money policy of the German central bank was intended to prevent the huge expenditure on reunification from creating a price spiral. Inflation was a problem elsewhere in Europe, but the German reaction to it was so historically sensitized and severe as to produce shock waves throughout the Continent.

German retrenchment and a policy that allowed unemployment to rise to levels approaching those of the years 1918–33 were ways to pay for reunification without inflation, but these tactics changed the economic landscape of Europe. And one of their most significant effects was to worsen the economic and cultural environment in which non-German residents of Germany lived.

In addition to the problems of alien workers and reunification, a third set of difficulties resulted from the influx to Germany of refugees and asylum seekers from eastern Europe and Yugoslavia. In 1980, 108,000 people sought asylum in West Germany, only 6 percent of whom came from eastern Europe. In 1991, 256,000 people sought asylum in the now reunited Germany, of which 47 percent came from eastern Europe, mostly Yugoslavia and Romania,[12] and in 1992, approximately 438,000 people followed, many from the same countries. The old German-Slav exchange of populations was a reality once more.

To appreciate the consequences of this influx of asylum seekers, we must distinguish among four immigrant populations recognized under German law. The first are "ethnic Germans," who are treated as citizens by inheritance when they return to the country and hence not included in totals of refugees or immigrants. The second are persons with the right of asylum according to Article 16 of the Basic Law in its pre-1992 form. The third are "Convention refugees," people who, according to the Geneva Convention of 1951, have a justified fear of persecution and cannot be deported to the persecuting country (see chapter 11). The fourth group are economic migrants who come to Germany to earn money and who do not enjoy the right of asylum or protection against deportation, although many claim asylum in order to gain residence or work permits.

There is some tension in Germany about the first and fourth categories, but on balance the consensus is that ethnic Germans are welcome (in moderate numbers) and economic migrants are not. Severe problems arise in the second and third cases, however, where questions of persecution are involved that become entangled with the painful history of the Holocaust. And a key problem is that there is often no clear boundary between the third and fourth categories, since many dubious asylum claims are filed by would-be economic migrants. Until December 1992, they were given the benefit of the doubt: that is, they had the right to reside in Germany and receive social welfare benefits while their cases were processed, which took years. In 1990, 3 percent of the 120,000 applicants were granted asylum status by the Federal Office for the Recognition of Foreign Refugees. But even initial failure to be given asylum status did not usually lead to deportation. Lengthy appeals procedures and confusion made this population very hard to find, let alone deport.

In addition, the nature of persecution in European nations is entirely different from that in African or Asian states. Yugoslavs fled to Germany even before the Yugoslav state disintegrated. Do Bosnian Muslims merit protection from a state persecuting them when that state has fallen apart? Do migrants from the former Soviet Union deserve protection from persecution? These are extremely complicated questions at any time, but especially in a period of economic austerity, when a nation's tolerance is likely to be strained.

That strain was expressed in two ways. The first was a resurgence of ugly incidents in German life. Although xenophobic violence had broken out before, sporadic violence against refugees and long-resident guest workers signaled a return of feelings reminiscent of the dark side of recent German history. The second was a change in Article 16 of the Basic Law, effectively the most liberal asylum policy in the world. The new formulation, for the first time, put the burden of proof of persecution on the asylum seeker, and those who applied were no longer given the benefit of the doubt and, with it, years of residence and social welfare benefits.

Some of the most serious incidents took place in what was formerly East Germany. In August 1992, five days of rioting by youths against refugees culminated in the firebombing of a hostel in the Lichtenberg quarter of the Baltic town of Rostock. Some of the assailants may have come from other parts of Germany, but they were cheered on by local people. Other Germans sheltered fugitive attackers in their apartments. Two hundred Romanian gypsy asylum seekers were moved away.[13] The violence was attributed to anger and resentment about unemployment, especially youth unemployment, about the empty promises of a good life following unification, and about the free housing and grants given by the state to asylum seekers. Xenophobia once again caused anger about domestic problems to be directed toward an identifiable alien group. Among those arrested after the trouble in Rostock were former agents of the Stasi, the East German secret police. Germany as a whole was paying the price for what one observer called "the breakdown of the economic and social infrastructure in Eastern Germany following reunification."[14]

In September 1992, attacks at refugee centers took place in Eisenhüttenstadt, near the Polish border. In Berlin, Jewish gravestones were desecrated, and a memorial to concentration-camp victims was destroyed by a bomb. Violence flared in the eastern town of Kolkwitz, where forty-three migrants from Romania, Bulgaria, Mozambique, and Angola had been given temporary accommodation. Refugee housing was attacked by protesters in ten German towns near Koblenz, in the southwest, to the Polish border. Two sleeping children were injured by a firebomb in the southwestern state of Baden-Württemberg, a day or two before a court in eastern Germany handed out light two- to four-year sentences to each of five youths found guilty of stabbing an Angolan immigrant to death in 1990. There were more than fourteen hundred attacks against foreigners in 1992 alone.[15]

The public debate over these events referred to all the issues examined in this book. "Of course we need foreigners," noted Kurt Kasch, senior vice president of Deutsche Bank in Berlin, "considering our low birth-rate, but how many? Our elites, political and business, have not been able to come up with good explanations for the fears people have about Germany's future. And when you have an entire country full of fear, you look for some place to focus those fears—a target."[16] Targeting asylum seekers was denounced time and again by the Federal President, Richard von Weizäcker. Joschka Fisher, a leader of the Green Party, noted that German unification had brought on "a surge of racism."[17]

To contain the anger and still the racism evident in a troubled population, German politicians took a number of measures. They concluded an agreement with Romania to repatriate those seeking asylum in Germany and to pay $20 million for transport and retraining costs. Similar pacts were signed with Czechoslovakia and Bulgaria. But once again, political statements did not stem the tide of violence. As we have already noted, three Turks were burned to death when their home in Mölln was firebombed. A man was burned alive near Wuppertal in western Germany because five youths thought he was a Jew.[18]

Two weeks later, on 6 December 1992, the leaders of the main political parties agreed to amend the Basic Law to make it harder for people without a strong case of political persecution to enter Germany. With the grudging agreement of the Social Democratic Party, the ruling conservative government tightened the provisions of Article 16 to align German policy with that of other European countries. The measure became law six months later.

There were five key changes in the new law. First, people from a country where political persecution was deemed not to be a problem would be turned away. Those from countries with a record of political persecution would have their cases considered as they were in the past and would have right of entry during the review period.[19] Second, officials were empowered to reject asylum seekers who claimed to suffer persecution in country A but entered Germany from country B, when B had no record of persecution and asylum could reasonably be sought there. In effect, an Iranian who came directly to Germany would have a case, but the same person going first to Switzerland and then to Germany would be turned back to Switzerland. Third, people fleeing a war zone would be admitted, in limited numbers, and only so long as hostilities continued. Fourth, the number of ethnic Germans admitted each year would not exceed a number 10 percent higher than those admitted in 1991 and 1992 (in 1991, it was about 220,000, thus the future ceiling is 242,000). Finally, guest workers, or those on temporary labor contracts, would not exceed 100,000 per year, and their work would be monitored. In recognition of the plight of Vietnamese and others who came as guest workers to East Germany before 1989, the new bill provided for "humanitarian solutions" to the problems of those whose contracts were about to expire. These new restrictive clauses, which came into effect on 1 July 1993, were aimed in part to bar the entry of eastern European asylum seekers, who had numbered about 250,000 in 1992. As Hermann-Otto Solms of the (liberal) Free Democratic Party put it, "It is clear that people from Afghanistan or Iran have a right to ask for asylum, and those from Turkey as well. The question is with countries like Bulgaria or Romania. People from there will probably be sent back."[20]

The broader implications of these changes for the future of German society are unclear, but in the short term the number of asylum seekers declined sharply, to 127,000 in 1995. The need to reassure a worried population, at a time of economic difficulty, that foreigners would not be a burden on the public purse clearly underlay this policy, but the profound problems uncovered by the controversy will not disappear with one constitutional change. Illiberalism has a way of sticking to the soil, especially in a country that still distinguishes the nationality of those of German descent from those who reside in the country without German lineage. It is important to note, though, that even after the reform of Article 16 Germany still has one of the world's most liberal asylum policies.

Below-replacement fertility, new patterns of family formation, economic instability, international migration, ethnic and nationalist tensions—these combustible materials are found in much of the developed world since the 1960s. Given the tragic character of the German past, it is not surprising that the configuration of these elements has especially disturbing echoes and features there. But Germany's population politics is not radically different from that of its European neighbors. Indeed, with the decision to eliminate passport controls among member states of the European Community—the Shengen agreements—the problem of controlling immigration passed from national to international jurisdiction.[21] Shengen has been repeatedly delayed, but it represents strong forces working to create uniform policies throughout the European Community. What the German story shows is the inexorable way demographic issues bring moral ones into public debate. The right of asylum evokes moral problems everywhere, but it is particularly difficult in a country that fifty years ago placed ethnic cleansing and genocide at the heart of its national life. The victims of the Nazis cannot be forgotten so quickly, and, when foreigners are burned to death in Germany, the memory of the death camps is bound to return.

One sensitive guide to the development of population politics in Germany is the work of Günter Grass. In one of his earliest novels, *The*

Tin Drum (1959), he chronicled the sufferings of German families in and around the Danzig region hit hard by forced resettlement after the war. In a later novel, *Headbirths; or, the Germans Are Dying Out* (1980), he mused on the obsession with fertility and ethnic identity in German affairs. More recently, he was one of the few to oppose immediate unification of the two Germanys, stand out clearly against ethnic nationalism, and raise serious doubts about the ability of Germany's civil society to resist the temptations of xenophobia. His voice is hardly representative of Germany, but he pinpoints the moral character of the nation's political and demographic problems.

chapter 2

"MARIANNE AND THE RABBITS":
THE FRENCH OBSESSION

The political explosiveness of population questions has taken many forms in western Europe since the 1960s. In France, population and ideology have become completely entangled. To illustrate this point, we recount here the story of a highly visible controversy in the Institut National d'Etudes Démographiques (INED). The quarrel is intrinsically interesting, but it also shows how debates about fertility and immigration express general currents of opinion about national identity.

In some respects, demographic issues have a higher political profile in France than in any other western European country, but not because of radically different demographics. Some brief comparisons with West Germany and Britain may help to show that what matters in population politics are not demographic trends per se but how they are located in the political culture.

Between 1960 and 1992, the population of metropolitan France grew by 25 percent,* rising nearly 12 million, from 45.7 to 57.4 million, an increase much greater than that registered by Britain (10 percent) or West Germany (14 percent). Annual rates of both natural increase and net migration were higher in France than in Britain, and French rates of natural increase exceeded those in West Germany (though Germany registered greater net migration). In short, the French population grew more rapidly than that of either of its historic rivals.

In 1960, the total fertility rate in France, 2.73, was almost identical to that in Britain, 2.71. Thirty years later, the fertility of both countries

---

*"Metropolitan France" excludes her overseas colonies and territories. However, Algeria was a French *département* until independence in 1962, and Corsica is still a *département*, hence part of metropolitan France.

had declined well below the notional 2.1 replacement level, to 1.73 in France and 1.84 in Britain. German fertility was lower still. A parallel decline in cohort fertility (the rate of reproduction among women during their fertile years) also occurred in the three countries. Marriage patterns—or nuptiality patterns, as demographers call them—were very similar too in the three countries. Between 1970 and 1993, out-of-wedlock births in France rose from 6.8 per 1,000 to 27.5; in Britain, the rise was from 8.0 to 29.8. The mean age at first birth was decidedly similar, too. In Germany, the same increases were registered (with higher ones in the East than in the West). Parallels occur in mortality patterns as well. Infant mortality declined from 18.2 per 1,000 live births in France in 1970 to 6.6 in 1992; in Britain, the decline was from 18.5 in 1970 to 7.4 in 1993. The West German figures were 23.6 in 1970 and 6.0 in 1992. Life expectancy was slightly higher for French than British women, 81 versus 78.5 years, while for men the two levels were almost identical.

So there were parallel changes in demographic behavior in France and Britain. In chapter 1, we discussed some special features of German development, but the general rule is that, in all three European powers, populations grew, life expectancy rose, and total fertility declined below the replacement rate. Yet the meaning of these trends and the significance attached to them were entirely different in the three countries. To understand why, we must turn again to historical experience and political culture.

In France, demography is front-page news. Readers of national newspapers are informed about the latest population trends. Occasionally, they also hear of demographic arguments that elsewhere would be restricted to the pages of learned journals and the handful of academics who read them.

A recent episode clearly illustrates the high profile of these issues and the striking mix of science and ideology in population debates in France. It was a quarrel within the hallowed walls of the Institut National d'Etudes Démographiques. Since May 1990, this body, which has an unparalleled reputation for demographic research, has been convulsed by a conflict over the alleged political and ideological character of its approach to population questions.[1]

The challenge came from within. Hervé Le Bras, a former editor of INED's scientific journal *Population* and a director of research there, launched a campaign in the press, on radio, and in books against what he took to be the bias in favor of high fertility rates of French demography in general and of INED in particular. The reactions were swift and personal. Technical exchanges gave way to mutual insult. While Le Bras obstinately refused to resign from an institution he believed to be infused with a repugnant ideology, he was condemned by his colleagues, removed from the editorial board of *Population*, and rebuked by the scientific committee of INED. It was a journalists' field day, with cartoons and editorials in the Parisian mainstream press.

Where else in the world would demography be so prominent? *L'affaire INED* highlights features of French political culture that account for the salience of these issues. While the Gallic flavor of this argument is undeniable, echoing the long-term French concern about *dénatalité* (a declining birthrate), the episode raises issues central to our understanding of population politics in recent years.

The occasion for the outbreak of *l'affaire INED* was a seemingly harmless article by the institute's then-director, Gérard Calot, published in an information paper INED circulates regularly. The article, published in April 1990, compared recent trends in French and Swedish fertility and showed that, while fertility rates calculated for a given year or time period (period fertility rates) in France were lower than in Sweden in the late 1980s, cohort fertility rates of French women born in the 1950s were higher than those of Swedish women. What is more, although period fertility rates were 1.8 in France—that is, below the replacement level—the cohort rate had risen to the replacement level in the mid-1970s and stayed there. Calot derived the following conclusions: first, French fertility was higher than Swedish fertility; second, in both cases, the recent recovery of fertility rates was attributable to births to women over the age of twenty-five; and third, this stabilization, following a period of fertility decline, was because of family policy, based on pro-natalist objectives in France and social objectives in Sweden.[2]

It is hard to believe that a learned and sober discussion of arcane statistics would occasion a public brawl among scholars of the same respected institution, but that is precisely what happened. Le Bras reports that he first learned of Calot's article in early May 1990 from the historian Andre Burguière. Burguière had been approached by a Paris journalist, Josette Alia of *Le Nouvel Observateur,* a prominent French weekly, who had been given proofs of Calot's article, had been surprised by its claim that French fertility had risen to replacement levels, and had consulted academic friends to make sure she understood the technical discussion about period and cohort measurements.

Burguière asked Le Bras if it was true that French fertility had reached the 2.1 level. Le Bras said that it was news to him and that, even if Calot said it was so, it was as unlikely as redating the opening of the French Revolution to 14 September 1790. To the journalist, Le Bras reiterated his skepticism: what had moved were not fertility rates but, rather, the way they were measured.

When he read the article himself, Le Bras reported, his incredulity grew. He noted that Calot suggested that the period rate, until then almost always used to generate fear about low fertility, might be misleading.[3] If so, then decades of alarmism about low fertility might also be based on such "misleading" data. Le Bras wrote later that at that moment he realized he had found for the first time in twenty years "a monumental error" made by French pro-natalists, an error enabling him to break the hold that pro-natalist ideology held over the French demographic profession. "The beast has come out of the forest," Le Bras mused, and, a true crusader, he stepped out to slay it.[4] The "beast" of pro-natalism (*natalisme*), a belief in the value of high fertility and of policy measures to achieve it, was an ideology, according to Le Bras, so pervasive that it could be found in every corner of French demographic research and was such an article of faith that it had been all but impossible to challenge. To demystify pro-natalism, he first had to strip away the mask of scientific neutrality and detachment that INED cherished.

For Le Bras, the way to do so was through provocation and polemic. In a tradition as old as the French Revolution, he mixed cautious criticism, invective, exaggeration, and insult in his efforts to make people question a key assumption of French political culture. He spoke on the radio, addressed the popular press, inspired parliamentary questions, and treated with utter contempt the niceties of academic exchange with his colleagues at INED.

Not surprisingly, they returned the compliment, attributing to him personal, self-aggrandizing motives, professional disappointments, a regrettable thirst for media coverage, a loss of touch with reality, and a taste for disinformation and defamation. INED demographers met repeatedly and vigorously reaffirmed their scientific integrity and independence from political influence. They condemned Le Bras's attempt to portray them as agents of a plot to mislead the French people about the true nature of French population movements.[5]

Le Bras's reputation as a social scientist is based on his sophisticated published work on historical demography and social geography. He was fortunate enough to have a second academic position in Paris, at the Ecole des Hautes Etudes en Sciences Sociales, the capital's highly respected graduate faculty of social sciences. As we shall see, even though he was severely reprimanded by INED and stripped of some formal positions, he could remain both within and outside it. Le Bras was not without support from some colleagues, who defended his right to be a maverick.

The press, some of La Bras's enemies, and later Le Bras himself made sure that the affair would continue. The chastising of Le Bras by his INED colleagues was hardly unexpected, given the ferocity of his criticism and the embarrassment his broadsides brought to a publicly funded institution. But to some of his supporters, notably Elisabeth Badinter, a feminist writer prominent in socialist circles, INED's treatment of him smacked of a "Moscow trial." Instead of favoring open debate, INED preferred silencing a critic by removing him from positions of responsibility. Nothing of the sort had occurred, she observed, when other members of INED joined right-wing campaigns against immigration or associated with the National Front. As Badinter provocatively put it, "Does the National Front want to infiltrate INED to lead it back to its original goals, as the Fondation Alexis Carrel for the study of human problems, created by [Marshal] Pétain?" The Fondation Carrel had indeed been the predecessor of INED, and its founder did have a questionable political past. But what matters here is her claim that Le Bras was being punished for exposing an extreme right-wing plot to manipulate France's leading demographic institution.[6] This unsubstantiated charge further poisoned the atmosphere.

One can see how quickly this dispute about the birthrate became personally acrimonious and politically heated. To the weekly *L'Express,* it was a war of "Christian demographers versus social demographers." To the more irreverent *Canard Enchaîné,* it was a cacophony of "Baby babadoum" (nonsense talk about fertility).[7] Such attention is the nightmare of most public institutions and was bound to shake INED to its foundations.

At a heated and lengthy meeting of INED's scientific committee on 15 June 1990, Le Bras's criticisms were aired. A substantial report by the distinguished demographer Roland Pressat was distributed, refuting all Le Bras's accusations about INED's supposed selective reporting of fertility trends. Le Bras was not present but was given a copy of the report; an hour later, he was invited in to explain his position. He maintained that his quarrel was not with INED but with French pro-natalism. He criticized INED for playing a "mediating role" in conditioning the public to think along pro-natalist lines. In particular, he objected to the concept of "the replacement of generations," which by definition excluded migration as a factor in population growth. He objected to the fact that a full debate on these matters had not taken place and that instead of confronting him in person the director of INED had gone on the air.

After Le Bras left the meeting, the committee reached a compromise. It did not condemn Le Bras by name but deplored that a technical discussion had degenerated into a nonscientific debate. Above all, it reaffirmed that INED was "a public establishment, both scientific and technological," that "had always diffused regularly and commented objectively in its diverse publications on the different indicators of the evolution of French fertility." A committee of three internationally respected demographers outside INED was nominated to clarify the technical issues of period versus cohort fertility. This anodyne report was written, filed, probably unread by all but a handful of people, and that, many at INED hoped, was the end of that.[8]

They were wrong. Only in Paris could this imbroglio have taken place. It had all the flavor of a war of intellectuals, which appears to be a regular necessity in the hothouse atmosphere of the French capital, but to understand the contretemps, one must step outside the circle of antagonists.

The morning broadcast of Radio Europe 1 on 4 May 1990 opened the hostilities. An exchange began with the interviewer, T. G. Burgeon (not Le Bras), offering these provocative remarks:

BOURGEON: If I were to tell you that the French have enough children, that the population is replacing itself and has done so since the war, you would laugh. Long ago, demographers assured us that the opposite is true. Well, they lied and they admit it. INED affirms in effect in its review *Population and Society* that the birthrate has never been threatened. One of the greatest French experts, Hervé Le Bras, makes his "mea culpa" and admits that the alarmist discourse has taken a serious blow.

LE BRAS: This fear of a weak birthrate and population decline has accentuated the fear of the foreigner. For certain politicians, the fact that there was a demographic decline and that some believed this to be so meant we were going to be invaded.

But the contrary was true, Le Bras noted, since, "by itself and without migration, the French population was growing and would continue to grow."[9] So much for the fear of both depopulation and the "alien wave." These were fighting words, though Bourgeon had coined most of them. Le Bras did not say INED had lied, but he passed over the statement when the interviewer made it. (On reflection, he thought the use of the word "lie" was a tactical mistake; the term was a little strong though "true enough."[10]) In subsequent interviews, he rejected the idea that INED had lied but insisted that the institution's pro-natalist bias affected its choice of indexes and its interpretation of data about fertility. Whenever possible, INED relied on data that raised the alarm about low fertility.

In Calot's article on France and Sweden, though, the opposite was true. When it suited his purpose, Le Bras suggested, Calot shifted attention from the period rate (below replacement) to the cohort rate (higher, and at the magical 2.1 replacement level). In Le Bras's view, Calot did so to show that the nation's investment in its future through family allowances and other supports of childbearing families was paying off.

According to Le Bras, the pro-natalist bias of French demography, as practiced by INED, unduly emphasized the negative consequences of low fertility, especially with respect to the aging of populations; preferred indigenous growth to immigration; and made an (unproved) assertion that French family policy increased fertility. These ideological positions were corrosive, he thought, because they formed a quasi-religious doctrine, which no one had had the courage to challenge, and pernicious, because they predisposed INED demographers to collect and analyze data that confirmed their prejudices. If they were innocent of lying, they were guilty of bad science.

This was harsh enough, but, after a brief lull in hostilities in 1991, encouraged in the interest of science by the Minister of Research and supported by the administrative council of INED itself,[11] Le Bras resumed the attack by producing a book titled *Marianne et les lapins: L'Obsession démographique* (Marianne and the rabbits: The demographic obsession), a broadside against the institutional and intellectual origins of the French pro-natalist consensus.

First, he analyzed the character and origins of INED. To Le Bras, INED, in its big concrete building in southern Paris, was a "bunker," a structure appropriate for an authoritarian institution. With its close press liaisons, its isolation from other disciplines, its domination of French demographic research, its denigration of foreign currents of thought on fertility, and its strong bureaucratic support from the French government, INED exercised a form of "thought control" on the way population issues were discussed in France. It was, he argued, a "narrow school of social engineering" committed to a political objective while claiming the mantle of disinterested science. Its monopoly was explicitly committed to maintaining a pro-natalist consensus.[12]

The origins of INED's authoritarianism he argued, lay in its early history. INED, a post-1945 creation, bore the marks of earlier initiatives in social biology. The most important was the Fondation Carrel, established in 1942 for "safeguarding, improving and developing the French population in all its activities." While remote from the sinister aspects of the Vichy regime, this institute revealed an antidemocratic authoritarianism embedded in the social biology of the time. It aimed, Le Bras argued, at the domination of the technician over the scientist and of both over the people. In 1946, the foundation was transformed into INED, according to

Le Bras, with the same aim and personnel; both were agencies of dirig-isme (guidance of the economy by the French state) and social engineer-ing. Over the years, the pedigree of its pro-natalism may have been obscured, but with the growth of new right-wing groups, especially the National Front, the links between INED's past and present have emerged, Le Bras said. From the 1940s to the present, we see "pro-natalist panic, fear of invasion, familial ideology, anti-parliamentarianism, anxious na-tionalism." It was not surprising, he argued, that INED detested the idea of its proximity to the extreme right, "because in reality, they are close on several points": they are obsessed with the graying of France; they dwell on fears of invasion (by North Africans); they prefer women as mothers rather than as active citizens; and they are committed to pointing out the dangers of low fertility and the merits of policies aimed at raising the birthrate. Precisely because of its implicit yet unacknowledged ideology, INED, in his view, had to be exposed as lacking scientific detachment and objectivity. Instead of advancing science, Le Bras charged, it fostered an "ideological nuisance" full of dangers: "It [pro-natalism] infests dis-cussions about pensions, it masks the role of productivity, it devalues immigrants when the opposite is urgent. Pro-natalism has withdrawn from the republican arena and has moved closer and closer to the ex-treme right." Note the emphasis on the devaluation of immigrants in a discussion of attitudes about fertility among French demographers. Our central thesis—the recent convergence of these two issues—here be-comes apparent. Because it clouded the subject of immigration and other social issues, pro-natalism had to be stripped of its scientific patina and exposed as a conservative ideology.

Le Bras made plenty of mistakes in his indictment of INED. His anal-ysis of the continuities between the work of the Fondation Carrel and INED was unconvincing. A similar case on the other side of the English Channel shows that origins and outcomes are not necessarily linked, as he claimed. Professional demography in Britain also developed in part out of eugenics. The Population Investigation Committee, affiliated with the London School of Economics, received (and continues to receive) financial support from the British Eugenics Society, whose aims in the 1930s were similar to those of the Fondation Carrel. But funding never set the agenda of the Population Investigation Committee or its journal,

Population Studies. This organization pioneered in teaching demography in Britain, and its director, David Glass, held a virtual monopoly on the subject. Hardly a man of the political right, his close control of teaching and research over four decades deeply affected the development of demography in Britain. But, despite the historical parallels, in Britain pro-natalism neither dominated demographic debate nor formed an intellectual consensus, either among experts or in the population at large.[13]

What gives pro-natalism its force in France is, rather, its appeal as a touchstone of French national identity. Le Bras was right to emphasize the nationalist assumptions of much French demography. Calot may indeed be a pro-natalist, but so too are most patriotic French men and women, and so were their fathers and mothers and grandfathers and grandmothers. Pro-natalism is a code, a mode of discourse through which French people express their Frenchness. INED did not invent pro-natalism, and its arcane publications have little force in the genesis or dissemination of the idea.

As Le Bras himself showed, INED was born at the moment of the most spectacular revival of the birthrate in modern French history. Indeed, from 1945 to 1990, France registered the most substantial rate of aggregate demographic growth at any time since 1700. But this development ran counter to more than two centuries of experience and explanation that linked slow population growth and declining fertility with economic and political decline. Old attitudes die hard, especially when they offer a convenient explanation for political and social failures, the origins of which lay well outside the demographic realm.

France, in fact, pioneered controlled fertility. In the eighteenth century, nearly a hundred years before Britain's or Germany's, French fertility began to decline and French population patterns diverged from those of its European neighbors. In 1700, the French population had been larger than that of Britain or the host of German states; two centuries later, that demographic primacy had been lost. Given sluggish rates of aggregate population growth, attributable to the early onset of fertility decline, and given the relative loss of political and economic power vis-à-vis Germany and Britain, it is hardly surprising that many French politicians and demographers found in fertility trends the key to the eclipse of French preeminence in European affairs. Once installed, this political language linking *dénatalité* with decline of every other kind matured into a hallmark of French political culture.

French politics has a long tradition of unstable political institutions and vitriolic conflict over political and social issues, but little overt division has occurred over pro-natalism and family policy. From the early twentieth century, learned bodies and political groups have engaged in an ongoing struggle to increase public awareness of the dangers of low fertility. This was in part an expression of conservative Roman Catholic opinion, but liberals and socialists contributed to the consensus in both political forums and the arts. The few anarchists and feminists who supported abortion were marginalized and subjected to prosecution.

The difference between rhetoric and reproductive behavior has rarely been clearer than in France. One reason for the longevity of the pro-natalist tradition is that decade after decade French fertility behavior refused to respond to it. The multiple campaigns against *dénatalité* are best understood as expressing a cultural code of nationalist anxieties rather than of personal commitments.

Even when fertility rates rose after 1940, pro-natalist ideas retained their rhetorical force. Even now, time-honored sentiments lie behind the pro-natalist consensus: a belief in the unique virtues of French civilization, a pride in its language and culture (expressed in a wish to expand the Francophone world), an intense attachment to the landscape of France. These nationalist ideas are too deeply ingrained in the political culture of France to be reduced to the language of technocratic or ideological manipulation. From the French Revolution on, France's republican regime has been intensely nationalist and committed to a universalist "civilizing" mission. It exported its republican ideas to the Low Countries and the German states; it threatened the hegemony of monarchical powers, supported the United States against Britain, and left a legacy of freethinking that has survived to this day.

On the French right, the very individualism of the Revolution was believed to be a solvent of family ties—herein lies one source of the French preoccupation with the "disappearance" of the family, for conservatives' cri de coeur on this matter was part of the rhetoric of reaction and extended to more liberal groups. And the widespread worry about the family reflected demographic realities. The decline of fertility in

42

France, a country still overwhelmingly rural as late as 1870, was unde-niable. In the countryside, French men and women were committed to family continuity and family pride, but they were also determined to avoid the downward social mobility that seemed inevitable when land was divided among a large number of siblings. This paradox was the bedrock on which pro-natalism rested: it was an ideology for the nation but not a prescription for the rural family. It pointed to what France should do but not, as it were, what we or our neighbors could or would do. This is why pro-natalism spanned the political spectrum but had no effect on fertility rates through the period of French fertility decline.[14]

Pro-natalism served other purposes too. The Third Republic, born after the catastrophic defeat by Prussia in the war of 1870–71, was weak, and it presided over a deeply divided nation. Religious divisions cut across class divisions, and there were complicated disputes over the re-lationship between the army and the state. What better way to paper over these problems and present the illusion of harmony than to develop an ideology of the French nation as a family, the growth and well-being of which were the interest and pride of all?

The military implications of pro-natalism were never far removed from the public gaze. Conscription was the rule in late-nineteenth-century France, and the greater numbers and military strength of Ger-many were a constant reproach to and reminder of French inferiority. The victory of France and the Allies in World War I did not change this obsession with numbers. On the contrary: the terrible bloodletting of the war, in which 1.3 million French soldiers lost their lives, was but further reason to advocate an increased birthrate as a national necessity.

This position has been as much a touchstone of left-wing opinion in France as of right or Roman Catholic opinion for historical reasons. The *levée en masse* (popular conscription) of the French Revolution is a sym-bol of republican militancy, and in the Franco-Prussian war of 1870–71 it was the revolutionary Communards (supporters of the Paris Com-mune) who wanted to continue the war; the right were the defeatists. With a brief hiatus during the Dreyfus affair at the turn of the twentieth century, French patriotism has been as much an article of faith on the left as on the right. After the second debacle of 1940, when the Third Republic fell and was replaced by the Vichy regime that collaborated with the occupying German forces, socialists and Communists were central in the Resistance to the Nazis and their allies. So left-wing patriotism was a powerful force at precisely the moment INED was formed.

The creation of that institution was much more an expression of the special and enduring features of French nationalism, stated in demographic terms, than of the sinister features of Vichy France. Vichy had simply embraced the pro-natalism of the Third Republic and then passed it on.

A key agent of continuity in family policy was the economist Alfred Sauvy. The author of many books on demography, nearly all of which proclaim the dangers of low French fertility, he is the real bête noire of Le Bras—and rightly so, for Sauvy's pro-natalism is inscribed in the 1939 Code de la famille (family law), in learned studies, in editorial columns he wrote for Le Monde and other newspapers, and in the public profile and policy papers of the institution where he worked until his death in 1993 at the age of ninety-one.[15] Behind INED and Calot stood the legacy of Sauvy, not of Alexis Carrel or a right-wing cabal.

INED is a public institution, charged with engaging in scientific research and analysis and informing the French government of the nature and consequences of demographic trends. Operating in the public realm and publicly funded, it must take note of political trends and broader political currents, of which nationalism is not the least important, especially given the pace of European integration. But this is not to say INED cuts its cloth to suit its master; rather, it shares a language of national pride with the French political elite and with most of the population.

Another flaw in Le Bras's assault on INED was his claim that evidence had been distorted to suit a prior commitment to pro-natalism. But this charge credits his opponents with a Machiavellian subtlety that does not bear close scrutiny. Calot's Franco-Swedish comparison, which precipitated l'affaire INED, is a case in point. The dispute was about which of two fertility measures to use: the cohort rate, which bears the weight of the past; or the period rate, which is a snapshot of reproductive behavior at a given point in time. Le Bras accused Calot of choosing a rate that suited his ideological purpose: the period rate below the notional replacement level of 2.1 will do for some purposes; the cohort rate at 2.1 will do for others. But the use of different indicators is hardly a sleight of hand or a conjuring trick; fertility is notoriously difficult to measure, and the utility of any given indicator depends on the questions being addressed.

Calot used a cohort measure to show that French fertility levels were less bad than those of other European countries and that this relative advantage was due to family policy. Both these assertions are suspect, and Le Bras was correct that the first reflects Calot's support for pro-natalism, a view he never sought to hide. The preference for higher fertility is ideological, not demographic. It is also true that the second claim, linking rising French cohort fertility to family policy, was made entirely without evidence. The best research shows that family allowances have a minuscule effect on fertility rates.[16] Otherwise, how can one explain the rough similarity of British fertility rates, with no substantial program of family allowances, and French fertility rates, supposedly buoyed by numerous pro-natalist measures? Calot's assertion once again is ideological, not scientific. But it reflects his considered opinion and is not a product of dishonesty, bad faith, or statistical manipulation. On this point, the conspiracy is in the eye of the beholder, a reflection of Le Bras's view that ideology and demographic science can and should be separated.

What is surprising is not that INED and its director are pro-natalist but that Le Bras believed they could operate outside the political culture of which they were a part. He noted that the idea for the book came to him during his participation in a meeting of the World Institute of Science, an organization built on the efforts of Russian scientists to obliterate their crippled past. But this admirable ambition flies in the face of the resurgence of nationalism not only in the former Soviet Union but in other parts of the world. In any case, internationalism is as much an ideology as nationalism, and whether internationalism would produce a value-free demographic science is a matter of opinion. Doubts must remain.

French pro-natalism is nationalism in demographic form. To destroy pro-natalism in the French context, one would have to strip it of its links with a nationalist heritage shared by left and right alike, and shared by the proverbial man in the street as much as by demographers.

If Le Bras's purpose was utopian, his methods suffered from many of the faults of the polemicist, including selective presentation of evidence.* He was surely wrong as well to see the hand of Vichy in the work of the current generation of INED researchers. The institution is staffed by people with many different approaches and outlooks. And among the range of scholars it employs, some suffered deeply in the war years; to accuse them of intellectual or political affinity to fascist ideas is both unwise and untrue. Most are French nationalists, but then so are the vast majority of their compatriots.

Still, in one area, Le Bras's position is strong. He notes the difference between *populationism* (a belief in population growth, whatever the source) and *pro-natalism* (a belief in indigenous growth). The exaggerated emphasis on the need to raise the birthrate, found both in INED writings and elsewhere, suggests an implicit consensus that the best way for France to grow is through its own native sons and daughters rather than through immigration.[17] At a time when the National Front has sponsored a quasi-racist campaign against immigrants, especially North African immigrants, the pro-natalist preference for the native-born is not politically neutral. As elsewhere, the coincidence of below-replacement fertility and large-scale immigration makes population politics in France an explosive issue.

In 1985, this problem was thoroughly aired after the appearance of a provocative article in *Figaro-Magazine* titled "Serons-nous encore Français dans 30 ans?" (Will we still be French in 30 years?). This "dossier on

---

*On one such point, we can speak with some authority. Le Bras cites as an example of the intellectual closure of the INED world the failure of efforts to translate our 1985 book, *The Fear of Population Decline*, into French. Le Bras's account is both true and incomplete. It is true that a contract was signed and later canceled by the publisher. It is true that the reasons given were questionable (allegedly, no translator was available, a highly implausible claim, given the facility in English of many French demographers). It is possible that our skeptical message about the dangers of predicted population decline offended some French scholars. But Le Bras failed to note that Gérard Calot himself agreed to write a preface for the French translation and that other scholars in INED took pains to try to bring the book out. They failed but not because INED refuses to hear divergent views, especially those of foreign scholars. INED has been a gracious host to generations of foreign scholars, whose views, to our knowledge, have never been scrutinized before the hospitality was offered.

immigration" had a color illustration of Marianne, the traditional feminine symbol of the Republic, wearing a chador, the Muslim woman's veil. One author of the article was Jean Raspail, the prizewinning author of a nightmare dystopia satirically titled *Le Camp des saints* (The camp of the saints). It is a novel about the arrival in the South of France of a flotilla of tramp freighters carrying hordes of starving Asians. The other author was Gérard-François Dumont, a self-styled demographer. Their purpose was to describe the future facing French children if nothing was done to alter French demographic movements and immigration policy. A dire future was virtually assured, the authors claimed, if France's political leaders did not lose their indifference to the swamping of the native-born by the "ENE" (non-European foreigners) living in France. The only answer, according to the authors, "other than the spectacular and rapid increase in French births, would be the immediate, radical, and final end of immigration, linked to a massive return of resident immigrants."

Part of the problem, Raspail and Dumont asserted, was that official statistics were false in that they seriously underestimated the number of ENE living in France. This error, on the order of 15–20 percent, occurred for "political reasons" and because inadequate account was taken of clandestine immigration.[18] Once a true statistical picture was formulated, it was obvious that the nation was changing color and character: "In 2015, if nothing is done to reverse the current trend, France will no longer be a nation in the sense [Joseph-Ernest] Renan intended ('the memory of great things which we did together . . .'). She will no longer merit her name. She will be no more than a geographic space."

Reactions to this sensationalist exposé were swift and predictable. The Socialist Prime Minister, Laurent Fabius, denounced the article in the National Assembly and elsewhere as an incitement to racial hatred and segregation. Three other ministers charged that it was "false, provocative, and racist." "A virus more dangerous than AIDS" was one left-wing characterization of the alleged racism of the *Figaro* article. On the center-right, there was cautious criticism, mixed with some anxiety over the electoral appeal of this message to the extremist National Front. Meanwhile the leader of the National Front, Jean-Marie Le Pen, benefited from the publicity and continued to profit from the nativist sentiment such arguments aroused. In 1987, he simply noted, "There's nothing wrong with the birthrate, except that we're not the ones who are making the babies." The royal "we" was unmistakably white and French.[19]

None of these reactions was unanticipated. But the role played by INED in the controversy is interesting: *au dessus de la mêlée*, or above the battle, and dismissive of amateur demographers trying to comment on subjects best left to professionals.

Michèle Tribalat, an expert on international immigration, demolished the assumptions on which the *Figaro* projections were based, and Le Bras was withering in his criticism of what he considered the preposterous nonsense that the Dumont-Raspail article passed off as demographic analysis. Although Dumont and Raspail answered their critics, and claimed standing as "scientific observers," the disdain of INED and other demographers was decisive in public debate.[20] The article, and the furor it stirred up, faded into obscurity. In the imbroglio, INED's standing was clear: It was a professional institute, employing dispassionate observers of demographic trends. A neutral and necessary part of the information-gathering processes of government, it offered a vital point of reference when anyone tried to pass off political argument as scientific evidence. Five years later, in May 1990, Le Bras challenged this neutrality. Is it surprising that in opening a debate about French fertility he wound up alienating most of his colleagues, who were shocked at his charges and determined to reassert their scientific authority?

For our purposes, this incident illuminates the admixture of political ideas and demographic measurements that infuses contemporary debate about fertility, immigration, and national identity in France. While the Gallic features of this story make it unusual, there is little doubt that— perhaps in less extreme form—similar quarrels over the nature and meaning of demographic indicators have occurred elsewhere and are likely to continue. Population politics in Britain, discussed in chapter 3, is a case in point.

BRITAIN AND THE "IMMIGRANT WAVE"

On 14 February 1989, an Indian-born British citizen and novelist, Salman Rushdie, was sentenced to death in absentia by the Ayatollah Khomeini of Iran. His alleged crime had been to slander Islam in his novel *The Satanic Verses*, published the previous year. The *fatwa*, or anathema, enjoined the faithful to seek out and kill Rushdie, who immediately received British police protection and is still in hiding. This affair has brought into relief the difficulties Britain faces as a multicultural society, difficulties exacerbated by developments in international migration and in British policy toward it since the 1960s. Whereas in Germany questions of refugees and asylum predominated and in France anxieties over fertility were widespread, in Britain issues of immigration and ethnicity increasingly came to the fore in this period.

The demographic history of Britain since 1960 resembles that of other western European countries. Whereas aggregate population totals grew from fifty-two million to about fifty-eight million in 1960–90, the total fertility rate declined from 2.71 to 1.84, placing Britain in the category of below-replacement states like France, Germany, and Italy (these latter two have much lower fertility rates than Britain). At the same time, annual net immigration remained stable at about fifty thousand. Though this is a small figure compared to the native population of about fifty-five million, immigration in 1990 nonetheless represented more of Britain's annual population increase than it had done before. In 1970, net migration had accounted for 16 percent of the population increase; in 1990, it accounted for 30 percent.[1]

Immigration flows had a distinctive ethnic character in terms of their origins and a distinctly regional character in terms of their destinations. About 15 percent of the immigrants came from countries of white settlement—Canada, Australia, New Zealand—and about 12 percent came from India and Pakistan. By the late 1980s, ethnic minorities numbered about 2.5 million people, or 4.5 percent of the population of the United Kingdom.[2] And the immigrants tended to settle in certain cities—traditionally London but also Yorkshire towns with immigrant communities like Leeds and Bradford, where earlier English population growth had either ceased or been reversed through emigration. The northern areas were among the hardest hit by industrial contraction and mass unemployment during the 1970s and 1980s; prosperous and well-educated people tended to move away from the cities, which reduced the employment opportunities and tax base for municipal social services when new immigrants settled there. In short, thousands of immigrants were absorbed into declining towns with concentrations of disadvantaged groups, who were progressively marginalized during the years of Margaret Thatcher's government (1979–90).[3]

International immigrants have always clustered in England's cities. When worrisome race riots occur, as in Bradford in 1994, everyone is concerned, until other problems come to the fore; then the well-to-do in both political parties trim expenditures in the interest of economic recovery and reduced inflation, decreasing benefits to those already marginalized. And when some in the immigrant community have larger families and a much higher birthrate than do their neighbors of British stock, the problems are magnified:

The Asian community has twice the proportion of under-16-year-olds the white population has. Only 2 per cent of the Asian population is over the age of 65, compared with 17 per cent of whites. The average British Asian family has about five members, compared with 2.4 among whites. Demographers predict, combining these trends, that the Asian community is set to double from around 1.5 per cent of the population. Most observers think that the practice of Islam will grow at least proportionately, if not more.[4]

Immigration in contemporary Britain has thus taken on a significance different from that in Germany and France. Eighty years ago, British opinion on population questions focused on two overlapping
problems: first, the high fertility of poor families, who lived in slum
conditions that bred disease, crime, and urban squalor that, many argued, were leading to what was termed "the deterioration of the British
race"; second, the low and declining fertility of well-to-do families from
which the leaders of British society were drawn. The future looked grim
to those who saw this as a demographic signal of national decline. And
in the 1930s, fears of "race suicide" accompanied reports of ongoing
fertility decline in Britain. A Royal Commission on Population was established in 1944 in order to suggest corrective measures. By the time
the commission reported in 1949, a postwar economic revival was under
way and so, too, was an upturn in the British birthrate.

Since the 1960s, when British fertility declined again, there has been
little public debate or anxiety over this feature common to western European countries.[5] However, the question of immigration has never
ceased to be a source of controversy, in this respect, as it is in France.
Immigration showed distinctive features of the British past still affecting
the present. Until the 1970s, all citizens of the British Commonwealth
had right of entry to Britain; this had been the case since its foundation
after World War II. On the other hand, there was a time-honored and
unrestricted ebb and flow of populations between Ireland and Britain.
Underlying much of the debate was an endemic racism, though it had
only once been central to a mass political movement: the New Party, led
in the 1930s by Oswald Mosley and quickly consigned by the electorate
to the remote margins of British politics. Other recent racist groups have
drawn more journalistic attention than votes.

Two developments made immigration a matter of major political and
social conflict. A combination of the British Commonwealth Immigration
Act of 1971 and liberalizing reforms in U.S. immigration law in 1965 produced a decline in Caribbean immigration to Britain, while immigration
from the Indian subcontinent remained stable (through admission of family members of current residents). This meant that more nonwhite immigrants to Britain were Hindu and Muslim than Christian. Most Muslim
immigrants to Britain quickly assimilated, but fundamentalists brought to

the fore questions about the compatibility of a devout Muslim outlook with the "norms" of British life, and they did so with a vengeance after the publication of Rushdie's novel.

The second development, potentially the most significant for the long-term future of Britain, was the formulation of European Community policy on immigration from outside the Community and free movement within it. Together, these two matters transformed the character and raised the temperature of population debates in Britain.

Salman Rushdie was born in Bombay on 18 June 1947, eight weeks before Indian independence, to a prosperous Muslim family; his father had attended King's College, Cambridge, and had brought his family up with a deep respect for British culture. Rushdie's childhood was spent, in the words of the title to his 1981 novel, as one of "midnight's children," those born in the shadow of the freedom and bloodshed attending partition of Hindu India and Muslim Pakistan. After attending the Cathedral School of Bombay, he traveled the time-honored path of the sons of well-to-do Indian families and continued his education at Rugby School, in the British Midlands, and at King's College, Cambridge, from which he graduated with a degree in history in 1968. By then, his family had moved to Pakistan, where Rushdie temporarily went after Cambridge.

Education at a renowned English public school and Cambridge produces in some foreign-born students an internal cultural divide, making them strangers in both Britain and their native countries. Rushdie had become, he said repeatedly, a non-Muslim Muslim, a British Asian, a non-European European. The ambivalence of his approach to both British and South Asian society and politics dominates virtually all his writing. In *Shame* (1983), he exposed the corruption of the military and political elite of Pakistan, "that fantastic bird of a place, two wings without a body, sundered by the land-mass of its greatest foe, joined by nothing but God." In light of future developments, it is indeed ironic that *Shame* was named Novel of the Year by Iran's Ministry of Islamic Guidance.[6]

In *Shame*, Rushdie presented a thinly disguised Benazir Bhutto, later to become President of Pakistan, in the form of the Virgin Ironpants.

In *Midnight's Children*, he conjured up the frightening figure of the Black Widow, easily decipherable as Indira Gandhi during the state of siege she introduced in 1977.[7] Following in the footsteps of the unlikely trio of Rabelais, Jonathan Swift, and Gabriel García Márquez, Rushdie brought to his fiction a flare for mixing the beautiful, the venal, and the grotesque in South Asian society. Awarded the prestigious Booker Prize in England for the best work of fiction in 1985, Rushdie had indeed arrived in English literary culture.

The casus belli between Rushdie and upholders of the Islamic faith was the publication of *The Satanic Verses* in 1988. This complex mixture of satire and fantasy presented two distinct stories. One concerns the degrading treatment nonwhite immigrants receive in British society. Rushdie portrays the plight of two unintentional immigrants deposited on British soil by parachute after their plane is blown up by terrorists. One of them, half goat, half man, is beaten and humiliated by police and immigration officials who scrutinize him on arrival. He enters the city of London, "a Crusoe-city, marooned on the island of its past, and trying, with the help of a Man-Friday underclass, to keep up appearances."[8]

No one escapes the caustic bath of fictional farce: Indians and West Indians in Britain are lampooned as wildly as the companions of the Prophet himself in the second narrative. This part of the novel—which has totally eclipsed the satire of Britain—sets the story of Muhammad in a dream of one of its characters, who wants to make his fortune by turning it into a movie.

All these literary devices and tricks were of no concern to the fundamentalist faithful: they took the text at face value, the last thing one should do with such a novel. Comedy, notes the Mexican writer Octavio Paz, "renders ambiguous everything it touches."[9] Maybe so, but in a religion where there is only one text, the Koran, and it is the voice of God himself, ambiguity is anathema to the devout.

What apparently was most offensive was Rushdie's elaboration of the medieval legend that Satan insinuated some lines into the Koran by whispering them surreptitiously in Muhammad's ear. These were fighting words, for the Koran is not like the sacred texts of Christians and Jews, part of an elaborate canonical tradition that has evolved over time. To the faithful, the Koran is *the* word of God, of unique integrity and sanctity, and to satirize its composition and sacred status is to undermine Islam itself. This challenge to the holy character of the Koran hit Islamic fundamentalists at the heart of their faith.

Rushdie added insult to injury: He named prostitutes after the twelve wives of Muhammad and called Mecca "Jahilia," or ignorance in Arabic. He gave Muhammad the name Mahound and conjured up an older non-Muslim tradition in which Mahound the Prophet is a charlatan or madman. What more did devout Muslims need to hear before concluding that Rushdie had moved from the field of fiction to a political polemic aimed to discredit Islam itself?

To mix the profane and the sacred in this way is a well-known conceit among Western writers: Nikos Kazantzakis's *Last Temptation of Christ* and Bertolt Brecht's *Good Woman of Szechuan* come to mind. In addition, the British comedy entourage Monty Python satirized numerous biblical stories in *Life of Brian*, a film that offended some devout Christians. This is hardly surprising: the film ends with a scene of dozens of men tied to crosses singing, "Always look on the bright side of life."

But limits still exist, even in Britain. It is likely that a British satire of King David, the sweet singer of Zion, as a pedophile would lead to Jewish protests and outraged accusations of anti-Semitism. And in 1976, musty statutes on blasphemy were exhumed to indict and convict the poet James Kirkup and the gay journal in which he published a poem, "The love that dares to speak its name," in which a Roman centurion has homosexual thoughts about Christ on the cross.[10]

British Muslims outraged by *The Satanic Verses* had no recourse to British laws on blasphemy, which did not extend to Islam. Instead, they took to the streets. On 14 January 1989, copies of *The Satanic Verses* were burned publicly in Bradford, home to a large population of Muslims whose origins were in poor rural areas of Pakistan. Two weeks later, thousands of Muslims demonstrated against Rushdie in London's Hyde Park. Overseas, the book also became a cause célèbre. It had already been banned in Bangladesh, Saudi Arabia, South Africa, and India. This is the background to the death sentence on Rushdie pronounced by the Ayatollah Khomeini on 14 February. Six demonstrators were killed in Islamabad in mass protests over Rushdie's supposed vilification of Islam, and he was barred from India.[11] A long diplomatic tangle ensued in which

British-Iranian and European-Iranian relations were put into question. As one journalist stated, "Rushdie and his book continue to inflame the world like the biting of an irrepressible flea."[12] Not until 7 September 1995, six years later, did Rushdie appear in public in England, at a Westminster City Hall in a debate titled "Writers Against the State."[13] He is still a marked man.

The Rushdie affair was explosive because it touched on a central question: Are Islamic beliefs compatible with citizenship in a European country? Britain has absorbed generations of immigrants, most of whom have faced prejudice and overcome it to contribute in diverse ways to British society. The unwritten social contract is that immigrants show tolerance and decency in their public affairs, prerequisites of assimilation for more than a century, ever since formal restrictions on Roman Catholic and Jewish participation in England's political life were lifted. The reaction of British Muslims to Rushdie's book challenged that contract, just as the treatment of other writers in Islamic countries represented an assault on what commentators, left and right, like to call "fair play."[14] It is the public morality of Charles Dickens and George Orwell, deeply ingrained in British culture, and the core of widely held beliefs that are no less strong because rarely articulated. This is why Prime Minister Thatcher, who disliked Rushdie and stood for everything he despised, provided police protection for him. A death sentence for publishing a novel was simply unthinkable in Britain.

But it was not unthinkable to many British Muslims. Here the vulnerability of their community may have played a part. Faced by the temptations of Western culture, British Muslims from South Asia feared losing their children to secularism. In 1990, the Muslim Institute published "The Muslim Manifesto—a Strategy for Survival," which announced that Muslims must obey the law "so long as that obedience does not conflict with their commitment to Islam and the *Ummah*."[15] And while this is a general stricture adhered to by many Christians and Jews, too, they have not in recent centuries called publicly for the death of a writer. Not speaking Arabic—the language of the Koran—as their native tongue, these Asian Muslims in Britain may also have been even more vigilant in defense of their holy text; they lacked the self-confidence to ignore a novel written by a Muslim-born writer who had ceased to be-

56

lieve in Islam. Since Islam is a total ideology, linking all behavior in a seamless whole, many Muslims agreed that life should be denied to a blasphemer.[16]

Thus did the Rushdie affair bring into high relief the issue of Muslim assimilation of British "values." Some extreme voices within the Muslim community in Britain took up the challenge. In August 1995, Hizb al-Tahrir (Liberation Party), a prominent radical organization of British Muslims, published an emphatic declaration: "Muslims do not believe in integration," it announced; "Muslims must continue to present their Islamic identity . . . In fact we are Muslims in Britain and we are not British Muslims."[17]

The question of the compatibility of non-European, non-Christian, or even nonwhite immigrants with British society had come to prominence earlier, in 1968, when Conservative Member of Parliament, Enoch Powell, delivered a dire warning to the British public. "As I look forward," he intoned ominously, "I am filled with a foreboding. Like the Roman, I seem to see the River Tiber foaming with much blood."[18] Powell was a classical scholar. His target was not the academy but the immigrant community in Britain, threatening (as he saw it) the peace and stability of the English people, especially in the cities, where they were concentrated. The answer, for Powell, was to end nonwhite immigration and to finance repatriation for those who wished it.

In 1973, Powell returned to this theme. Immigrants, he said (without specifying their race or religion), were "an active volcano" ready to erupt in urban Britain. One of his political opponents, Roy Hattersley, remembered the reaction of his Asian constituents in Birmingham. To be described as dangerous simply because you were black was bad enough but, "when a man who has been a professor, a brigadier, and a minister attacks racial minorities, racism begins to look respectable."[19] The language was jarring to international observers, too, who heard Powell's first speech just before the assassination of Martin Luther King, Jr., in the United States and a few months before Northern Ireland flowed with Irish blood. But what was most intriguing was the reaction of the Conservative Party: simply put, Powell was run out.

The reasons were twofold. First, the Conservatives, then in opposition but in power in 1970–74 and 1979–97, were unwilling to tolerate a populist campaign from their right wing. The ruling center, then under Edward Heath and in 1990–97 under John Major, had no tolerance for extremist views or for the divisions they would bring, knowing that Powell spoke for a fraction of the party (and nation) but not its ruling part. Second, and more important, Powell was committing the same "sin" that the Muslim demonstrators against Rushdie were to commit twenty years later: he broke the social contract of tolerance and decency, the rule that public discourse in Britain is conducted within boundaries, which exclude many (though not all) of the vicious calumnies about one's opponents that mar political discourse in "Other Countries," as Dickens's Mr. Podsnap would have put it.

The same treatment was meted out to another maverick Conservative M.P., Winston Churchill III, grandson of the wartime Prime Minister, when, in February 1995, he told the Association of Conservative Graduates in London that the "relentless flow" of immigrants "was threatening Britain's traditional way of life." He charged that officials were intentionally understating immigration, which instead of the official figure of fifty thousand was at least a hundred thousand a year, thereby producing one million immigrants each decade. Race relations were bound to be placed under an "intolerable strain" unless action were taken, he said.[20] Churchill's views were denounced by the party leaders, who handled him with the same disdain shown to Powell in 1968.

As we shall see below, populist conservatives in Canada have been able to mount a serious challenge to national elites, but they needed a regional basis to do so. Such an alternative power base within England was unavailable to Powell, whose subsequent career as a Northern Ireland M.P. relegated him to the political wilderness, or to Churchill, who faced the same fate; how he will respond is still an open question.

Between 1968 and 1995, this already difficult issue of immigration became increasingly tangled with the issue of European integration. It is hardly surprising that Powell remained a strident voice in England's campaign against joining Europe. In 1974, just before voting began in national elections, he intoned in Birmingham:

> This is the first and last election at which the British people will be given the opportunity to decide whether their country is to remain a democratic nation, governed by the will of its own electorate expressed in its own parliament, or whether it will become one province of a new European superstate under institutions which know nothing of the political rights and liberties that we have so long taken for granted.

This was a direct attack on Prime Minister Heath, the pro-European leader of his party; as it happened, the Conservatives lost the election.[21]

Fifteen years later, Powell stood his ground. Leaving the Conservative Party, he stood as a Unionist (Protestant) M.P. in Northern Ireland. His two bêtes noires remained the European Community and immigration. The 1972 European Communities Act "cast a curse on all those who were responsible for it, or who supported it, or who defend it," and as for immigration, he was not "surprised by the persistence if not the growth of the same alarm to which I gave voice in 1968."[22]

The link between the two issues was that the European Community gives a right of free movement within it, a right that threatened to take from British officials the authority to control entry into Britain. In 1971, immigration had been restricted to dependents of people already resident in Britain and people with work permits, provisions that applied to citizens of the New Commonwealth (India, Pakistan, and Nigeria, among others) in the same way they did to anyone outside the European Community. In 1987, the right of dependents of bona fide residents to entry was made subject to proof that they could be supported.

Both measures tightened restrictions, but it is important to note that net immigration was negative between 1966 and 1982, since migration to Canada, Australia, and New Zealand continued to exceed immigration from those countries to Britain. Moreover, a new destination was now Europe: by the 1990s, about 350,000 British citizens were living in the European Community, perhaps half of them having arrived since Britain entered the Common Market in 1973. Some Europeans moved to Britain, though in smaller numbers: in 1995, 38,000 French and 42,000 Germans were living in Britain.[23]

Entry into the European Community challenged British sovereignty in many ways—the issue of a common currency is one—but control over refugees, asylum seekers, and immigrants was the most salient. The nightmare of anti-Europeans was that officials in Brussels would enable migrants turned away from Britain's tight immigration controls to enter Britain through the back door, by successful application to more lenient Community members. The Conservatives responded by separating control of migration to Britain from membership in the European Community and then tightening British rules on refugees and asylum seekers. Much publicity attended the repatriation of illegal immigrants and those whose right to entry was denied.[24]

Still, the terms of the debate in Britain are framed to stop poor and unskilled people (many, though not all, of whom are not white) from adding to the rolls of those supported by the Unemployment Benefit and the National Health Service. The fact that most immigrants who come to Britain to work are highly skilled and stay only briefly is ignored.[25] Images hold more sway than realities.

Such fears of the putative burden of supporting immigrants have been exacerbated by a second worry: that hordes of Russians and eastern Europeans desperate to move west for a better life might be let in to Germany or another European country and, through the Community's open borders, arrive in Britain. Britain has reserved the right to restrict immigration from third countries via Europe, but the European Parliament has taken Britain to the European Court for failing to uphold the principle of the free movement of peoples.[26] This issue became prominent in the spring of 1995, with the resignation of the minister responsible for immigration at the Home Office, Charles Wardle. "I believe Brussels threatens to push this country down a dangerous road" was the way he put it. Unless forceful action was taken, he argued, "the trend towards a frontier-free Europe will be unstoppable . . . That is why I have decided to stand aside so I can argue and fight openly on an issue which affects every one of us."[27] He wanted an ironclad guarantee that European Community membership would not preclude passport checks at British ports of entry. Such assurances may not be politically practicable; if so, he asked, where does British sovereignty stand?

The treatment of asylum seekers is also a subject of intense political debate. The former head of the immigration service, Peter Tompkins, said in 1995 that Britain was a "soft touch" for asylum seekers, because they retained the right to welfare benefits and medical care there while their cases were being reviewed. He also claimed that official statistics played down the scope of the immigration problem. The press took up the charge. "More than 100 immigrants a day have claimed political asylum in Britain this year," reported the conservative *Daily Mail* in September 1995, and, worse, the flow was rising in Britain while it was falling on the Continent. Each asylum seeker costs "the taxpayer £100 per week in income support and housing benefits," though "many" applied "only when they were arrested for criminal offenses." The Home Office moved to deny these benefits to applicants appealing negative judgments on their claims, but the courts threw out such action as arbitrary and unjust.[28]

Other voices were raised to defend asylum seekers. The lawyer Chris Randall noted, "People in Britain have become so indoctrinated that they cannot hear the word 'asylum-seeker' without thinking 'bogus.' " Even when the grounds for seeking asylum appear firm, as in cases of people from the former Yugoslavia, the bureaucracy works to the disadvantage of those in need. In November 1992, such applicants rose to more than five thousand. The British government announced that no Bosnian could travel to Britain without a visa, but there was no British embassy in Sarajevo to issue one; if a Bosnian reached a British embassy somewhere else, he or she would have to stay there. The result: a drop in asylum seekers from the war zone of the former Yugoslavia.[29]

Most of the remaining applicants for asylum are from Africa (Zaire and Nigeria) and Asia (Turkey, Sri Lanka, and Pakistan). The son of a Nigerian dissident executed by the military regime was denied asylum, though his case was reopened after a public outcry. For asylum seekers from Turkey, Pakistan, and other nations of the Middle East and Asia, there is the additional fear that fundamentalist Muslims will use tolerant Britain to launch attacks on West-leaning dictatorships. For example, the Home Secretary ordered one Saudi dissident, Muhammed al-Masari, expelled from Britain for compromising Britain's friendly and very profitable relations with the Saudi regime. As one commentator put it, "Arab ambassadors welcomed the move against Dr. al-Masari as the first step in making London a more hostile environment for Islamic activists"—a statement that appeared in the right-wing *Times*, which also printed one of Dr. al-Masari's statements with the comment that it mixes "fact, rumor and libel."[30] In case readers didn't get the point, below the article was a picture of the international terrorist "Carlos," who was neither Muslim nor Arab but still signified all the fears that Britain now attached to Middle Easterners. Dr. al-Masari was eventually allowed to remain in Britain, but his case has all the elements of the politics of immigration: conservative fears of dark-skinned foreigners, their worries about the importation into Britain of Middle Eastern violence, and, above all, the vilification of fundamentalist Islam.

Though British politicians have tried to relegate immigration to the margins of politics, it keeps creeping back to the center. That is because it involves questions not of technical administration alone but of principle. To this extent, Enoch Powell was right: "Whose Britain?" is a legitimate question. Some of the answers express conservative yearning to preserve the British way of life. Others are nostalgic, conjuring up a mythic time when Britain was a homogeneous, peaceful place. Immigration threatens this largely fanciful construction of British history.

Other reactions are more sinister, some racist, others xenophobic. But, given the vulnerabilities of the British economy, British finance and industry need the European Community, and in it Britain has less political weight than its stronger neighbors. We have seen how France and Germany benefit from the European Community, first and foremost, by ending the adversary relationship that deformed both countries in this century. Britain lost one million men in the two world wars but was slow to join the European Community; native traditions die hard. Yet too much is invested in Europe and by Europe to change the direction of affairs. The critics are right: a revolution is in progress, changing the character of the British state, and it is largely a silent revolution, kept that way by the leaders of both political parties, who do not want a nativist backlash against full integration in the European Community.

Connecting the European dimension of population politics with the racial and religious one are concerns that Britain will be swallowed up in a European conglomerate and that "the British way of doing things" will be eclipsed by (mostly colored) immigrants, who dress differently, cook differently, pray differently, and act differently from the English majority. In the context of two decades of high unemployment, only recently (1998) abated, one can see the potential for severe political and social conflict in which immigration issues are likely to be at the center of the storm.

PART TWO

EASTERN EUROPE

chapter 4

THE YUGOSLAV TRAGEDY:
FORCED MIGRATION AND ETHNIC CLEANSING

The most clear-cut, most tragic example of an intersection of demographic and political elements in international affairs is offered by Yugoslavia, where the presence of different national and ethnic groups in specific geographical areas has mattered in a very brutal way. Between 1990 and 1995, Bosnian Serb militias and irregulars cleared whole swaths of Bosnia of Bosnian Muslims, who had lived there for centuries. Croat atrocities followed Serb atrocities. Rape became a political weapon used to debase and terrify people of a different ethnic makeup—Croats, Serbs, and, above all, Muslims—and to expel them from land their adversaries claimed. Ethnic cleansing occurred time and again. Forced migration of terrified noncombatants brought the evidence of savagery to every observer with eyes to see.

In late 1995, the warring parties agreed to a partition of Bosnia into a Bosnian Serb area and a mixed Muslim-Croat area. NATO and other troops entered to enforce this agreement, but many territorial claims and ethnic quarrels remained unresolved, as did the indictments of Bosnian Serb political and military leaders at the International Court of Justice at the Hague on charges of crimes against humanity. The bitterness of this war will not vanish like a puff of smoke: too many lives have been brutally crushed; too many civilians have been murdered or abused. And even when a cease-fire was agreed to in 1995, the politics of numbers, ethnicity, and migration created flash points with the disturbing potential for future conflict. For example, four times as many Albanians as Serbs live in the Serbian province of Kosovo, in the south of former Yugoslavia. How will their communities avoid the disastrous spiral of violence that engulfed Bosnia in earlier years?

How did it happen? To answer that question, we need to describe the breakup of Yugoslavia into six independent republics in 1991. Superficially, this fragmentation of an internationally recognized state seems similar to the nearly simultaneous breakup of the Soviet Union, but the two events have different origins and present different problems to their successor states and to the international community.

With the end of the Cold War came an end to the balance of power that had kept the eastern European satellites of the Soviet Union—and even Yugoslavia, though it had broken with the Soviet Union in 1948—from adopting Western political institutions. And the collapse of the Communist Party in the Soviet Union naturally enough weakened the power of other Communist Parties and regimes. In Yugoslavia, this was expected to be less significant than elsewhere, because of its relative independence in international affairs and because the Soviet army was not in place there to enforce Soviet interests; an indigenous Communist Party faced alone the forces tearing the country apart.

Those forces were numerous—ethnic, religious, rural, urban, ideological, political—and each conflict amplified the others. Once violence broke out and war began, the primitive responses of individual and group barbarity were added to an exploitation of these forces by cynical leaders. The result was a seemingly never-ending spiral of cruelty and suffering.

How and why did the breakdown of legitimate authority occur in this European state? First, demography. There is little in Yugoslav demographic history to indicate why the level of ethnic conflict became so lethal. Demographic trends in Yugoslavia have paralleled those in other eastern European countries. In common with the rest of the region (and Europe in general), both period and cohort fertility declined in Yugoslavia—from above the replacement level (2.81) in 1960 to 1.88 in 1992. In 1960, the republics in Yugoslavia varied in fertility levels and rates of fertility decline, fertility in Bosnia, Macedonia, and Montenegro being much higher than in Serbia, Croatia, and Slovenia. Thirty years later, fertility in Bosnia (1.70) was lower than in all the other former Yugoslav republics except Slovenia (1.48) and Croatia (1.69), while Serbia was still at the notional replacement level of 2.1. In effect, Serbian fertility had declined by one-sixth over the thirty years, while Bosnian fertility had halved (though this apparent disparity must be treated cautiously, since

Serbia absorbed the autonomous region of Kosovo during this time, with its large Albanian population of relatively high fertility).[1]

The mortality rate, too, was higher in Serbia than in Bosnia, which had not been the case before. In 1970, infant mortality in Bosnia had been 69.1 deaths per 1,000 live births; in Serbia, 56.3; in 1990, the former had declined to 15.3, the latter to 23.2. Once again, Bosnia had made greater progress and in a key datum. (Croatian and Slovenian infant mortality rates were lower than in Serbia and Bosnia both in 1970 and in 1990.) By the 1980s, such differentials among all former Yugoslav republics were relatively minor.

Given the brutality of the armed conflict that attended the breakup of Yugoslavia and the volatility of population movements since then, it is unwise to claim precision for demographic data of the 1990s, but it is important to note that throughout the 1960–90 period the population of many parts of former Yugoslavia was socially and ethnically heterogeneous. For example, one can obtain no reliable statistics on the relative numbers of Serbs, Croats, and Muslims, one reason being the frequency of intermarriage across ethnic lines. Sarajevo, the capital of Bosnia, was and is filled with mixed-origin families, and, even in some rural areas, where the divisions are clearer, purity of ethnic identity is a figment of the imagination. The most obvious conclusion to make is that the demographic profiles of Serbs, Croats, and Bosnians in Yugoslavia converged in 1960–90.[2] Bosnia became more western European, registering an even more striking decline in fertility and mortality rates than Serbia.[3]

So Yugoslavia's recent demographic history resembles that of many other European countries: fertility and mortality declines, decreasing variations among regional and "national" groups. This convergence of vital trends contrasts sharply with the divergence of political trends. It was not demography but how demography was used in increasingly brutal ethnic politics that drove Yugoslavia to disaster.

The political history of the Balkans is fraught with conflict but perhaps no more so than in other parts of eastern and southern Europe. After all, different ethnic groups lived together in the South Slav lands long before the founding of the Yugoslav state in 1919, when, after the war, the imperial holdings of defeated Austria-Hungary were dismantled and reassembled and the Kingdom of the Serbs, Croats, and Slovenes was born. (Notably, Bosnians were not included and received no special treatment in the peace negotiations.)

Three imperial vectors had converged in the Balkans: the German-Austrian vector, pointing south and east; the Russian vector, pointing south and west; and the Turkish vector, pointing north and west. The Allied victors held no brief for any of these powers or their interests: the first and third had been defeated; the second was in the throes of a revolution and civil war. Serbia, on the winning side, had suffered proportionately the highest military losses of any combatant country (37 percent of Serbian men in uniform had died in the war [4]), and what later became Yugoslavia was a post-imperial entity with a powerful Serbian core: initially a monarchy linking Serbs, Croats, and Slovenes in a territory whose boundaries were disputed by all its neighbors except Greece. The new state had neither a homogeneous population nor the sense of a national destiny capable of rallying many ethnic groups. According to the census of 1921, of its 12 million citizens, 1.5 million had a mother tongue that was not Slavic. Ethnic patterns cut across town and country, occupations and families, and ethnic differences became part of the increasingly corrupt politics of the new state. In addition, there were roughly 1.5 million Muslims alongside about 4 million Roman Catholics and 4 million Eastern Orthodox Slavs.

The attempt to create order by establishing a dictatorship under King Alexander in 1929 was the occasion for the birth of Yugoslavia. The name Kingdom of the Serbs, Croats, and Slovenes was dropped as part of Alexander's effort to attenuate the hold of local loyalties and consolidate the powers of the central state, but this effort failed, and the king was assassinated by an agent of Croat extremists—the Ustashe—in 1934.[5]

Yugoslavia was politically frail; it had no chance to survive the disintegration of the European order following the Nazi accession to power in Germany and the creation of a German-Italian-Japanese axis. The fall of Czechoslovakia in 1938, the Russo-German pact of August 1939, and Italy's invasion of Albania in 1940 convinced the Yugoslav government that it had little option but to accede to Germany's relentless pressure to join the Axis. The announcement of this decision on 26 March 1941 led to massive public protests; when the Yugoslav Air Force intervened, the government was overthrown and sent into exile.

Defiance was one thing, effective defense another. Eleven days after the coup d'état, the German army invaded Yugoslavia, and, within a few weeks, the Wehrmacht's victory was complete; the Italian and German armies divided military control of the country. The northern areas of Slovenia were annexed to Germany, Dalmatia and much of the south to Italy; Hungary and Bulgaria swallowed up other morsels. An enlarged Croatian state, covering all of Bosnia and Herzegovina, was created under the aegis of the Nazis and led by Ante Pavelić, head of the Ustashe.

This infamous political formation initiated genocide in Yugoslavia. There was nothing hidden about the crime, which was perpetrated by killers and thugs who were terrorists first, fascists second; the Germans did not force the murder plan on the Ustashe. The massacres began after June 1941, when most of the German forces in Yugoslavia departed for the Russian front. Controversy surrounds the extent of the crime. Some estimates exceed 300,000. Others suggest that the total killed by the Ustashe was much lower.[6] In any event, if there is an analogy, it is to the genocidal campaign waged by Turkey against its Armenian citizens in 1915. Twenty-six years later in Yugoslavia, the victims were Jews, gypsies, and, above all, Serbs.

Resistance to the occupiers and their local allies took many forms. Former units of the defeated Yugoslav army, the Chetniks—mostly Serbs under General Draža Mihailović—took to the hills, but they were not alone in the guerrilla war that ensued. They were flanked by Communist Partisans led by Josip Broz (who took the code name Tito), whose outlook and character were very different, since the Chetniks were royalists (by and large Serbians) whose more cautious tactics the Partisans opposed. So they worked and fought against not only the Germans and Italians but also each other in a war of stupefying cruelty and hardship. At least sixty thousand Bosnian Muslims were killed by various Chetnik groups in eastern Bosnia. The only winners were Tito and the Partisans. By 1944, Tito, leading the most effective antifascist force in the Balkans, secured Allied support for his political position and his claims to postwar power. On 20 October 1944, when Belgrade fell to a combined force of Partisans and Soviet troops, the civil war did not end. Caught between the Communists and the Germans, the Chetniks were doomed; in effect, theirs was a lost cause from the start. Mihailović evaded capture until March 1946. Four months later, he was tried for treason, convicted, and shot.[7]

While initially tolerating non-Communist collaboration in the new Yugoslavia, Tito cleverly positioned the Communist Party as the dominant force within the new Federal People's Republic, a state that comprised six autonomous republics and two dependencies. Over time, the trappings of federalism gave way to the dominance of the Communist Party and its bureaucrats.

Conflicts with Stalin arose over trade agreements and the activities of Soviet advisers in the Yugoslav army. A breach came on 28 June 1948, when Stalin expelled Yugoslavia from the Communist International and ordered it boycotted. Stalin could not have given Tito a more effective political weapon, for his action enormously strengthened Tito's position. Tito defiantly consolidated his power throughout Yugoslavia on the basis of a tripartite political platform: first, the memory of the Partisan struggle and the importance of Communists in it; second, the suppression of ethnic quarrels through a commitment to Yugoslavia's federal state structure; and third, the struggle for independence from the Soviet Union. As Ivo Banac has put it, "Without communism there would have been no postwar Yugoslav state. Tito's rule was held together by the use of fear: fear of Great Serbian restoration, fear of a return to the wartime massacres, and (after 1948) fear of the Soviet Union."[8]

This government survived for the thirty-four years that Tito was in power (1946–May 1980), but its weakness was obvious. The Partisans grew old and passed away; ethnic consciousness did not. And when in the mid-1980s the Communist movement everywhere faced massive economic problems, little held the Yugoslav state together except the bureaucracy and the army. (There were approximately seventy thousand career soldiers in the Yugoslav army, of which 70 percent were Serb or Montenegrin.[9])

The reality of Yugoslav power was that it had institutionalized ethnic inequalities. The state was Serb-dominated, though Tito himself was a Croat and the Communist Party tried to mask ethnic divisions under the cloak of federalism.[10] In part, this was a clever trade-off. Tito had come to power after defeating Serb royalists and conservatives; creating a multitude of Serbian apparatchiks within the regime effectively converted Serb nationalists into loyal Communists. But the tactic was double-edged, for the Communist Serbs turned into nationalist Serbs with breathtaking speed once the federation started to unravel. Slobodan Milošević became head of the ruling League of Communists of Serbia in 1986; as President of Serbia beginning in 1987, he masterminded the projection of Serbian interests on the other constituent republics in the former Yugoslavia. The result was the formal breakup of Yugoslavia between 1989 and 1991.

Political atrophy and soaring inflation created the conditions that led to civil war. Communist authority unraveled at every level, with party membership and activity shriveling fast in towns and villages and no national leader able to control inflation. (Some estimates put the annual increase in prices then between 800 and 900 percent, others above 1,000 percent.[11]) Everywhere in eastern Europe, people were suffering from political instability and searching for more democratic systems, but in Yugoslavia, for many Serb nationalists, democracy increasingly meant securing Serb rights at the expense of other ethnic groups' rights.

This quickly became apparent when Serbia annexed the autonomous province of Kosovo in March 1989, which showed that the Serbs were willing to intensify the complex ethnic tensions between them and the Albanian majority in Kosovo. That decision transformed the nature of Yugoslav politics. Tito's system had managed to balance ethnic claims when it was unable to deflect ethnic quarrels. By 1989, many prominent Communist politicians had decided the time for deflection was over and placed ethnic or "national" issues at the top of the political agenda. The most conspicuous individual identified with this calculated strategy of confrontation and of generating nationalist fervor and fear was Milošević. But he was not alone. What turned ethnic conflict in Yugoslavia into civil war was the mobilization of fear by cynical politicians, who deliberately stirred up ethnic anxieties and bitterness to justify and tighten their grip on power. Milošević, the Croat President Franco Tudjman, and the Bosnian Serb leader Radovan Karadžić were masters of the politics of ethnic hatred.[12]

All three were professionally trained to deal with memory—Milo-šević studied law, Tudjman is a historian, Karadžić is a psychiatrist—and each ensured that history came back with a vengeance. In the hands of these men, history became shibboleths draped in rancor and the language of folk memory, while ethnic history became a recurrent nightmare. For some Serbs, the quarrels conjured up the return of the fascist Ustashe; for some Croats, the Serbian threat brought memories of retribution by the Partisans or Chetniks, or the cynical brutality of Communists wearing nationalist garb. Others saw in the conflicts an enduring Muslim threat. It turned into a generalized politics of fear, worsened by the crimes committed in increasing numbers.

The threat of armed conflict, generated by the resurgence of Serbian nationalism, was a deliberate strategy of Milošević and his supporters, who focused on the most sensitive element in the Yugoslav equation: the treatment of Serbs in Croatia and other non-Serbian republics and their position in the areas associated with Serbia—Kosovo in the south and Vojvodina in the northeast. Since he controlled 70 percent of the former Yugoslav army, Milošević could put weight behind his claim that Serbs outside Serbia deserved armed help when threatened. The old, dormant quarrels and memories of atrocities inflicted on Serbs by Croats (and vice versa) were taken up by irregulars—often farmers whose ethnic consciousness was more vivid than that of city dwellers used to living with Serbs or Croats without trouble—who commonly had private arsenals and whose deployment of guns was not controlled by an independent police force or judiciary.

This was the background to Slovenia's formal secession from the Yugoslav federation. Slovenia's President, Janez Stanovnik, was deeply suspicious of Milošević and his strongman pose: "When you start worshiping a leader, you no longer have a population that is able to act democratically" was the diplomatic way he expressed his disgust for Serbian "Stalinism."[13] When Slovenia's Writers' Union sided with striking Albanian miners in Kosovo, Serb nationalists were further angered and pressed for the adoption of constitutional amendments affirming their right to self-determination in the Slovene Assembly. Meanwhile, secessionist pressure increased in Roman Catholic Croatia, which was bound to cause tension among the many Serbs there.

This was the atmosphere in which Slovenia and Croatia moved to form a confederation in October 1990. Slovenia opened its first diplomatic mission, in Brussels, and then, on 3 December, the largely Serbian Yugoslav army entered the fray: the Yugoslav minister of defense, General Veljko Kadijević, ordered Slovenians and Croatians to disarm their local militias. They refused, and Slovenia prepared to annul all federal laws. After a confused period of negotiation and standoff, Slovenia and Croatia seceded from Yugoslavia on 25 June 1991. The Yugoslav army invaded Slovenia but failed to gain control. By July, the Serb military had withdrawn. Western powers largely acquiesced in these developments, with the newly reunited Germany leading the way. Germany's foreign minister, Hans-Dieter Genscher, announced German recognition of both Slovenia and Croatia on 15 January 1992.[14] Yugoslavia was dead.

In late 1991, a harsh struggle had broken out in Croatia: Serbian irregulars clashed with Croats, and a series of ugly street battles followed. Heavy weapons and artillery, mostly used by the Serb-dominated rump of the Yugoslav army deployed in confined areas, took their toll on civilians and combatants. Torture, mutilation, and atrocity on a grand scale brought parts of late-twentieth-century Europe back to the dark ages (or the equivalent in the 1940s).

Fighting soon spread to Bosnia, where roughly 40 percent of the population was Muslim, 30 percent Serbian, and 17 percent Croat. Bosnian Serbs, controlling the heights around Sarajevo, subjected the city to an artillery barrage that killed thousands of defenseless civilians—Serbs, Croats, Muslims, and Jews alike. Mortar shells landed in hospitals, on breadlines, among mourning relatives burying the dead of the previous day—and these were the lucky ones. Much, much worse was the fate of Bosnian prisoners taken in the fighting, some of whom were tortured, and the Muslim women among them, who were humiliated and raped.

However the Yugoslav civil war ends, one thing is clear: what *has* come to an end is the vision of a federal state presiding over a multinational population that once produced some of the finest art, poetry, and scholarship in the world; in its place are various fiefdoms deploying militias that seek revenge for mass atrocities. The Yugoslav tragedy describes the terrible space carved out by ruthless politicians intent on mobilizing greed and fear for personal advantage. The ascendant warlords have brought the darkness of ethnic hatreds to the remains of Yugoslavia.[15]

There are many ways to categorize the objectives, crimes, prejudices, and nightmares of the war in Yugoslavia, but one stands out: the ambiguous phrase "ethnic cleansing" evokes eugenics, military mopping-up operations, and the extermination of vermin. Banac cites a Chetnik document of June 1942, expressing determination to "cleanse Bosnia of everything that is not Serb."[16] One scholar traces the term to the Soviet Union, where it was used in 1993 to describe one group's attempts to drive out another in the contested area of Nagorno-Karabakh, in Azerbaijan. William Safire recounts a July 1991 statement by a Serb in Croatia: "Many of us have been sacked because they want an ethnically clean Croatia." The phrase recurred the same month in an accusation made by Croatia's Supreme Council that Serbian expulsions of Croats were aimed at "the ethnic cleansing of the critical areas . . . to be annexed to Serbia." A *New York Times* correspondent observed a year later that the "precondition" for the creation of a "Greater Serbia" "lies in the purging—ethnic cleansing in the perpetrators' lexicon—of wide areas of Bosnia."

The term suggests a simple formula: an ethnically mixed population is "purified" by "changing the demographics" through expulsion, atrocities, and killings. Purification thus entails "the expulsion of an 'undesirable' population from a given territory"; the justifications or causes are "religious or ethnic discrimination, political, strategic or ideological conditions or a combination of these."[17]

Forced migration is intrinsic to ethnic cleansing. "Undesirable" people are induced to leave. Intimidation, humiliation, and torture create a politics of fear that is powerful enough to convince people to abandon their homes and property to others. Thoroughness matters. The purpose of ethnic cleansing is to remove everyone in the proscribed group. This was at the heart of the Nazis' attempt to make Germany *Judenrein* (free of Jews). Other precedents include the forced relocation, under conditions of appalling brutality, of American Indians in the nineteenth century and of Armenians in the Ottoman Empire in 1915, when, in both cases, thousands of men, women, and children were exiled from desirable territory because others wanted it.[18]

Yet economic motives have been less evident than political ones in this century. Revenge and fear rather than greed underlay the forced relocation to the west of ethnic Germans living in Russia, Poland, and Czechoslovakia at the end of World War II, as we have seen in chapter 1. Similarly, the migrations that accompanied the creation of India and Pakistan in 1947 were initially planned political efforts to separate, at least in part, the Hindus and Muslims, who lived in danger of extremists on either side. The flight of tens of thousands of Palestinian refugees from what is now Israel to adjacent Arab states during 1947–48 was not planned by Israelis but happened in the fog of war and was brought on by mass fear and dissolution of Palestinian society during the fighting. Some Israelis cultivated those fears; most did not yet nevertheless benefited from the exodus of Palestinians.[19]

In contrast, ethnic cleansing in Yugoslavia was the result of deliberate calculation and a political strategy based on maximizing fear. Though limitless in their cruelty, these measures may not permanently alter the overall ethnic balance Bosnia, Serbia, or Croatia. Ethnic cleansing is perhaps more a tool for political mobilization, a means whereby certain leaders create and re-create their justification for holding power, than a program with a predictable or intended outcome. The suffering it entails is evident; the logic behind it is neither religious nor ethnic but cynical and political.

It is instructive to examine three aspects of the Yugoslav tragedy from this point of view: the politics of massacre, of rape, of ethnic confrontation. The locus for each was different, but the origins were not. Each was the outcome of a political vision mobilized by mass support: ethnic supremacy.

The distinction between civilian and military targets had been erased long before the Yugoslav civil war began, but the barbaric policy to kill noncombatants and prisoners became especially important.

In Croatia, Croat forces in control of the city of Vukovar in 1991 withstood a three-month siege, but Serb artillery and airpower made their position untenable, and on 19 November, with hundreds dead and the city in ruins, the Croats were forced to capitulate. Serb forces took control of all important points, including the Vukovar hospital (which also served as Croat crisis headquarters), where two hundred wounded Croat soldiers were being treated. The hospital was seized before the International Red Cross arrived to supervise the handover. There were reports that these soldiers and about thirty Croat medical attendants were taken out of the hospital, driven to the nearby village of Ovcara, beaten in a warehouse, then transported to a wooded spot, where they were shot.[20]

The capture of Vukovar involved not only murder but another feature of ethnic cleansing: the deliberate leveling of churches and cultural institutions. In Vukovar, the Bauer collection of thirteen hundred Croatian paintings, the Municipal Museum with its ancient and medieval artifacts, and the History Museum with its contemporary history archives were destroyed. "The aim is not only to expel the ethnically 'unclean' population from the desired territory but also to destroy all possibilities for their return," and so tanks targeted museums, libraries, churches, and mosques. The objective was "completely to dismantle the spiritual and material structure of the civilization of the unwanted population."[21]

The murder of prisoners and noncombatants as well as the destruction of cultural records and artifacts—"cultural cleansing," or what one observer called "culturecide"[22]—had been Nazi specialities and had also been widely practiced by the Nazis' collaborators, including the Ustashe. In Vukovar, past crimes were linked to present ones. The city had a long history of atrocity. In the 1940s, Croat forces had killed more than ten thousand Serb civilians in and around the city. And in 1991, Croats imprisoned Serbs once again, this time at the Borovo footwear factory on the city's outskirts and at the Rowing Club of Vukovar, where perhaps a thousand Serbs died under the eyes of the Croatian National Guard. Thus, the Serb attempt to break through to Vukovar was intended to free endangered Serbs, but at the cost of implicating Serbs in the execution of prisoners. The spiral of violence seemed clear, indeed sufficiently clear for United Nations officials to investigate the incident as a war crime worthy of judgment by tribunal.[23]

Vukovar stood as a symbol of Serb suffering in this as in earlier conflicts, a point highlighted by one of the Serb nationalists' controversial supporters, the Russian nationalist leader Vladimir Zhirinovsky. On 31 January 1994, Zhirinovsky visited the wreckage of the "heroic town, a symbol of the defense of the Slav world, a monument against the barbarians who destroyed it." Recalling dreams of nineteenth-century Pan-Slavism, his Serbian hosts called Zhirinovsky the hope of the "reawakening" of the "great Orthodox spirit." In return, Zhirinovsky pledged that, should "a single bomb fall on a Serbian town, that will mean a declaration of war on Russia."[24] Such wild threats by a Russian political maverick presumably were aimed at deterring Western military action against the Serbs.

The course of atrocity, counter-atrocity, and retrospective justification in the conflict between Serbs and Croats was sickeningly predictable. In neighboring Bosnia, an additional dimension to ethnic cleansing was the systematic rape of Bosnian Muslim women by Croats and Serbs. Croatian women suffered similar assaults, but only in Bosnia is there evidence of systematic policies of rape, first by the Serbs, then by the Croats.[25] In the Kalinovik camp, for example, 185 Muslim women were imprisoned and repeatedly raped by their Serb captors. Among the many motives was the intention to create a permanent wall between groups that had coexisted peacefully for years. "We can never live with Serbs or Croats again after what they've done to us," said a rape victim in Mostar. She was one of a group that took the name Miriam, the Islamic name for the Virgin Mary, to embody the need for healing and purification. Coexistence would take much longer than individual healing, which was precisely the point.[26] These were not silent crimes, and they were intended to humiliate and terrify. Little was done to prevent them or to punish the criminals. No one has established a clear link between the Serbian leaders and the men who raped from thirty thousand to fifty thousand Bosnian women. The chain of command worked indirectly, because of the loose relationship between the former Yugoslav army and its satellite system of militias. Suffice it to say that news of these crimes was widely known. Either Serbian leaders used rape to terrify the Bosnian population into submission and flight and are guilty of a war crime, or they failed to control their men and must take responsibility for their criminality.

Many commentators supported the contention that rape was an intentional policy. The United Nations Commission on Balkan War Crimes reported in June 1994 that "command responsibility can be established" for systematic crimes "particularly brutal and ferocious in their execution." The "magnitude of victimization" was so great that it showed planning, not random and isolated incidents. "Ethnic cleansing" was carried out "with extreme brutality and savagery in a manner designed to instill terror in the civilian population, in order to cause them to flee and never to return." To that end, mass murder, torture, looting, and destruction of property were accompanied by rape. This also had been the conclusion of an earlier investigation, conducted by the International League for Human Rights in 1992.[27]

Sexual crimes committed as acts of war are particularly barbaric, but time and again in this century the boundary between private and public actions has been blurred when fertility is linked to political strife. Sexuality becomes politics when fears are induced about different fertility rates among states or factions within states. The Balkan wars, too, descended to this level of political hysteria. Population decline here meant having a fertility rate lower than that registered by a hated neighbor. There were in fact no grounds for fearing that Muslims (except in Kosovo) were more fertile than Orthodox Christians: such differences as had existed in the past were rapidly disappearing. But a general Serb fear of being swamped by Muslim hordes in Serbia was easily translated into more general terms.

The ideological and political link between national power and fertility became especially evident in Kosovo, a province with a largely Albanian population (most of it Muslim) that is a dependency of Serbia. Kosovo was the seat of the medieval Serbian patriarchate and the site of the unforgotten Serbian defeat by the Turks in 1389. Serb shrines and monasteries there, as it were, are in the belly of the whale. In 1986, the Serbian Academy of Sciences and Arts decried the "physical, political, legal, and cultural genocide against the Serb population" of Kosovo, and it was here in 1989 that Slobodan Milosević gathered the Serbian faithful in a mass demonstration to affirm their claims to Kosovo and announce the beginning of a new confrontation between the Albanian majority and their Serbian rulers.[28]

The dominant Serb administration has the power to harass Albanians in many ways; job discrimination is one of the most prominent, though other measures breed resentment too. Albanian newspapers have been banned, the use of the Albanian language in schools is forbidden, and arrests have been frequent. But each community blames the other for making coexistence impossible. Both trade accusations of brutality and rape. The Albanians reply with passive resistance and a parallel infrastructure that includes clandestine hospitals and schools.[29]

Mercifully, ethnic cleansing is not an option in Kosovo. There are simply too many ethnic Albanians and no way to produce a Serbian majority. Moreover, the birthrate among Albanians is substantially higher than that among the (mostly Orthodox) Serbs. In 1950, there was a rough balance in Kosovo between Albanian and Serbian births; by 1996, there were four times as many births to Albanian women as to Serbian women. This is gloomy for those who dream of a greater Serbia encompassing most of the former Yugoslavia. As Ivo Banac has put it, "The high Albanian fertility is frequently explained as a conscious program. In the words of a member of a Belgrade research institute, 'This is not a case of some alleged Muslim tradition, but of a deeply conceived infernal plan to force the Serbs to emigrate from their age-old hearths by all means available.' "[30]

One way that war brutalizes is by creating and disseminating distorted images of and assumptions about ethnic or national groups. That such notions are remote from reality has no bearing on their effectiveness. The more vicious the conflict, the more likely it is that people will resort to such simplifications to account for atrocities in the past or to justify them in the present. Another instance in the Balkan conflict illustrates how stereotypes develop.

In May 1989, before the breakup of Yugoslavia, the literary magazine *Knijiževne novine*, organ of the official Association of Serbian Writers, published a caricature of Tito—then dead nine years—surrounded by dozens of Albanian children. The implication was clear: unless something is done, they will eat *us* alive. The artist who created this image, Milenko Mihajlović, later turned to other aspects of the conflict. In September, he offered his readers the image of two Croatian men, identified with the *U* for Ustashe, fishing for the eyes and body parts of Serbian children. As if this were not vile enough, in January 1990, he sketched

Tito surrounded by populous Muslim Albanians, 1 May 1989

Ustashe fishing for Serb children, 1 September 1989

Illustrations by Milenko Mihajlović from "The Fearful Asymmetry of War" by Ivo Banac (*Daedulus*, Spring 1992)

a Roman Catholic bishop holding a rosary made of Serbian children's eyes, with the blind victims arrayed behind him. And to show the ecumenical nature of his prejudice, he added another dimension: a September 1990 caricature shows a priest and a Muslim cleric fighting over the body of a Serbian child. The priest gouges the child's eyes out while the Muslim prepares to circumcise him.

The fevered workings of one artist's mind are not significant in and of themselves, but they do indicate the historical context. In this case, the language of ethnic cleansing moved rapidly from fantasy to political debate to implementation. Even in the partial success of this project, we can see how unscrupulous leaders appealed to crude demographic fears.

Ethnic conflict always entails counting the size of groups whose growth rates are low or negative and who are threatened by assimilation. These

Catholic Bishop with rosary made of the eyes of Serb children, 15 January 1990

Serb children being blinded by a priest and circumcised by a Muslim, 1 September 1990

groups, feeling besieged, respond by cultivating a collective consciousness, and this frequently includes pro-natalist campaigns—nonviolent conflicts fought over the long term. This kind of demographic ethnic conflict—a culture war about numbers—harms no one, but as soon as cynical politicians and their followers try to take a shortcut and redress the imbalance by forcible eviction of another ethnic group, demography becomes lethal. Talking about the need to raise fertility stimulates fears; talking about the desirability of an ethnic group's migration creates an atmosphere in which crimes occur.

Destinations of Refugees from the Former Yugoslavia, 1995

Country	Number of Refugees
Australia	14,000
Austria	52,000
Belgium	5,600
Bulgaria	250
Canada	11,640
Croatia	228,000*
Czech Republic	6,730
Denmark	17,500
Finland	2,200
France	15,900
Germany	350,000
Greece	150
Hungary	8,900
Ireland	370
Italy	54,600
Liechtenstein	400
Luxembourg	1,000
Netherlands	45,000
New Zealand	200
Norway	11,000
Pakistan	380
Poland	240
Portugal	60
Slovak Republic	1,900
Spain	3,700
Sweden	48,500
Switzerland	32,100
Turkey	30,000
United States	12,820
Rump Yugoslavia (Serbia and Montenegro)	300,000†

*Bosnian refugees only. The figure does not include internal Croatian refugees.
†Bosnian Serbs.

In 1995, the United Nations High Commission on Refugees placed the three million people who fled the fighting in Yugoslavia in thirty countries, as indicated in the table opposite. The numbers in the table do not indicate how many of these immigrants were illegal and how many were legal.[31] European policies on asylum seekers and refugees changed for many reasons, but the Yugoslav civil war made it imperative that the nations of Europe reassess their rules about international migrants. The most powerful repercussions of the Yugoslav civil war, however, are likely to be felt farther east, in the republics of the former Soviet Union, where a patchwork of ethnic settlements has already produced bloody armed conflicts. As the Roman historian Tacitus put it, only fools cheer when a giant falls. The collapse of Soviet power has created its own form of population politics, to which we turn next.

chapter 5

THE END OF THE SOVIET EMPIRE

The former Soviet Union is a house of many mansions inhabited by a heterogeneous population facing severe difficulties. Some of these difficulties can be seen in demographic trends that are disturbing to many Russians. Russian life expectancy fell from 63.9 in 1990 to 58.9 in 1993, the lowest level among all industrialized countries.[1] In December 1995, Mikhail Lemeshev, chairman of the Ecology Committee of the Russian Duma, said, "In the last four years Russia's population has fallen by 2 million. Last year, 900 births were noted for every 1,000 deaths. Statistics would look even worse were it not for the nations inhabiting the southern republics making up the Russian Federation. In North Caucasus and Asian republics, families with many children are a widespread, integral element of local tradition."[2] Declining fertility, rising mortality, ethnic differences, and internal and international migration are salient issues in Russian social affairs today.

International and interregional migration further complicates the demographic picture. Illegal immigration is rampant, given the porousness of Russia's borders, and many immigrants live in appalling conditions. Some bring disease; others are criminals. In addition, perennial political quarrels intersect with these migratory patterns. This is particularly a problem in Asiatic Russia. Three Russian commentators write:

> From the standpoint of Russia's geopolitical interests, [immigration] could assume particularly threatening proportions in the Far East. There, a large area of Russia borders on densely populated regions of northeast China, which have a population several scores of millions of people greater than that of the whole of Russia. The problem is compounded by a border status that

85

86

lacks full legal enactment. And on top of this, there is an economic incentive stimulating immigration and a geopolitical interest in it on the part of the country of origin of the immigrants.[3]

Migration, fertility, mortality—each has a social and political meaning, and in the former Soviet Union, together they constitute one of the most volatile demographic situations in the world.

The recent demographic history of the nations of the former Soviet Union, like that of Yugoslavia, is incomprehensible without reference to its extraordinary political history. The fracturing of the Soviet Union into fifteen states in 1991 did not come suddenly.* The unraveling of the last great European empire has a torturous history, about which historians have not yet reached a consensus, but three interpretations have dominated: The first has been termed the Sleeping Beauty argument, which posits recent developments as "eruptions of long-repressed primordial national consciousness" or "expressions of denied desires liberated by the kiss of freedom." A second, alternative approach is the Bride of Frankenstein view, positing nationalism and national movements as " 'imagined' construction[s] actively cobbled together from actual social and historical material" by writers and activists who project back onto the past a narrative enabling them to galvanize present action,[4] action that sometimes goes well beyond their intentions. A third may be termed the nationalist fugue argument, since it posits that nation building happens repeatedly over time in different registers, when different social and political groups face (or think they face) fundamental threats to their vital interests or existence. Thus, nations coalesce during and after wars, when their propagandists and journalists proclaim the arrival of a moment that history prepared over generations, if not centuries; when the next war or crisis occurs, the nation is "reinvented" and a new historical chorus proclaims its ancient lineage. The second and third approaches have affinities, since they both refer to "inventing traditions,"[5] though the Bride of Frankenstein school concentrates exclusively on the period

---

*The fifteen republics are: Armenia, Azerbaijan, Belarus, Estonia, Georgia, Kazakhstan, Kyrgyzstan, Latvia, Lithuania, Moldova, Russia, Tajikistan, Turkmenistan, Ukraine, Uzbekistan.

1870–1910, whereas the fuguists see national units and their histories appearing anew generation after generation.

There is some truth in each of these positions. But the first is too timeless and abstract for most historians, because it relies too much on a belief in the enduring, immutable, or transcendent properties of people, nations, and races; the second is too rigidly tied to one phase of European history. Analysts tend to favor the third, the nationalist fugue approach, according to which national units under specific pressures "invent" the histories they need to survive. The materials out of which these histories are created are ethnic, as Benedict Anderson has put it, in that they are "distinguished by the collective names by which they were known to themselves and to others" and share "a common myth of descent, some notions of history, usually a language and religion, a sense of solidarity or kinship, and often an association with a specific territory."[6] Each successor state of the Soviet Union created a national identity out of such materials.

The dissolution of the Soviet empire and the flowering of peripheral nationalities are all the more surprising given the authoritarian character of the Soviet state, not only built by Lenin and Trotsky but also inherited in 1917 along with much of the institutional structure of the tsarist state. Prerevolutionary Russia was the largest land empire in the world, a "mixed, contradictory system" of indirect rule, direct military government, and formal associations with satellites such as the Grand Duchy of Finland and the Kingdom of Poland. The tsarist system sponsored what one scholar has called "an intermittent policy of forced cultural homogenization" and blatant prejudice against some ethnic groups, in particular Poles and Jews.[7] The revolution of 1917 and the subsequent civil war drew populations with dramatically different class structures and degrees of national consciousness into the Soviet Union. At one extreme were peasant-dominated Belorussia, Lithuania, and Azerbaijan, all without fully developed nationalist movements. (For instance, the first grammar of the Belorussian language appeared only in 1918.[8]) At the other extreme was Armenia, whose people were long and deeply devoted to a nationalist cause. In the middle were Ukrainians, Estonians, Georgians, Latvians, and Finns. All had difficult and complicated relations with the Russians, whose sense of national character also shifted over time. With all of them, the new regime at once fostered and suppressed their nationalism. In each nation, social and class loyalties jostled with national sentiment, recognized by the regime from its earliest days.

Lenin's commitment to national self-determination shocked other Marxists. To the Polish-born theorist of the German Social Democratic Party, Rosa Luxemburg, it was a betrayal of everything Marxism stood for.[9] But it is hard to see how the new regime could have survived without recognizing that not only the tsarist system but also the Russian empire had already collapsed. There was a degree of cynicism in the pronouncements of the first People's Commissar of Nationalities, Joseph Stalin, affirming "the rights of the toiling and exploited peoples"; but whatever the motives, the new state fostered from the outset a federal structure embracing numerous constituent national elements. The federation fooled few: it was an empire dominated by Russians.

Nothing like it had ever been seen in the past. Its intrinsic instabilities are so obvious that now that the edifice has collapsed the question has become what kept it together for so long. One answer is terror, but more important was the dialectic between centripetal and centrifugal forces in the development of core-peripheral relations in the Soviet Union.[10] As Ronald Suny has shown, the creation of the Soviet state and "the long and difficult years of Communist party rule actually continued the 'making of nations' of the prerevolutionary period." At times harsh and hostile, at other times supportive of national claims, the Soviet Union created the conditions for the emergence of its successor states; in short, it was a victim of its own ambivalent approach to the national question.

The first sign of this ambivalence was legislation establishing "equality of languages in courts and administration, the free choice of language in schooling, and the protection of minority languages." By 1927, 82 percent of the schools in the Ukraine were permitted to teach in Ukrainian and relieved of the old tsarist obligation to teach in Russian; this expressed the Communist Party's commitment to "nativization" in its membership. In the process, as Suny argues, "national identity was both transformed and reinforced in its new form."[11] The promotion of national languages throughout the Soviet Union increased the political awareness of non-Russians, who in their turn would be more susceptible to nationalist messages.

At the same time, forced collectivization and industrialization promoted a "generalized Soviet culture" in which by the 1930s ethnic interests were subordinated ruthlessly and murderously to the interests of the U.S.S.R. Thus, the liquidation of kulaks (landowning farmers), in the Ukraine from the late 1920s, through the first man-made famine in history, was a reversal of the commitment to national forms of expression. By 1939, the Stalinist terror had eliminated all alternative centers of power, including national ones.

It took a severe crisis to reverse this trend. This occurred within twenty-four hours of Germany's invasion of the Soviet Union in 1941, when a systematic policy of extermination waged by the German army in the Ukraine and other parts of the Soviet Union managed to undo some of Stalin's damage to both ethnic sentiment and Soviet patriotism: by the time the first shock of the German assault had been absorbed and much of European Russia lay behind Nazi lines, it was apparent that only through a revival of both national and Soviet loyalties could the invader be expelled, at whatever the cost. And what a cost! Recent estimates have increased the loss of life, officially reported as twenty million between 1941 and 1945, to perhaps forty million, or 20 percent of the population of the U.S.S.R.[12] But the survivors found in the struggle a renewed sense of Soviet identity.

The upheavals of industrialization, domestic terror, and war profoundly affected the ethnic composition of regions within the Soviet Union. Migrations along the southern border, well established over time, helped to consolidate ethnic groupings in the Soviet Union's peripheral regions, though within these more and more homogeneous areas, enclaves of other populations remained. (One instance is the concentration of Armenians in the Karabakh region of Azerbaijan.) And this migration highlighted national and linguistic differences: Witness the case of the Georgian capital of Tbilisi, more than half of whose population was either Russian or Armenian before the revolution; only in 1960 did it come to have a Georgian majority. Similarly Yerevan, capital of Armenia, became more Armenian over the century, as ethnic Armenians from other parts of the Soviet Union increasingly moved there.[13]

These migrations also left intact traditional social and familial forms, which stubbornly survived the transformations of state, religion, and economic life. In parts of Central Asia, for example, the Soviet republics did little to obliterate the traditional Muslim subjugation of women; wearing the veil is still common practice today. Such traditionalism shows the unevenness of Soviet development, which from the start was more effective in cities than in the countryside,[14] and the dialectical character of ethnic histories. That is, the process of ethnic concentration was tempered by an opposite and parallel tendency to promote Russian settlement in areas outside the Russian republic. By the late 1980s, approximately sixty million people lived outside their homeland, twenty-five million of them Russians. Soviet policy both tolerated and repressed national consciousness, then, and within some regions ethnicity conferred benefits, while others were not so lucky.

Jews suffered discrimination in being identified ethnically. The word "cosmopolitan," or nonnational, was the Soviet euphemism for a Jew, and even during World War II, Soviet anti-Semitism thrived, as Vassily Grossman's epic novel *Life and Fate* testifies. After the war, Stalin cultivated these ugly lines of continuity in Russian history. But Jews were not alone in facing the incongruities and inconsistencies of Soviet policies. All national groups were subject to the fluctuations between iron rule from the center and respect for the wishes of supposedly autonomous republics. After Stalin's death in 1953, the Kremlin's grip loosened. Ethnic and national Communist Parties on the periphery came to have more and more power, forging ties with local nationalists and other elites. Once again, the shadow of the past can be seen in the way regional power spun off into the hands of power brokers not very different from prerevolutionary barons. Kickbacks and corruption were rife, further weakening the authority of the central state, which was either unwilling or unable to interfere with the rule of local bosses.

The crisis of legitimacy that ultimately brought down the Soviet Union flowed from these disparate and contradictory sources. Dissent flourished during a disastrous war in Afghanistan that exposed the military weakness of the regime, and the insufficiencies of Soviet agriculture and industry increased when expenditure for arms soared. What languages could be used to express this dissent? Precisely those half encouraged, half repressed by the Soviet regime itself: the languages of the republics within the Soviet Union.

When Mikhail Gorbachev took power in 1985, his effort to reform the political system was initially opposed by the Soviet *nomenklatura*, the Party and state officials who had benefited from the old regime. But within a few years, many of these Party leaders had been removed from power; their successors faced mass nationalist movements that did not want to live within the old federated Soviet system. Some of the new pragmatists were old-line Communists who subtly made their peace with nationalists; others were out to change the Soviet system altogether. Whatever their views, all were intent on dismantling the old structure. Given Gorbachev's unwillingness to use power to enforce the will of the center on the periphery, it was only a matter of time until the Soviet Union fell apart, which it did when the Russian-dominated central government lost its hold on both its eastern European satellites and its internal nationalities.[15] Gorbachev had hoped to create a real federation of states in place of the mockery of self-determination over which Stalin and Leonid Brezhnev had presided, but democratization doomed his policy of "revolution from above," giving space and ammunition for a "revolution from below" of nationalities.[16] That revolution was in motion long before the formal end of the Soviet Union in 1991. As in 1917, an effort at reform led to the breakup of the state and the reconfiguration of the empire it controlled.

The successor states of the Soviet Union are composed of nationalities shaped by the Soviet experience. Contrary to the Sleeping Beauty metaphor, Armenia in 1994, for example, was not simply the Armenia of 1917 revived through the kiss of democracy. Each republic of the former Soviet Union has its own minorities and ethnic conflicts, which are the legacy of an imperial system that lives on years after its demise.

Empires always contain very different constituent parts, and imperial history always entails complicated demographic histories. To appreciate the volatility of population politics in the former Soviet Union, one must

survey its salient demographic trends. This is meant not to be comprehensive but merely to indicate those areas where population trends have
intersected directly with broader social and political trends.

Soviet fertility rates at the time of the 1917 revolution are unknown,
since data collected under the old regime are incomplete,[17] but we know
that fertility rates in 1920 were almost certainly high. Abortion was legalized by decree on 18 November of that year, and subsequent Soviet
fertility rates are believed to have declined steadily, though still estimated at a remarkably high 6.4 children per woman for 1927. Following
the disastrous famine of 1933, reported fertility fell sharply, reaching a
prewar nadir of 3.8 in 1934; by the onset of World War II, it had re-
bounded—4.9 in 1939—in part due to recovery from the 1933 crisis and
to official pro-natalist policies that included a ban on abortion adopted
in 1936.[18]

In common with the other countries whose recent demographic history is surveyed in this book, the period 1960–90 was one of declining
fertility, though in the end total fertility was still well above the notional
replacement rate of 2.1. Overall rates were reported at 2.80 in 1960 and
2.26 in 1990.

The most striking aspects of Soviet fertility trends can be found,
however, not in the national aggregates but in the high degree of regional
and ethnic diversity. Wide disparities, entirely in line with prior Russian
imperial history, continued throughout the seven decades of the Soviet
regime, when the western and northern regions took on the demographic
characteristics of the developed countries of Europe, while demographic
patterns in the Central Asian republics continued to resemble those of
south Asia.[19]

The American demographer Ansley Coale, who has examined historical trends in both marriage age and total fertility for the Soviet Union,
divides the Soviet republics into four groups: the Baltic states; the non-
Baltic European republics; the Central Asian republics; and the three
other non-European republics—Kazakhstan, Armenia, and Azerbaijan.

Three of these four, he noted, "shared similar patterns of change in
age at marriage or overall fertility or both with different neighboring populations outside the Soviet Union."[20] First, Latvia and Estonia showed
marked similarities to Scandinavia in 1900 and followed similar trends

until World War II. After 1960, however, trends in Estonia and Latvia diverged from those of Scandinavia, which registered increasing rates of nonmarital cohabitation and divorce and a rising age at first marriage. Second, the non-Baltic European republics shared demographic trends with most of eastern Europe except Hungary. In the first half of the century, they both registered early first-marriage ages (around twenty as the average) and high total fertility (5.9 and above). After World War II, marriage patterns remained unchanged, but fertility declined to around 2, stabilizing after 1970. Fertility decline in eastern Europe and the European republics of the U.S.S.R. was parallel, though the timing varied, with the decline in the U.S.S.R. occurring later. Third, until around 1970, the Central Asian republics showed demographic trends similar to those of China and, especially, the neighboring Chinese province of Xinjiang. Age at first marriage rose gradually from an extremely young initial level. Total fertility was high and remained so until the 1970s, when it declined sharply in China but not in the Central Asian republics.

But the demographic history of the three other non-European republics of the U.S.S.R.—Kazakhstan, Armenia, and Azerbaijan—diverged from that of their neighboring regions. They showed a very low mean age at first marriage (generally less than 18.5 years) at the turn of the century and until the 1930s, but subsequently the marriage age rose and fertility declined more rapidly than in the Central Asian republics.

Urban fertility rates in European Russia were on the decline before the 1960s but then stabilized; within a decade, rural fertility there was at a similarly low level. Over the same period, however, fertility remained high in much of the Asian southern tier. Although fertility in Armenia had fallen sharply after the 1920s and 1930s and declines had begun in Azerbaijan and Kazakhstan, there was little if any sign of fertility decline under way in the other four Central Asian republics. By 1980–81, the total fertility rate for the Russian Federation was 1.9 and for the Ukraine 1.9; during this period, however, total fertility was still as high as 5.6 in Tadzhikistan, 4.9 in Turkmenistan, and 4.8 in Uzbekistan.[21]

A decade later, on the eve of the breakup, fertility averaged 2.3 for the U.S.S.R., but this number covered an enormously wide range among the republics: 1.9 in the Russian Federation and in the Ukraine, but 5.1

in Tadzhikistan, 4.2 in Turkmenistan, and 4.1 in Uzbekistan. Since the collapse of the U.S.S.R., fertility has declined in all of the former Soviet republics, but large differentials persist: for example, in 1993, estimated fertility in Russia was 1.4 and in Ukraine 1.6 versus 4.3 in Tadzhikistan, 4.0 in Turkmenistan, and 3.8 in Uzbekistan.[22]

Analysis of mortality data for the U.S.S.R. and its component republics is also problematic. Publication of detailed data was intermittent before 1975 and essentially suppressed between 1975 and 1986.[23] Certain technical procedures, and changes in them, affected the Soviet statistics but were never explained. There is strong evidence that deaths, especially in rural areas, were substantially but differentially underreported. Parts of the former Soviet Union, especially the Central Asian republics, show clear signs of statistical imprecision, due to the well-known tendency of people in many developing countries to report their ages in round numbers (thirty, forty, or fifty, for example) or to claim to be older than they are. Also, the Soviet definitions of live birth and infant mortality differed markedly from those recommended by the World Health Organization and used by most other countries; notably, this affects their accounting of deaths of newborns, with the result (as estimated by two research groups) that Soviet infant-mortality rates today are understated by roughly 25 percent.

Still, one can compile a gross summary of overall mortality trends in this century. The onset of a modern decline in mortality occurred almost a century later in the Soviet Union than in other developed countries: whereas control over mass famine and epidemic had been achieved in much of Europe by the end of the nineteenth century, the structure of mortality in the U.S.S.R. as late as 1938–39 corresponded to that typical of Europe in the 1840s; Soviet life expectancy was only 37.5 years in 1927, from which it fluctuated irregularly until the early 1930s, when it plummeted to an astonishing 11.6 during the 1933 famine; by 1939, it had risen to 43.6 years. Similarly, infant mortality, estimated at an already-high 182 per 1,000 live births in 1927, rose to 317 per 1,000 in 1933, before recovering to 168 by 1939.[24]

Wartime conditions were horrendous for much of the European population of the Soviet Union. Leaving aside the disasters that afflicted those behind Nazi lines, the war years were a time of acute deprivation for millions of noncombatants in the rest of the country; perhaps one million people died in and around Leningrad alone.[25] Short-term increases in civilian mortality were dramatic; after World War II, mortality conditions improved substantially, and by 1980, male life expectancy was reported to have risen to 62.2, female to 72.5, while infant mortality was reported at 27.2 per thousand.[26]

During the late 1980s, the perestroika and glasnost policies of Gorbachev brought about greater access to mortality data. Beginning in 1988, original statistical tables (mostly in manuscript form) were made available to Russian researchers by the U.S.S.R. State Statistical Committee (Goskomstat) and the Russian State Archive of Economics. For the first time, one could obtain detailed information on deaths by sex, age, cause of death, and republic. Analysts of these data have expressed considerable skepticism about their quality for many of the Soviet republics. However, the data for Russia have been analyzed in some detail and corrections made for identifiable mortality underreporting, especially for infants.[27] Both male and female life expectancy was rising until the mid-1960s. Indeed, reported mortality improvements in Russia from the end of World War II to 1965 rapidly narrowed the long-standing gaps between Russian life expectancy and that of Western countries.[28] Beginning around 1965, however, there was a break in this trend, as Russian mortality improvements stagnated while those in the West continued. Moreover, whereas male and female life expectancy had been improving in tandem, they now parted company with a vengeance: female life expectancy fluctuated and then fell sharply beginning around 1990; meanwhile, male life expectancy began a long decline that continued into the early 1980s, followed by an astonishing short-term rise around 1985–86, and then a renewed and subsequently accelerated decline to 1993.

The availability of detailed data on cause of death has led to a (perhaps surprising) consensus among researchers as to the sources of these recent deteriorating mortality conditions for Russian males. First, they note, the principal age-group experiencing rising mortality is that of adults. Second, there are slow increases in cardiovascular mortality. Third, the short-term dramatic fluctuations in the late 1980s and early 1990s were due to rising deaths attributable to alcohol and violence.[29]

One more element in the mortality history of the Soviet Union requires notice. On 25–26 April 1986, a catastrophic nuclear accident occurred at the Chernobyl nuclear-power station, about sixty-five miles north of Kiev, in the Ukraine. Large amounts of radioactivity were released into the atmosphere after an explosion blew the roof off the reactor. The mortality immediately attributable to the accident was relatively slight: about thirty people died from the explosion or from exposure to radiation, and several hundred other people developed radiation sickness. But the full effects of the accident are harder to calculate. About eight tons of radioactive material were carried into the atmosphere and detected as far away as Scandinavia and western Europe. Water and milk supplies were contaminated, which required evacuating a twenty-mile penumbra around the disaster site and endangered those living in a much wider and unspecified area. This disaster highlighted not only the questionable safety record of the Soviet nuclear-power programs but also the subject of environmental pollution and its health effects in the Soviet bloc. Worse, perhaps, bureaucratic incompetence and shocking irresponsibility were shown with respect to informing the public as to the nature of the disaster and taking steps to protect the health of the population.[30] The bankruptcy of the Soviet regime as a whole was illustrated in many ways in this period, but the Chernobyl incident was one of the most salient and troubling. As an indication of the links between health questions and political power, it has no equal in this or any other period.

There was another demographic element of potentially even greater explosiveness: the changing ethnic composition of the population.

It is always misleading to deal with Soviet demographic history as if it were seamless; the seams are everywhere, and many of them are ethnic. What is more, questions about ethnic composition are difficult to answer, because of changing definitions of minority status used in Soviet censuses and vital statistics and because the categories used in these records have changed over time. The 1926 census, for example, reported on ethnicity (narodnost') while subsequent censuses asked for nationality (natsionalnost'), a shift that may have produced apparent declines in Ukrainians and increases in Russians due to assimilation. Consequently, these data must be handled delicately. Still, major changes in ethnic and national composition have occurred since the founding of the

U.S.S.R.[31] There was, for example, a sharp drop in the percentage of the aggregate population recorded as Ukrainian (however defined) between 1926 and 1939—from 21.2 to 16.5 percent. Forced agricultural collectivization proved especially harsh in the Ukraine, the northern Caucasus, and Kazakhstan, and the famine of 1932–33 produced much higher mortality and lower fertility.

Though the empirical evidence available is sparse, it seems likely that another major element in Soviet population change was the differential effect of World War II. Direct and indirect mortality due to the war was probably much higher in western and central areas, particularly those subjected to siege-induced starvation (Leningrad) or German occupation and extermination. In addition, boundaries changed very substantially because of the war. Poland was divided; the Baltic states were annexed by Russia, and combat produced large emigrations of Russians, Ukrainians, Latvians, Lithuanians, and Estonians from German-occupied territories. These massive shifts overwhelmed whatever fertility differentials occurred in this period.

While the proportion of particular nationalities significantly shifted in the overall population, in the period 1920–59 the relative size of major cultural groupings—Slavs, other Europeans, and Muslims—did not change much. The dominant Slav group declined only from 78.0 percent in 1926 to 77.1 percent in 1959; a sharp drop in the Ukrainian percentage was balanced by a large increase in the Russian percentage.

This thirty-year pattern of relative stability in gross ethnic composition altered dramatically during the 1960–95 period we examine in this book. In particular, the Muslim percentage increased sharply within only twenty years (from 11.5 in 1959 to 16.7 in 1979), while the Slav percentage declined from 77.1 to 72.8. The available data make it clear that the dominant factor here was higher fertility among the Muslim populations coupled with declining rates of mortality. The result: average annual rates of demographic increase among Uzbeks, Tadzhiks, and Turkmen approached 4 percent during the 1960s—an extraordinary growth rate similar to that registered in the Arab Middle East and Kenya.

These dramatic growths did not go unnoticed among Soviet and Western analysts. The subject being politically delicate within the U.S.S.R., commentary about fertility differentials there tended to emphasize low European and Slavic fertility rather than high Muslim fertility. But in the West, specialists and journalists began to speculate that, if then-current rates were to continue, the politically dominant Russians would inevitably—and quite soon—become a minority of the Soviet population.[32]

But these fertility rates were unstable: Soviet Muslim fertility began to decline, sometimes rapidly, during the 1970s, and by 1990 Muslims were only 20 percent of the population, much less than had been projected on the basis of the very high 1960s fertility rates. The percentage had indeed increased since 1960 but by a smaller magnitude than forecast.

A survey of differential fertility among ethnic groups is incomplete without reference to its effects on the age structure of the population. A high-fertility Muslim population inevitably produced a high proportion of young men. As fertility declined in the non-Muslim population, these differentials would affect the ethnic composition of the army, as well as the balance of ethnic demands in education, housing, and social services. Once again, shifting ethnic composition presents political and social challenges of real significance.[33]

How have these political upheavals and demographic patterns intersected in recent years? Policy debates about fertility in what was once the Soviet Union have a long, convoluted history that is marked by at least three distinctive features: shifts in the official discourse, the evolution of patterns of economic change, and fluctuations in nationalist politics and nationalities policies. At one or another time, these three forces have worked in concert or in contradiction, but they are all essential.

It is highly misleading to equate Russian Communist doctrine on population with Karl Marx's writings on the subject. The key factor, rather, was how the Party bureaucracy made use of or ignored Marx's writings when it suited them. In only the broadest sense can we call Soviet population policy Marxist.

Marx's writings on population questions are meager, and it was solely in reaction to the ideas of Thomas Malthus that some of his thoughts on demographic themes became clear. Marx was unprepared to share Malthus's vision that human happiness is limited strictly by the intractable relation between numbers and resources. For Marx, anyone who supported this analysis accepted a social regime in which millions were sentenced to a life of extreme poverty without hope of reprieve; it was for him a scientific justification for mass passivity,[34] since the path was short between resignation to the causes of poverty and the servility Marx despised. Not only were Malthus's conclusions abhorrent; so too was the state of mind induced by acceptance of his conclusions. To acquiesce in a system producing extremes of poverty and wealth was, in Marx's view, a crime.

But Marx the polemicist was a poor guide to the content and sophistication of Malthus's thought. Like many of his followers to this day, Marx succeeded only in caricaturing the thought of "Parson Malthus" as a man who blamed the poor for their own poverty, and a Malthusian as a mean-spirited miser who wanted to force working people to marry only when they could provide for a family.

But in reality, Malthus was an advocate of what he termed the "prudential" check on fertility: that is, late marriage in hard times. Although the term "Malthusian" in common usage came to mean anyone who saw controlling fertility as essential to the well-being of the population, it should be distinguished from the later (neo-Malthusian) advocacy of birth control within marriage, a practice Malthus rejected as abhorrent.

Marx was neither a Malthusian nor a neo-Malthusian, though he tended to blur the distinction between the two. He saw population change as following economic change and granted demography no independent status. In light of the evolution of Marxian views on the population question, two overarching assumptions tended to dominate Soviet discussion: that population trends are essentially a function of economic trends; and that under socialism (unlike capitalism) fertility would adjust "naturally" to an appropriate level.[35] In addition, for reasons embedded in Russian intellectual history, Soviet leaders tended to believe that the freedom to have abortions was a woman's right, whereas contraception was paradoxically viewed as a demographic policy associated with shabby Malthusianism and reaction.

The logic of state building and the bureaucratic institutions it produced quickly turned these positions into official dogma. Lenin used the Marxist elements he thought essential for the Soviet regime's survival; so did Stalin and Stalin's successors. Official dogma was whatever the Communist Party needed at the time. And its statements were composed from the materials used throughout Soviet history: materials with a socialist past, not always but frequently torn from their initial context— and this was as true at the end of the Soviet experiment as it was at the beginning.

It is not surprising, then, that Soviet officials discussed demographic issues in the context of debates on economic development. On the eve of the 1917 revolution, patterns of economic growth within the Russian empire were already diverse. The cities of European Russia had undergone rapid economic change, and Russia was becoming a superpower; meanwhile, in the hinterlands of Central Asia, long-established Islamic tribal cultures went on with their nomadic or subsistence economies. The differences persisted through the century—through the Stalinist and post-Stalinist periods, and indeed into the post-Soviet era. Even with the profound disruptions of the past decade, it remains generally true that a vast difference can still be seen between the economic prosperity of the major cities of European Russia and former republics, on the one hand, and the republics of Central Asia, the Transcaucasus, and other peripheral areas, on the other hand. This is the bedrock on which much demographic discussion rests.

Population debates unavoidably revealed and contributed to larger issues about nationality conflicts, especially those dividing the Baltic states, the Ukraine, Belorussia, and European Russia from the southern tier of the Soviet Union, where deep economic differences overlapped with distinct ethnic boundaries. One can say generally that the more developed and prosperous regions tended to be Slavic, European, and Russian Orthodox, while the less developed regions tended to be non-Slavic, Asian, and Islamic. As we have noted, the explosive uncertainty of national self-determination within the world's largest land empire created a field of force in which demographic issues were used time and again for political advantage, and it is hard to see how this could have been avoided.[36]

Demographic debate also showed special features of the history of

Soviet demography, both as a scientific discipline and as a branch of the state bureaucracy.[37] The Soviet Union inherited a paucity of data on and analysis of population phenomena; indeed, there had been only one modern population census (1897) in Russia before the revolution. Within a decade, three censuses were undertaken by the new Soviet authorities: in 1920, 1923 (urban populations only), and 1926. This decade was equally favorable for the intellectual development of demography: prominent Soviet demographers emerged, and the Academy of Sciences founded Institutes of Demography in the Ukraine in 1919 and in Leningrad in 1930.

The demographic catastrophes of the 1930s, caused by Stalin's policies of agricultural collectivization and the resulting famine, were disastrous for the demographers who studied them, and Soviet demographic science did not recover until the 1960s. Publication of the politically embarrassing demographic data on mortality was suppressed by the state, the Leningrad Institute of Demography was closed in 1934, while Soviet officials gave the press what we now know were deliberate overestimates of population. When the 1937 Soviet census produced lower but more realistic figures, the regime denounced it, and many statisticians and demographers who had worked on it were shot.[38] The Ukrainian Institute of Demography was closed in 1938.

Given the general trends toward political and social liberalization in the 1960s, providing accurate demographic information appeared in a new light. Soviet demographers now focused on analyses of demographic behavior, attitudes toward fertility, and the behavior of different age cohorts. With the enormous diversity of demographics within the Soviet Union, they were drawn toward comparative analyses of regional fertility and mortality trends. Yet Soviet political leaders continued to believe that demographic data and analysis were politically and ideologically sensitive. Until 1988, statistical tables excluded certain causes of death: cholera, plague, suicide, homicide, and work accidents. The published tables combined deaths due to these "hidden causes" with all "ill-defined causes." The Soviet government did, however, have a separate tabulation of such deaths in "a top secret special table, [whose] . . . data make clearer the reasons why they were kept so secret. In 1970, for instance, the standardized death rate by homicide was about 8 times as

high as the European average rate. We can understand that Soviet officials searched to hide such 'criminal' facts from the foreign and domestic
observers."[39] Russian demographers have written recently about the political uses made of often defective or distorted data. It was common at
international gatherings for Soviet officials favorably to compare the low
infant-mortality rates they reported for the Soviet Union, especially in
its more rural and less industrialized republics, with those of other countries. Yet it is now generally agreed that the differences between Soviet
and World Health Organization definitions produced a 25 percent un-
derestimate of Soviet infant mortality in the 1980s, and there is evidence
of "deliberate falsification of data in the [more rural] locales to mask the
true infant mortality rates."[40]

An earlier example of such political manipulation occurred in 1954,
when Anastas I. Mikoyan, the Old Bolshevik who later became Stalin's
confidant and the Soviet Union's first deputy premier, wrote, "While
prior to the Revolution mortality in Russia was double that in the USA
and England and almost double that in France, at present it is lower in
the USSR than in the USA, England and France. The Soviet Union's
achievements in the field of health and longevity speak for themselves."[41] The Russian demographer A. Vishnevsky has commented bit-
ingly on such misuses of demographic data:

> Demographers know well that the crude death rate is of little use
> for the judgement of real mortality level, as it too much depends
> on the age composition and is always much lower for the
> "young" populations than for the "old" . . . In reality, mortality
> in the USSR was never, even in the most favorable years, lower
> than in most developed countries, to say nothing of the ex-
> tremely unfavorable, catastrophic periods. The truth of the de-
> cline of mortality due to its modernization was tightly interlaced
> with the lie.[42]

It is no exaggeration to conclude that the entire history of demography
and demographic data in the U.S.S.R. was "tightly interlaced" with the
powerful political and ideological forces of Soviet history.

. . .

Slavic (especially Russian) dominance of the Soviet elite led to much discussion of the large fertility differentials between the European and non-European populations in the Soviet Union. During the late 1970s and early 1980s, these comments tended to be sotto voce, the focus of attention being not on the continuing high fertility levels of non-Europeans but on the low fertility rates of Europeans. Such worries conflicted with the official line, and there was real ambivalence about proposals to change the situation. If fertility was a product of economic forces, then direct interventions aimed at raising fertility levels (without working through economic elements) were suspect. Similarly, any effort to regulate fertility in the Central Asian republics was deemed likely to appear Malthusian. If having an abortion was a woman's right, then restricting it so as to increase fertility (as Stalin had done in the 1930s) was at best problematic.

Expert opinion on the subject divided into two camps. One group of Soviet analysts foresaw a grim future if fertility levels in the European republics did not increase, and they tended to advocate strong pro-natalist measures modeled after those that had been adopted in eastern Europe.[43] The attitudes of these pro-natalists were similar to Western ones: low fertility would produce aggregate population decline, an aging population, a decline in the growth of the labor force, an increase in the aged population dependent on state pensions, a decrease in occupational mobility, and a smaller share of the world population. But the second group of analysts was more sanguine: fertility decline was a natural consequence of successful Soviet economic development; continued economic growth depended more on improved productivity than on the size of the labor force; demographic aging was inevitable unless one wanted a return to the very high fertility levels of the interwar period; and as fertility continued to drop in developing countries, there would be less cause for concern about the forecast decline in the percentage of the world population in the Soviet Union.[44]

Yet both groups agreed that the ideal Soviet family size was two or three children. Achieving this ideal would require major changes in European and Islamic regions: in the former, the trend toward single-child families would have to be reversed, while in the latter the trend toward very large families would have to be moderated.

How could such disparate goals be achieved with what was termed a unified policy, that is, a set of policies applied uniformly across the whole country? Soviet demographers from non-European republics tended to favor such a policy,[45] and the forces promoting it were strong. First, all Soviet support programs had to meet a test of economic equalization by promoting a minimum floor on living standards; it followed that policies relating to family size would favor higher benefits for large families in poor regions rather than encourage families in higher-income regions to raise their fertility. Other demographers argued for a differentiated policy, which would promote fertility increases in some settings and declines in others. Such an approach would tend to shift resources away from high-fertility groups toward those with small families, located primarily within the European regions. This point was not lost on demographic analysts in Kazakhstan and other non-European republics.[46]

The debate was between regional and overall claims, one well known in the West. Given that the thrust of the arguments was similar to long-standing official Soviet commitments to equalization and the minimization of poverty, there was really no contest: the proponents of the unified policy prevailed. Revised policies adopted in 1981 for the eleventh Five-Year Plan included little incentive for fertility increase in low-fertility settings, and most benefits accrued to high-fertility families in lower-income regions, though there was a two-year delay in implementing the new, extended work-leave for working mothers in high-fertility regions. Nowhere in these policies were there provisions to encourage second and third births among low-fertility urban women.[47]

Toward the end of the 1980s, however, the debate became more unrestrained, the Slavic alarm more strident. In many ways, the debate became similar to the one that occurred in France a century earlier. In 1900, Émile Zola wrote a novel celebrating the virtues of high fertility. In September 1990, both *Literaturnaya Gazeta* and *Komsomolskaya Pravda* published Aleksandr Solzhenitsyn's "Rebuilding Russia," which contained the gloomiest of demographic forecasts. "Everyone knows," wrote the exiled Russian nationalist author, "our mortality grows and surpasses the births, and thus we shall disappear from the earth." *Moskva* magazine had published an article in 1986 by an exiled Russian economist, Mikhail Bernstam, titled "How Long Will the Russian People Live?" which deployed the extraordinarily long-range projections favored in such polemics to argue that, if then-present trends were to continue, there would be only twenty-three million Russians left by 2200. (The American pro-natalist journalist Ben J. Wattenberg made a similar argument about the future of the West: should the lower fertility of the West vis-à-vis the Warsaw Pact nations continue for a century, he suggested, the result would be a shift of power and influence from the former to the latter.)[48]

Particularism is deeply embedded in many Russian views in this field. Responses to Bernstam's article suggest that many people were unaware that Russian fertility levels were similar to those of other industrialized countries. Instead, they stressed the uniqueness of the Russian situation, as in the original editors' foreword to Bernstam's article in *Moskva*:

> Of problems inherited by us from the epoch of stagnation, the most serious is the demographic crisis of the European populations of the USSR, the Russians in the first place, the people who, to tell the truth, have commenced to die out. It has the lowest fertility potential in the world, and if present-day trends continue, in the next century all Russians, i.e., East Slavonic peoples—Russians, Ukrainians, Belorussians—will cease to be a major world population group and become a small insignificant ethnic group scattered in territory settled by other peoples . . .
>
> Bernstam's forecasts may plunge one into despair. He has forecast ethnic death, a fast demographic catastrophe . . . But despair is the lot of the weak . . . The Russians were on the brink of a national, including demographic, catastrophe not [only] once . . . But every time it resurrected, its number grew. The Russian people possesses specific metaphysical properties not grasped by rational thinking, which permitted it to honorably get out of the most difficult situations. The scale of the threat menacing it increase[s] tenfold its strength, energy, and vitality.[49]

As for the high fertility of the Central Asian republics, the focus continued on the difference between the unified versus differentiated policies that had been so heatedly debated during the 1970s. Though the debates were rendered moot by the breakup of the Soviet Union, concern about low Slavic fertility by no means disappeared, especially as economic and political instability produced further fertility declines. According to Russian press reports, the Commission on Safeguarding the Health of the Population, established by the Security Council of the Russian Federation, held a July 1994 meeting "devoted to the drastic worsening of the demographic situation in Russia." Two reports prepared for this meeting (by the State Statistics Committee and the Ministry of Public Health and Medical Industry) pointed to "one thing: a demographic catastrophe in Russia is no longer a potential possibility, it is a fait accompli."[50] The total fertility rate had reportedly declined from 2.2 in 1987 to 1.3 in 1993. During 1993 alone, male life expectancy fell by 3.6 years to fifty-nine, and female by 2 years to seventy-two; the gap between lower male and higher female life expectancy widened, so that on average women lived 13 years longer than men. As a result of declining fertility and life expectancy, it was reported, the most likely demographic prediction for 2005 was that the population of the Russian Federation would decrease by some nine million, or 6 percent, with twelve million more deaths than births.

There is, however, good reason to doubt the accuracy of these forecasts. They assumed that the Russian total fertility rate would not rise above the current 1.3, although the decline in Russian fertility since 1991 bears all the signs of a deferment of births by couples facing political and economic uncertainties that may be temporary and transitional. (A similar period of very low fertility during the Great Depression in Western countries led to forecasts of sharp population declines that proved wildly wrong when the postwar baby boom appeared.[51]) In addition, that some twenty-five million Russians reside outside the current boundaries of the Russian Federation and may seek to return suggests the need for real caution in making aggregate population forecasts, as we shall see.

Nonetheless, demographic trends in Russia have "aroused fears among nationalists who lament that it will soon begin to affect Russia's status as a great power."[52] One of the most passionate of such responses emanated from the ultranationalist Liberal Democratic Party of Russia (LDPR). In September 1994, the party announced that its outspoken chairman, Vladimir Zhirinovsky, had decided to take things into his own hands. "The catastrophic demographic situation creates a direct threat to the Russian nation," he declared. Consequently, Zhirinovsky had given orders "to ensure that at least one child by the chairman of the LDPR personally be born in each regional branch of the LDPR in 1995," for which purpose the party would make "appropriate monetary allocations" from its budget.[53]

In the old Soviet Union, there was nothing distinctive about the government's control over the entry of nonnationals. This kind of power is universally seen as a core element of state sovereignty, and no state has opened its borders to unlimited immigration (notwithstanding the repeated advocacy by *The Wall Street Journal*'s editors that the United States enact a constitutional amendment about this[54]). The Soviet policy was distinctive in its control over the *departure* of its citizens. Most Soviet citizens were unable to obtain the passports necessary to enter another country lawfully, and even those who were granted passports were often denied permits to depart.

There were exceptions, of course—in particular, some members of ethnic or national groups with external homelands (Jews, Armenians). Often the granting of permits was the result of international pressure, such as the Jackson-Vanik Amendment, which prohibited the United States from giving most-favored-nation trade status to centrally directed economies that impeded the free departure of their citizens. Yet overall, Soviet policy on emigration oddly reflected the views promoted by the eighteenth-century political economists known as mercantilists. To these writers, an exodus was a hemorrhage of the state's human capital. Following this logic, Soviet departure taxes were imposed to recover the state's investment in the education and upbringing of those leaving. As a result, there had been but a trickle of Russian emigration abroad from the 1930s to the 1980s.

Within the U.S.S.R., however, Russian migration to the non-Russian republics continued, especially after World War II. Such population transfers were part of Soviet economic policy: skilled personnel were needed to industrialize the Soviet Union's less advanced regions, and to some (unknown) degree, the migrations were encouraged as a means of strengthening Slavic, especially Russian, influence on non-Slavic or non-Russian republics. By the late 1980s, an estimated twenty-five million Russians were resident in non-Russian republics, most of which were to become independent sovereign states.

Subsequent events have shown that the presence of such large numbers of Russians in the "near-abroad"—newly sovereign states of the former Soviet Union—has profound implications for human rights, minority rights, and the relations among the Russian heirs of the Soviet state and its former non-Russian republics. The government of the Russian Federation has expressed concern about any mistreatment of Russians living in former Soviet republics and asserted its right to intervene—militarily, if necessary—to protect them from abuse. At the same time, a large number of Russians have returned to the Russian Federation.

Following the collapse of the Soviet Union, then, the demographic differentials between Russia and the other former Soviet republics probably grew, as fertility rates among Slavs dropped sharply. These differentials are now mainly *international*, though large differentials among the nationalities of the Russian Federation persist. Current Russian fertility approximates that of Italy, Hong Kong, and Germany.

The fall of the Soviet empire has freed demographic discussion from some of the conditions that restricted it in the 1960s and 1970s. But the end of one set of ideological constraints has been a prelude to other ideological readings of population issues. The Russian debate has entered the historically familiar terrain of fear of population decline. Demographic discussion thus marries some of the old with some of the new. How it will evolve will depend on the needs of the new Russian state and its neighbors, as well as the uncertain future of demographic trends themselves.

chapter 6

THE POLITICS OF THE BIRTHRATE
IN SOCIALIST ROMANIA

Romania provides another, and most striking, illustration of the mixture of political and demographic issues during the past three decades. Here, a politically determined campaign focused almost entirely on fertility, and unlike in many nations, international migration was a marginal concern.

In 1966–67, Romania experienced what is surely the greatest fertility increase in a large population in recorded human history—100 percent in one year, from 1.80 to 3.66. (Month to month, Romanian fertility nearly tripled between November 1966 and September 1967.) The effects on Romanian families, especially women and children, were dramatic: newspapers reported cases of three pregnant women sharing the same hospital bed and of doctors urging their patients to give birth at home. Quantitative evidence showed sharp increases in mortality among pregnant women and newborn children.[1] The number of children younger than a year was twice that of one-year-olds; eventually, this tidal wave of children overwhelmed the nation's day-care facilities, primary schools, secondary schools, and entry-level job markets.

How can this remarkable and unprecedented surge of fertility be explained? The answer is in no doubt whatever: it was the consequence of policies adopted by the repressive Communist government of Nicolae Ceausescu. In 1957, before he came to power, the government had made abortion on request freely available but discouraged the use of contraception as Malthusian. (We have noted the Marxian origins of this peculiar paradox.) Romanian women seeking an abortion needed no official approval and were assured of privacy. The fee was low (less than two dollars), the medical danger slight. The only requirement was that the pregnancy be of less than twelve weeks' duration. Demand for effective means of fertility control was apparently strong among Romanian women at that time, for the birthrate declined more than a third by 1965, from 22.9 to 14.6 per 1,000. According to estimates by the Romanian Ministry of Health,[2] almost all the decline was attributed to abortions, which had become the socially accepted method of family limitation. By 1966, Romania's total fertility rate had fallen to 1.8, clearly below the notional replacement rate of 2.1.

In 1965, when Ceausescu took power, he expressed alarm about the implications of Romania's low fertility rate. In October 1966, apparently with little public discussion, his government abruptly reversed its policy on abortion, strengthened its discouragement of contraception, and adopted new pro-natalist measures. On 1 November, legal abortion was limited to only a few circumstances: those involving risk to the mother's life; congenital malformation of the fetus; rape; pregnancy to women more than forty-five years old or already supporting four or more children; and rigorously defined physical and psychological conditions. To get permission for abortion required completing a series of bureaucratic applications and obtaining approvals. The importation of oral contraceptives and intrauterine devices (IUDs) from Hungary was discontinued (though a black market supplied some at high prices). Condoms and contraceptive creams continued to be produced and sold, the former intended principally to control venereal diseases.

Finally, the Ceausescu government adopted a full array of pro-natalist measures aimed at increasing family size. A propaganda campaign was initiated to encourage Romanians to bear children in the interests of the socialist state. Special tax benefits, housing rights, maternity leaves, and retirement provisions were given especially to parents of two or more children. Generous premiums were paid to mothers of newborns. Meanwhile, divorce was made more difficult; the divorce rate dropped sharply.

By all accounts, the Ceausescu government did not consult demographers and health planners before adopting this policy and did not realize several important facts. First, in a low-fertility population dependent on abortion, which is an atypical situation, very few women are not at risk of pregnancy in any given month. In a more typical population, most women will likely not become pregnant because they are using contraceptives, are already pregnant, are in the postpartum period, or are lactating. But there were few women in these categories in Romania. As a result, a high proportion of women became pregnant in those first three or four months after the new policy was implemented.

A second reality ignored by the Ceausescu government was that roughly half of all Romanian physicians, and even more nurses and midwives, were women of reproductive age who, like other Romanian women, had become dependent on abortion for fertility control. The sudden policy shift therefore meant that many physicians and nurse-midwives were on maternity leave at the time of most childbearing, during late 1967. Together, the clustering of additional births within only a few calendar months and the unavailability of critical medical personnel contributed to an unexpected increase in maternal and child mortality.

This extraordinary episode cannot be understood in solely demographic terms. To account for this violent oscillation in fertility rates, we must consider the political history of the regime that brought it about. Population politics was like all other forms of politics in Ceausescu's Romania: it was dominated by the exercise of totalitarian power in all phases of personal and public life. Communist views on abortion had led to its legalization in Romania in 1957, within a decade of the Communist takeover and shortly after the same action was taken in the post-Stalinist U.S.S.R. in 1955.[3] The Soviet measures, emulated by all eastern European states, were based on the Leninist view that abortion was essential to women's rights to control their own bodies and the worry that illegal abortions adversely affected women's health. In the U.S.S.R., abortion had been legalized by decree in 1920, a decree that Stalin reversed in 1936. But in the years 1921–36, contraception had hardly been encouraged—indeed, it was discouraged—because of suspect status in Communist ideology as shabby Malthusianism and the Stalinist belief that, since a growing workforce was essential to economic growth, it was important to encourage fertility.

Strong Romanian nationalism was compatible with this Stalinist advocacy of population growth. Compared to the U.S.S.R. or Yugoslavia, postwar Romania was quite homogeneous; in the 1956 census, nearly 86 percent of the population reported themselves Romanian. (The next largest groups, Hungarians and Germans, were only 9 and 2 percent of the population, respectively.[4]) Romanian nationalists claim, with good reason, that the Romanian nation is one of the most ancient in Europe, and the Romanian language is testament to the fact that the early population of this Carpathian region was linked to the Roman empire; though overrun by subsequent Germanic and Slavic migrations, the Romanians remained culturally and linguistically distinctive.[5]

In the hands of the Communist government, particularly under Ceausescu, popular beliefs in the unique origins and destiny of the Romanian nation were mobilized. When fertility levels declined, within a decade of the legalization of abortion, the Communist economic model's need for a growing labor force might have been met by importing labor from abroad or by making changes in other policies, but there was really no contest among the options: a decline in the proportion of the Romanian population or an increase in other nationalities within the boundaries of the Romanian state was profoundly threatening.

An understanding of the special features of Romanian Communists helps to set this politics in perspective. According to one historian of the period, "In 1921 the [Romanian Communist] party had been founded at a socialist congress in Bucharest. The decision to set up a communist party was largely the work of police *agents provocateurs,* who had infiltrated the congress with the aim of identifying extremists. Once the vote to set up the party had been taken, the genuine enthusiasts were arrested."[6] From the beginning, the membership base was narrow, never exceeding a few thousand, of which almost half were ethnic Hungarians and Jews; ethnic Romanians were less than a quarter. And this tiny party was riven by internal disputes, which continued into and were exacerbated by World War II. One faction decamped to Moscow to escape the murderous oppression of the pro-Nazi National Legionary State of the *conducator,* Marshal Ion Antonescu. A second, the "prison-Communists" led by Gheorghe Gheorghiu-Dej, was jailed. A third maintained the Party secretariat in hiding. Although the Romanian word *conducator* has a meaning roughly equivalent to "führer" or "duce," in practice Antonescu exercised little control over the country. But the mythic terms deployed to herald the *conducator* were eerie harbingers of Ceausescu's style: "the leader, visionary, philosopher, apostle, father-savior, synthesis of Latin genius, personification of the Daco-Roman tradition, and superman of dizzying simplicity."[7]

After Soviet troops entered Romania in April 1944, King Michael brought together a Patriotic Front that initiated a coup in August against the Antonescu regime. The prison-Communist and secretariat factions of the minute Communist Party were only minimally involved, but they were on the spot and well ensconced before the Moscow faction returned. There followed a half year of coalition government that included all the parties of the Patriotic Front. Then, after a series of violent protests allegedly engineered by the Communists in February 1945, Soviet Deputy Foreign Minister Andrei Vishinsky came to Bucharest to convey an ultimatum that King Michael establish a new coalition government led by the Communists; otherwise "the Soviet Union could not . . . guarantee the sovereignty of Romania." The result was a "bogus coalition" government in which Communists controlled the key ministries of defense, justice, interior, and economy; other parties were systematically harassed.

In December 1947, the Social Democratic Party was forcibly merged with the Communist Party to form the Romanian Workers Party; other parties were outlawed and their leaders arrested. On 30 December, King Michael agreed to an audience with Gheorghiu-Dej and the Communist Premier, Petru Groza. Under threat, he agreed to abdicate and leave the country for Switzerland. On that same day, Romania was declared a people's republic. This Communist takeover, guided by Gheorghiu-Dej, was followed by considerable violence against political rivals and a period of state terror, with irregular trials and the execution of an estimated sixty thousand people. Factional infighting among the now-dominant Communists continued until 1952. The ultimate victory of the prison-Communists is attributed to Stalin's confidence that Gheorghiu-Dej was both ideologically reliable and of Romanian ethnicity. (For Kremlin tastes, the secretariat faction was too flexible and hence presented the risk of a Romanian Tito, while the Moscow faction was overly dominated by Jews.) By 1948, membership in the Communist Party had swollen to more than a million.[8] Opportunism rather than commitment had much to do with this growth; from 1947 onward, only Party members were eligible for government bureaucratic appointments.

The new Communist leadership closely followed the economic policies of the Kremlin. All businesses were nationalized, and state investment was shifted toward heavy industry. Conditions were harsh: forced labor, barrack accommodations, a virtual absence of consumer goods. A policy of forcible redistribution of agricultural property from large landowners to landless peasants was reversed in 1949; the Stalinist model of collective farms in which laborers worked on collectively owned land and received a share of the profits was instituted. Though there was strong opposition to this plan from tens of thousands of newly landed peasants, agrarian collectivization was completed by the early 1960s. The result, according to official statistics (likely inflated), was impressive rates of growth in aggregate levels of economic production—for example, 13 percent growth in gross domestic product (GDP) during the 1950s.

Beginning in 1958, the regime moved toward more liberal economic policies involving a gradual reorientation of the nation's foreign trade toward the West. In 1960, negotiations were concluded with Western governments on compensation for property nationalized in 1948. In part, this shift expressed Gheorghiu-Dej's strained relations with Nikita Khrushchev's regime in the Soviet Union: since coming to power, Khrushchev had systematically courted European socialists with détente and peaceful coexistence while promoting economic specialization ("socialist division of labor") in which the northern "socialist" countries would concentrate on industrial production and the southern states would focus on raw materials and agriculture. Khrushchev's plans presented a profound challenge to Gheorghiu-Dej's image of a sovereign, industrial Romania. The national autonomy issue also appeared, with policies aimed at de-Russification—specifically the termination of a host of institutions established in 1946–48 with the express intent of furthering Russification. The leader of the liberalizing movement was one of Gheorghiu-Dej's new "barons," Ion Gheorghe Maurer, chief of state from 1958 to 1961 and premier from 1961 to 1974.

When Gheorghiu-Dej died suddenly of cancer in 1965, he was succeeded by a troika consisting of Maurer, the new head of state, Chivu Stoica, and Gheorghiu-Dej's protégé, Nicolae Ceausescu, who became Party leader. Although Ceausescu had spent part of his wartime years in prison with Gheorghiu-Dej, he was seen in 1965 as a "gray blur," little known but thought to be a good administrator. His elevation to Party leader was an interim measure to hold the government together while other, better-known politicians jockeyed for power. But Ceausescu proved more politically effective and durable than expected, and within several years he had outmaneuvered his rivals and established a dominant position. His success depended heavily on support from the Party rank and file, many of whom he had earlier appointed to positions of minor influence. He also played the nationality and class cards: his pure Romanian, rural proletarian origins versus the disproportionately Jewish or Hungarian, urban, and professional origins of his competitors.

Ceausescu accelerated the economic and political liberalization initiatives begun earlier by Maurer. State-controlled investment and economic activity were directed away from heavy industry and toward improving the living standard of average Romanians. In 1967, private shops and restaurants and the construction of privately owned homes were legalized. (Within six months, 183 privately owned restaurants had opened.) These economic reforms were effective, at least in the short term: wages rose; food supplies increased; the prices of consumer goods declined; the number of private cars rose; and persistent housing shortages were addressed by massive investments in blocks of high-rise workers' flats around major cities.

The 1965–70 reforms were in some respects more than economic— they included what all agreed was a substantial political liberalization. Ceausescu invited public complaints about poor managers and acted on them. He criticized the excesses of the security police and promised reforms. He even posthumously rehabilitated the Party members who had been executed during the 1940s and 1950s and blamed his patron, Gheorghiu-Dej, for their "criminal frame-ups." He also allowed new freedom for intellectuals and artists, which produced a late-1960s literary renaissance.

Ceausescu's demographic policies, however, departed markedly from his economic and political ones and in many ways came to be a central, often bizarre example of his regime's most peculiar beliefs and commitments. While Ceausescu's reliance on economic models drawn from the Soviet 1930s may have waned somewhat, at least for several years, he continued to adhere to the Stalinist view that an increasing workforce was essential to socialist economic growth. Coupled with his commitment to nationalism, it made him see declining Romanian fertility as a direct threat to the future of socialism and the nation.

Though it is impossible to be sure about the popularity of Communist leaders, it appears that these early years of Ceausescu's regime were marked by considerable popular support. This was enhanced by his decision to defy the Soviet Union after the 1968 invasion of Czechoslovakia, which for a time made him a national hero. Ceausescu evoked latent but powerful feelings of Romanian nationalism when he talked of independence, sovereignty, "fighting to the last man," and "the lesson of 1968."

His early economic and political reforms were short-lived, however, and the late 1960s were the high point of his popularity. Soon he reverted to the economic and political policies of his predecessors, which brought him into conflict with Maurer, who favored slower investment in heavy industry and more attention to consumer goods. In 1970, Ceausescu imposed—over Maurer's objections—revisions to the 1971–75 Five-Year Plan adopted only a year earlier. The revisions reduced the share of GDP for consumption and increased that reserved for government investment. Consumer goods became scarcer as investment was again directed toward centrally controlled industries with impossibly high production targets. Political opponents again were suppressed by the security police. In 1971, Ceausescu returned from China to issue his "theses," in which he denounced technocrats and cosmopolitanism and exalted ideological purity. A few months later, he accused Maurer of economic defeatism and a lack of faith in Party policy. That same year, Ceausescu denounced "liberal" and "intellectual" trends and called for a return to "socialist realism." In 1973, he appointed his wife, Elena, to the Executive Committee of the Party, beginning a career that led her to become the second most powerful person in the country. In 1974, Ceausescu contrived to have himself elected President of Romania, and Maurer was replaced as premier (he later lost his position on the Central Committee).

The last of Gheorghiu-Dej's barons had been overcome, and the cult of personality began. Images of Ceausescu shifted from portraying him as a hero of the working class to one in a long line of Romanian kings and potentates. Even academic researchers joined in: Romanian scientists suddenly discovered remains of the "first European man" at a site near Ceausescu's birthplace in Oltenia and designated it *Australanthropos olteniensis*. In ensuing years, no book could be published without appreciation of Ceausescu's guidance. His portrait appeared in every public building and on signs praising him along every main road. Increasingly enthusiastic epithets accompanied any mention of his name. Martyn Rady has listed them: "the Architect; the Builder; the Creedshaper; a Danube of Thought; an Epoch; Father; Genius of the Carpathians; our secular God; Wise Helmsman; Sweet Kissing of the Earth; Lawgiver; Tallest Mast; Nimbus of Victory; Oak Tree; Prince Charming; the embodiment of Romania (hence, 'When we say Ceausescu, we say Romania'); Son of the sun; Titan; and Visionary." In short, Ceausescu had become a new *conducator*.

For two long decades, Romania had registered one of the highest economic growth rates in the world. Its industrial output (at least according to official statistics) had shown average annual growth of more than 10 percent. During the 1970s, however, that rapid growth slowed appreciably, due in part to problems internal to Romanian economic policy and in part to external forces, particularly the dramatic increase in world oil prices in 1973–74. The 1980s were years of harsh austerity for Romanians, and the Ceausescu government promulgated increasingly extreme policies. In 1981, the economy recorded negative growth for the first time since the Communist takeover in 1947. Soon, even the modest official goals could not be achieved, despite the Ceausescu government's falsifying data more and more. Romania, once a rich breadbasket, began to import food. Bread and gasoline were rationed; imported staples such as sugar, rice, and coffee were often unavailable. Prices for other household commodities tripled in 1982. By the late 1980s, many pharmaceuticals were unavailable, and the use of refrigerators and vacuum cleaners was banned to conserve electricity. For the same reasons, street lighting in rural areas was banned, and in Bucharest streetlights were dimmed; restaurants were closed at night.

The Ceausescu government also embarked on an extraordinary and expensive redevelopment of central Bucharest that involved destruction of the old quarter of the city, including twenty-six churches and two monasteries; the displacement of forty thousand residents; and the construction of a colossal House of the People designed (despite its name) to house the office of the President, the Central Committee, and the Executive Committee, at an estimated cost of between $750 million and $3.3 billion. Nor were rural areas spared these grand redevelopment plans. Indeed, perhaps the strangest innovation was that of "systematization," a rural redevelopment plan announced in March 1988 that involved razing more than half of Romania's thirteen thousand villages and resettling the eleven million rendered homeless in low-level apartment blocks clustered in "agro-industrial complexes."

On the demographic front,[9] the sharp fertility increases of 1967 had been followed by gradual declines, though overall fertility levels remained high for more than a decade. By the early 1980s, however, they had fallen again to the 1966 levels. It appears that abortion continued to be the preferred means of regulating fertility, though it was now largely obtained illegally or at least informally (including by bribing physicians). Probably as a result of this clandestine process, the mortality of Romanian women during childbirth continued to rise: from about 85 deaths per 100,000 births in 1966 to about 150 per 100,000 in 1984, 85 percent of which were attributed to illegal abortion.

In 1984, the Ceausescu government issued a forceful declaration on demographic trends: the birthrate decline to 14.3 per 1,000 and abortions exceeding live births by more than 30 percent were "intolerable." A new set of measures was promulgated to restrict access to abortion, and an invigorated propaganda campaign asserted that "normal demographic growth in the population is a high honor and a patriotic duty . . . to ensure for our country successive new generations that will contribute to the prosperity of our socialist nation and to the triumph of socialism and communism in Romania." State security police agents were stationed in obstetrics and gynecology clinics. Working women under the age of forty-five were required to undergo monthly gynecological exams in their workplaces; if they refused, they lost their pensions and health-care benefits. Meanwhile, factory physicians were docked wages if the factory's birthrate did not meet a set quota. Unmarried persons over the age of twenty-five were assessed a special tax of 10 percent of wages. The strength of Ceausescu's views on fertility may be measured by his 1986 declaration: "The fetus is the socialist property of the whole society.

Giving birth is a patriotic duty, determining the fate of our country. Those who refuse to have children are deserters, escaping the laws of natural continuity."

These harsh new measures had some effect on Romanian fertility, but they were very unpopular. Ceausescu's demographic policies of the 1980s were among the first to be dismantled after his fall in 1989; abortion was formally legalized again in 1990. (Corroborative demographic evidence of their effect is provided by data on live births by birth order: though nearly two-thirds of all births in 1988 were still first- or second-order, three-quarters of the increase between 1983 and 1988—an increase of 69,000 births—had been at third- and higher birth orders, suggesting that these were births that otherwise might not have occurred.[10])

Romanian Births, 1983 and 1988

Year	Total	1st birth	%	2nd birth	%	3rd birth	%	4th+	%
1983	321,498	135,573	42.2	96,847	30.1	41,554	12.9	47,497	14.8
1988	390,043	143,479	36.8	109,485	28.1	56,546	14.5	80,533	20.6

Source: Romanian Statistics Board.

Although there is evidence of organized opposition to the drastic political, economic, and demographic policies implemented in the early 1980s, including murky indications of army coup attempts in 1983 and 1984, the first popular uprising occurred in the Transylvanian city of Brasov in November 1987 and was quickly suppressed by the army, with subsequent small disturbances in other cities, such as Timisoara and Bucharest. Opposition to the rural systematization program produced further dissidence, notably among intellectuals led by Doina Cornea and among "old Communists," culminating in a March 1989 open letter from six eminent members of the Party old guard, all of whom were promptly placed under house arrest.[11]

In 1989, the Communist regimes of eastern Europe began to collapse from within. In August, Solidarity took over in Poland; in October, a nonsocialist government came to power in Hungary; in November, the East German government fell and so did the Berlin Wall. Both Czechoslovakia and Bulgaria seemed well on the way to similar changes. Only Romania and Albania remained in control of unrepentant Communist regimes.

The incident that precipitated the Romanian "Christmas Revolution" was due to forces gestating for several years in Timisoara, a city in western Transylvania with a mixed population of ethnic Romanians and Hungarians. There, Laszlo Toekes, an ethnic Hungarian and (like his father and earlier ancestors) a pastor of the Reformed Church, began in the early 1980s to criticize human-rights abuses in Romania. He was predictably harassed, but when his story came to the attention of the U.S. Senate Foreign Relations Committee, American diplomatic pressure led to his appointment as assistant pastor in Timisoara. By the late 1980s, Toekes had become an outspoken critic of the systematization program, which he believed threatened the peasantry of Hungarian and Romanian origin. A campaign of intimidation by the security police intensified, and Toekes was accused of working as an agent of Hungary. Threats became increasingly violent but were restrained when the Hungarian government officially protested. Still, two violent attacks occurred on Toekes's flat in November 1989, and then on 15 December an effort forcibly to evict him was prevented only when a human chain of several hundred of his parishioners stopped the action. The next day they were joined by several thousand more, mostly young ethnic Romanians. Toekes explained it this way:

> The crowd was mostly Romanian and it was there again the next day . . . I could not have imagined this. Hungarians and Romanians had always been opposed to one another. The regime had fostered real hatred between the two peoples. The support I received from the ethnic Romanians during these days was an overwhelming experience. How moving to see the Romanian crowd under my windows chanting their national anthem. Until that day, that hymn had separated us. From that day on, it united us.[12]

Ultimately, the security police evicted Toekes and removed him to a village two hundred miles away, but a train of events had been set in motion that proved impossible to halt. The crowds in Timisoara continued to swell, burning books written by Ceausescu and demanding an end to rationing and to systematization. Ceausescu attributed the disorder to the work of "foreign agencies and . . . anti-socialist and anti-Romanian circles in East and West alike" and ordered his defense minister and internal affairs minister to suppress the disorder even if mass slaughter was necessary. The alternative, according to Ceausescu, was "the liquidation of communism."[13]

The suppression began on 17 December, with government forces in armored vehicles firing on crowds and others bayoneting and running over protesters. About seventy people were said to have been killed in Timisoara, though European media accounts put the number of fatalities in the thousands and these numbers were reported in Bucharest. When, on 21 December, Ceausescu tried to show that his government remained in control by assembling a hundred thousand workers bused in from outlying districts to the Square of the Republic in central Bucharest, he was answered by cries of "Timisoara" and "Murderer." Stunned, he attempted to regroup by promising wage increases and later calling in water cannon and tear gas, but the crowd refused to disperse. Armed police units opened fire from rooftops, though army units under orders from Defense Minister General Vasile Milea did not fire on the demonstrators and assumed a passive posture. The next day, Ceausescu ordered General Milea to take decisive military action, which the general refused to do; he was summarily shot—by either the President's personal security force or by his brother Ilia, according to alternative accounts—though official reports had it that he committed suicide.

The news of the death of Milea, a respected professional soldier, led to open rebellion in the army. Unimpeded, demonstrators flooded into the Central Committee building, and Nicolae and Elena Ceausescu beat a hasty retreat from the roof by helicopter. That afternoon, a new National Salvation Front, led by Ion Iliescu with support from the military, was announced. Confused fighting continued for several days, but the Ceausescus were apprehended that same day by militiamen in the town of

Tirgoviste, fifty miles northwest of Bucharest, and transferred to the town's military prison. After a quickly organized military trial, Nicolae and Elena Ceausescu were convicted and executed by firing squad. So, against a prison wall in 1989, ended the increasingly bizarre regime of Nicolae Ceausescu.

One of the first actions of the successor government of Premier Ion Iliescu was to dismantle the prohibitions on abortion and to legalize contraception. Yet Ceausescu's demographic legacy lives on. Though the abortion rate declined between 1990 and 1995 from 3.2 to 2.2 abortions for every live birth, it remained the highest in Europe. Reports during 1990 of the desperate circumstances of unwanted Romanian children brought Western financial assistance for family-planning services within Romania's state-run health system, but the Iliescu government was reluctant to promote these, and the minister of health, Iulian Mincu—who had been a personal physician to Ceausescu—publicly stated his opposition. Romanian doctors continued to recommend abortions to their patients, sometimes repeating stories from the Ceausescu era about the alleged health dangers of contraceptive pills, and while the state still paid for abortions, imported contraceptives were too expensive for many women. The pregnancy-related mortality rate in Romania declined substantially between 1990 and 1995 but remained among the highest in the industrialized world. After a public outcry, Mincu was dismissed during the summer of 1996 in the buildup to the Presidential and parliamentary elections. And during his campaign for the Presidency against Iliescu, Emil Constantinescu vowed to improve health services; with his election, a more supportive policy on family-planning services was expected. Though reliable data are hard to obtain, there is evidence that Romanian fertility rates have declined since the fall of the Ceausescu government. The rate of natural increase dropped from +0.3 percent in 1990 to −0.16 percent in 1995.[14]

Over the same period, Romania has become a country of significant emigration as well as a springboard transit country for illegal immigration to western Europe. Israel admitted tens of thousands of Romanian workers on temporary visas (intended as replacements for Palestinians, who were prohibited from Israel after the rise of terrorist bombings in 1994). Israeli police reported that Romanian and other foreign workers "contributed to a steady rise in violence, alcoholism, prostitution and crime." Many have allegedly overstayed their temporary visas or have paid to enter into fictitious marriages with Israeli women, and the subject has become contentious in Israeli political circles. In November 1996, Israel announced it would deport 2,000 illegal immigrants each month in 1997 (up from about 150 per month in 1996) and opened a detention camp near Tel Aviv to facilitate such deportations.[15]

Many Romanians have also moved to Germany. During 1995, about half of the illegal aliens apprehended along the German-Polish border were Romanian. Many of them claimed political asylum, but the German government considers post-Ceausescu Romania a "safe country" that does not persecute its people and has negotiated an agreement with the Romanian government for their return. In 1996, the Romanian government also began to crack down on would-be illegal immigrants who were in transit to western Europe and at that time reportedly numbered about twenty thousand, mainly from Africa and Asia.[16]

The history of Romanian demographic change since 1965, in many ways unique and even bizarre, nonetheless shares important elements with developments elsewhere in eastern Europe. The Marxist ideological commitments combined with authoritarian regimes and state-controlled economies led to fertility declines that depended heavily upon abortion, and to forceful, sometimes harsh government interventions when political leaders decided that fertility rates had fallen too low. And we can now see that competition among ethnic groups, allegedly extinguished during the Communist period, was smoldering below the surface all along.

With the end of Communist rule, fertility rates in much of eastern Europe have again declined to very low levels, with important effects on the age structure of the population. Moreover, the ethnic tensions so long suppressed have burst into flame, resulting in volatile, sometimes violent mass migrations across often new national boundaries. Future demographic trends in eastern Europe, and debates about them, will long reflect these special historical circumstances.

PART THREE

NORTH AMERICA

chapter 7

A GENERATION OF DEMOGRAPHIC DEBATE
IN THE UNITED STATES

Politics and demography in the United States differ in a number of ways from the European developments we have discussed in earlier chapters. True, the United States shares many of the underlying demographic trends we have been examining—fertility has declined, and migration has been an increasingly divisive issue, with its attendant concerns about national identity—but the form and substance of American debates are very different from those in Europe.[1]

In particular, anxiety about low domestic fertility rates in the United States has been muted, while ideological confrontations about other population issues have been almost ferocious. Immigration has risen in prominence as a political issue, yet little attention has been paid to the fertility behavior of immigrant groups. American debate on these and other matters has unavoidably borne the legacy of the country's history of race and ethnicity, and these issues have tended, again in a characteristically American manner, to wind up in the courts, where they are considered in relation to the Constitution.

In the 1960s, the United States led in the international effort to moderate high fertility, especially in the developing world. Then came a reversal, as the U.S. government, under President Ronald Reagan, took the position that population growth was "neutral" in the development process. In the 1990s, the wheel turned again: the Clinton Administration embraced earlier concerns about rapid population growth and added that international action to empower women was the best way to moderate fertility.

On the issues surrounding international migration, there were also radical discontinuities. Between 1980 and 1990, Congress passed laws that greatly increased the numbers of legal immigrants and refugees admitted to the United States for permanent residence. It also legalized the status of 2.7 million illegal aliens, while adopting measures intended to reduce future illegal flows, though these measures were so constrained as to be easily circumvented with fraudulent documentation. By 1995, policies toward immigration seemed again to be shifting direction: a strong populist backlash against the policies of the previous fifteen years emerged in California, a principal destination of many migrants, and the U.S. Congress debated and acted upon measures to reduce the inflows of both legal and illegal immigrants.

How can we best understand such dramatic reversals of policy in a liberal democracy that is both politically stable and averse to drastic policy change? The answers must be sought in the complex politics of public advocacy. Population issues were central to the work of many groups dedicated to mobilizing public opinion around matters of conscience and self-interest. The driving forces behind this pressure-group politics and opinion formation whipped up passionate political debate. Population questions became tangled in complicated webs of ideological commitments, religious beliefs, ethnic identities, and the pro-life, feminist, libertarian, and ethnic-rights movements. In this swirling atmosphere, the science and statistics of demography became inseparable from philosophical and political arguments. Fertility and migration touched first principles, and new forms of population politics emerged that are likely to be with us for the foreseeable future.

In the United States as in most other Western countries, fertility rates reached record lows during the Great Depression. This fertility decline evoked some anxiety in political and intellectual circles, though discussions never had the depth and fervor that they did in France. By the 1950s, however, a powerful postwar American baby boom had extinguished any such worries, as fertility rates rose to levels not seen since the turn of the century. From about 2.2 in the mid-1930s (and about 2.5 at the end of World War II), American total fertility rose to nearly 3.8 in 1957.

Demographic growth rates in Asia, Latin America, and Africa rose during the same postwar period, with declining infant and child mortality, but U.S. opinion was slow to respond. A few commentators—the philanthropist John D. Rockefeller 3rd and the Princeton University economist-demographer Frank Notestein—pointed to these international trends as problematic for economic and social development, but by and large Americans maintained innocent unawareness or deliberate indifference. Some attributed U.S. inaction on this front to the sustained opposition of the Roman Catholic Church, and the Presidential candidacy of John Kennedy was opposed by some who feared his election would enhance Church influence on such issues. But the opposite turned out to be the case. His Administration implemented the first U.S. policy initiatives on population matters, quietly beginning to financially assist developing-country governments that requested support for population programs. The Administration of Lyndon Johnson continued and expanded these initiatives. As part of the domestic social-policy agenda of Johnson's Great Society, 1968 laws provided, for the first time, voluntary no-cost family-planning assistance to those unable to pay for it.

Similarly, the Johnson Administration expanded U.S. foreign assistance for family planning in developing countries, through a program administered by the Agency for International Development. The United States also tried to mobilize the United Nations and other multilateral organizations to be involved in population activities, but these efforts were blocked by an unlikely alliance of the Soviet Union and other Communist states and the Holy See and its supporters, forcing the United States to settle for a voluntary UN Fund for Population Activities, to which it quickly became by far the largest contributor.[2] These domestic and international initiatives received strong endorsement from informed American public opinion—Republican and Democratic, conservative and liberal alike. Indeed, public discourse about population issues often sounded distinctly apocalyptic, some writers conjuring up the disasters of *Famine 1975* and *The Population Bomb.*

President Richard Nixon, the conservative Republican who succeeded the liberal Democrat Lyndon Johnson, also gave energetic support to population initiatives. A blue-ribbon Presidential commission, the Commission on Population Growth and the American Future, was established, with John D. Rockefeller 3rd as chairman, and the Administration lobbied strongly and successfully for a global UN conference on population (it was held in Bucharest in 1974). The delegation to this conference appointed by Nixon was chaired by Caspar Weinberger and dominated by political conservatives who endorsed population programs and loudly urged global initiatives to reduce high fertility, including specific demographic targets against which each nation's progress could be measured over time—an agenda rejected by most Third World governments.

Executive and legislative backing for international initiatives on population continued through the Republican Administration of Gerald Ford, who was defeated in 1976 by a moderate Democrat, Jimmy Carter. Although Carter supported population activities in principle, fractious quarrels about the independence and ultimately the directorship of the Agency for International Development's Population Office produced an extended bureaucratic stalemate and loss of momentum. In retrospect, the standoff in the Carter years was a calm before the political storm that broke during the Reagan Presidency.

The election of the Republican Ronald Reagan in 1980 ushered in a period of dramatic revisionism, marked by zealous ideological commitments. The Administration rejected not only the apocalyptic "population bomb" arguments of the 1960s and early 1970s but also more moderate worries about the deleterious effects of high fertility and rapid population growth. Population increase instead was seen either as a universal boon promoting human welfare and prosperity or as a neutral matter of no policy interest.

This volte-face derived from passionate domestic debates on issues no less transcendent than the definition of human life, to which were added an overlay of fundamental disputes about the role of the state in relation to the marketplace and the impacts of demographic patterns on economic trends.[3]

In the debates about human life, the crystallizing stimulus was the 1973 Supreme Court ruling in *Roe v. Wade*.[4] The Court ruled that, as a matter of constitutionally protected privacy of the individual woman, abortion within the first twelve weeks of pregnancy could not be restricted; abortions in later pregnancy could be restricted only within specified bounds, delicately balancing the interests of the state in protecting viable fetuses against the rights of pregnant women. This ruling not only legalized early abortions nationally (some states, such as New York, had previously done so) but also stimulated those opposed to abortion to mobilize against it. Initially describing themselves as "right-to-life" (later "pro-life"), these groups found considerable grassroots support among conservative religious communities both Roman Catholic and Protestant. The National Conference of Catholic Bishops, assemblies of fundamentalist Protestant denominations and evangelical churches, and television ministers gave institutional and financial support. The pro-life movement gathered its resources during the mid-1970s and emerged in full flower by the 1980s.

At first, the pro-life movement focused on domestic issues and limited its opposition to abortion as such. However, some of its leaders were also opposed to "artificial" contraception, even as others supported it as a principal means of limiting the use of abortion. Gradually, those opposed to contraception other than by "natural" methods, such as periodic abstinence, became dominant. Pro-life groups extended their lobbying into opposition to contraception, initially to certain methods (such as IUDs) they considered abortifacients and later to government-funded programs for family planning, whether domestic or international.

Reagan's Presidential campaign in 1980 included a strong pro-life platform, and his candidacy was supported by many pro-life groups and voters. During the eight years of his Presidency, the pro-life movement lobbied to limit or eliminate domestic funding for abortion and contraception. It had considerable success eliminating public funding support for abortions, but related efforts on publicly financed family-planning programs were blocked.

In the international arena, there was more success for the pro-life camp. The lack of powerful domestic constituencies for foreign aid in general made international population assistance more vulnerable to concerted attack. A few high-ranking foreign-policy officials in the early Reagan years were deeply committed to the pro-life agenda. One, Under Secretary of State James Buckley, tried to eliminate all U.S. funding for international population assistance, but his efforts were frustrated by others in the Administration and Congress. Later, President Reagan appointed him to head the U.S. delegation to the 1984 UN International Conference on Population in Mexico City. Other active members included the neoconservative writer Ben J. Wattenberg, who passionately proclaimed the dangers of the "the birth dearth" in the West.[5] Thus, there was a confluence—not without turbulence—between the pro-life activist stream and largely unrelated (and to a degree antithetical) ideological arguments emanating from the New Right.

American conservatives had long believed that rapid demographic growth impeded economic improvement in developing countries, but during the 1970s a handful of libertarian conservatives had begun to argue otherwise. They held that the state should not facilitate or prohibit contraception or abortion; these matters lay in the distinctly private realm.* Instead, it should restrict itself to establishing the structure and rules allowing a "correct" economic system to develop. For them, this meant a free market wholly unconstrained by "statist" interventions, including conventional laws in most industrialized countries such as those guaranteeing minimum wages, social-insurance programs like Social Security, and transfer payments (welfare). With such a free market, they argued, no economic limits or problems could be posed by demographic increase, no matter how rapid, since the numbers produced by even very rapid population growth were not only of consumers but also of producers. Moreover, they argued, there were no limits to the natural-resource base, as proved by declining real prices of raw materials. Some enthusiasts of this revisionist New Right perspective went so far as to claim that, the more people living, the more Einsteins would emerge, thereby enhancing human technological dominance over the natural environment and accelerating increases in prosperity and welfare.[6]

The people prepared to propound such views were few indeed—a dozen might be an overestimate. However, their ideas overlapped with

---

*They therefore opposed in principle the efforts made by pro-life forces to prohibit legal abortions. Their opposition tended to be muted, however, in deference to the pro-life support for much of the Reagan agenda and because it would place them in coalition with liberal and feminist groups with which they otherwise had little in common.

the policy agendas of both the rising pro-life movement and the increasingly influential think tanks of the New Right. The Heritage Foundation and the Cato Institute (and, to an extent, the larger American Enterprise Institute) were especially effective during President Reagan's first four-year term (1981–85). They prepared brief backgrounders, concise enough for busy policy makers, that summarized the rationale for their positions; they organized seminars, workshops, and television shows; they developed networks of associates in influential government positions; they wrote numerous Op-Ed pieces in newspapers and magazines; and they actively promoted ideologically compatible books through press releases, lecture and talk-show tours, and free distribution to policy-making elites. The views of the Heritage Foundation and the Cato Institute were also given national prominence in the New Right editorial and Op-Ed pages of *The Wall Street Journal,* one of the few American newspapers with a national distribution. The New Right did not necessarily always agree with the pro-life movement's abhorrence of abortion, but their views converged on the significance (or, rather, lack of significance) of population trends.

As chairman of the U.S. delegation to the 1984 UN International Conference on Population in Mexico City, Buckley insisted on a complete review of U.S. foreign policy on population matters. This task was assigned, paradoxically enough, to the *domestic* policy staff of the White House—whose leadership was ideologically more congenial to Buckley than that of the foreign policy staff—and it essentially excluded demographic experts from the Census Bureau, the State Department, and the Agency for International Development, whose views Buckley saw as politically awkward or suspect.

This review process produced a draft policy statement for the conference that departed radically from the positions propounded by all American administrations since 1960. There ensued an energetic internal struggle between the proponents of the draft statement and those supporting long-standing U.S. government policy. The outcome was a hastily stitched-together compromise that was heavy with internal contradiction: the first section consisted essentially of the revisionist New Right pronouncements initiated by Buckley; the second was a bow to the pro-life movement, arguing that abortion is morally unacceptable; and the third embraced the views of those in the administration who remained committed to population programs.[7]

As to the first of these, the main assertions were summarized in the Policy Statement itself:

> First and most important, population growth is, of itself, a neutral phenomenon. It is not necessarily good or ill. It becomes an asset or a problem only in conjunction with other factors, such as economic policy, social constraints, need for manpower, and so on.
>
> The population boom [in developing countries] was a challenge; it need not have been a crisis . . . [I]t coincided with two negative factors which, together, hindered families and nations in adapting to their changing circumstances.
>
> The first of these factors was governmental control of economies . . . One of the consequences of this "economic statism" was that it disrupted the natural mechanism for slowing population growth in problem areas . . . That pattern might be well under way in many nations where population growth is today a problem, if counter-productive government policies had not disrupted economic incentives, rewards and advancement. In this regard, localized crises of population growth are, in part, evidence of too much government control and planning, rather than too little.
>
> The second factor that turned the population boom into a crisis was . . . an outbreak of anti-intellectualism which attacked science, technology and the very concept of material progress.

Official adoption of this amended statement by the Reagan White House was accompanied by a decision to exclude the senior professional diplomat responsible for population matters—Ambassador Richard Benedick, the State Department's coordinator for population affairs—from the U.S. delegation to the conference. (Benedick resigned forthwith.) Other civil servants with expertise in demographic matters were similarly held at arm's length.

At the conference itself, the U.S. delegation's positions could not have diverged more drastically from those of its predecessor ten years earlier. Whereas the delegation appointed by Nixon was at the activist pole of the 136 national delegations attending in 1974, the delegation appointed by Reagan was clearly at the other pole of the 168 attending delegations in 1984. And the American views found little support from the other national delegations in Mexico City. Despite the strongest urging from the U.S. delegation's chairman, foreign policy officials in Washington refused to allow a formal negative vote to be registered in opposition to the consensus declaration adopted at the Mexico City conference. (Buckley reportedly went over the heads of his State Department superiors with a personal appeal to President Reagan, but to no effect.)

At the same time that the domestic American consensus on the virtue of active support for family limitation programs at home and abroad broke down, a number of other groups contested the new position adopted by the Reagan Administration. These alternative views were well disseminated in the 1980s and became the core of policy initiatives in the 1990s.

The intellectual origins of the modern feminist movement date back to long before the 1960s, but that decade witnessed a resurgence of thinking and action along feminist lines.[8] Modern contraceptives had at least something to do with liberating the lives and minds of women from the reproductive cycles of their bodies: the oral contraceptive and the intrauterine device (IUD), both of which were later criticized by some feminists, became readily available during that decade. But access to effective contraceptives was only one of many forces supporting the resurgence of feminist thinking. Others included the example of the civil-rights movement; the radicalizing effects of the Vietnam War and the opposition it engendered; anger about the prevailing sexism not only of conservatives but also of liberal and left civil-rights and antiwar movements; the increasing participation of women in the labor force; rising divorce rates and their implications for women's economic security; intellectual and literary currents both American and European; and the reactions of young women born during the early years of the postwar baby boom to the limitations in the lives of their mothers, many of whom had returned to domestic life after participating in the wartime production effort. Several organizations established during the 1960s and still rather small at the time of the 1973 *Roe v. Wade* decision now mobilized to oppose the rising chorus from the pro-life movement. The National Organization for Women, founded in 1966, highlighted the right to legal abortion on its agenda. The National Abortion Rights League, founded in 1969, was closely tied to feminist organizations and led by forceful, articulate women. Other groups promoting women's rights and describing themselves as pro-choice joined in opposition to the pro-life movement.

In a uniquely American style of politics, much of the activity on both sides of this debate was directed not toward electoral politics but toward the appointed federal judiciary. The pro-life movement sought to make commitment to reversing *Roe v. Wade* a litmus test for appointment of new justices to the Supreme Court. Throughout the Reagan and Bush Administrations, judicial nominees' views on the vexed question of abortion rights were prominent in an increasingly fractious process of Presidential nomination and Senate confirmation.

The matter came to a head at the nomination of Clarence Thomas to the Supreme Court in 1991. Feminist and pro-choice groups were convinced that Thomas's confirmation would shift the Court toward restricting or reversing *Roe v. Wade,* and they urged their supporters in the Senate to reject the nomination. The volatile politics of abortion were in this case coupled with the combustible politics of race, since Thomas is an African-American conservative who was being nominated to succeed the only previous African-American Supreme Court Justice, Thurgood Marshall, a prominent liberal who had been a leading civil-rights advocate. At the Senate Judiciary Committee hearings on the Thomas nomination, convened hastily after word was leaked to the press of dramatic sexual-harassment accusations against Thomas by one of his former staff members, Anita Hill, the issue of abortion and the ideological composition of the Supreme Court loomed conspicuously in the background. After Justice Thomas's confirmation, feminist groups mobilized public and congressional support on the issue of reproductive freedom, and the *Roe* decision remained the law of the land.

. . .

With the election in 1992 of Bill Clinton as President and Al Gore as Vice President, U.S. policy again shifted, though it did not return to that of the 1970s. Rapid population growth continued as an important issue, but access to abortion was also supported as a basic human right, and improvements in women's status and roles became pivotal. What might be termed the "Gore position" emphasized the need for aggressive environmental protection and identified rapid population growth as one of several forces tending toward environmental degradation.[9] And a more general feminist position was conveyed by the political power and prominence accorded by the new President to his wife, Hillary, and by his explicit policy of appointing women to high-level government positions.

One of the first moves made by the Clinton Administration was to reverse the Mexico City policy of the Reagan and Bush Administrations. Clinton reorganized the State Department to give higher-level attention to population and environmental issues and appointed ex-Senator Timothy Wirth as the first Under Secretary of State for Global Affairs, with responsibility for such matters.

The political process leading up to the 1994 International Conference on Population and Development in Cairo produced a consensus among U.S. interest groups that supported the Administration's programs; these were principally groups concerned with population policies and with women's health issues. Although in many respects this represented an uneasy alliance of groups with disparate agendas, the Administration successfully established common ground, and since the groups concerned with population and those focused on women's issues both had strong support within the Administration, neither could exclude the other; in any case, the compromise furthered the goals of both. The promised financial support was important to both, and it avoided the inevitable struggles in a zero-sum game fought over fixed resources.

In the preparatory meetings and at the Cairo conference in September 1994, the U.S. delegation took a leading role, as it had in Bucharest in 1974 (though not in Mexico City in 1984). Its position—that reproductive health must be central to any approach to population issues and that the empowerment of women was essential if high fertility levels were to decline—was supported by many other delegations, if strenu-

ously opposed by the Vatican and some Islamic governments. Reproductive health and women's empowerment became the leitmotif of the
Cairo consensus.

Flushed with success, the delegation returned to the final stages of
a fierce congressional election campaign that was to produce—yet
again—a sharp political reversal. The triumph of Republican candidates
brought about, for the first time since 1954, a Republican majority in both
houses of Congress, and individual Republican members of Congress
who for years had opposed population programs and feminist agendas
came suddenly into leadership positions on key committees—most notably, Senator Jesse Helms as chair of the Senate Foreign Relations Committee.

Governmental budgets everywhere were being stringently cut, and
U.S. foreign assistance to developing countries, especially aid directed
toward population goals, was seen as ripe for reduction if not elimination. Strong, ultimately successful efforts were made to reimpose the
Mexico City policy reversed only two years earlier. The level of funding
allocated for U.S. population assistance was severely limited, and legislation was introduced (but failed to pass) to eliminate the newly created Under Secretary position. The reversal of direction in the legislative
(though not executive) branch could not have been more striking. Meanwhile, debates on immigration became newly vituperative.

In the early history of the United States, immigrants and refugees were
powerful political and demographic forces. There were no quantitative
legal limitations on immigration until 1921, though qualitative restrictions imposed during the preceding half century had excluded categories
such as paupers, criminals, illiterates—and most Asians. In a complex
process of political mobilization and legislative action, numerical limits
on immigration were imposed after World War I, and visas were allocated according to a National Origins Quota System intended to prevent
immigrants from changing the national and ethnic composition of the
United States. Due both to these restrictions and to the deep economic
distress of the Great Depression, immigration flows dropped to very low

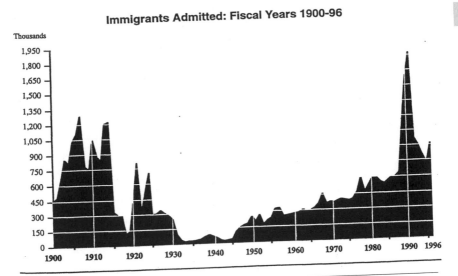

Immigrants Admitted: Fiscal Years 1900-96

Source: U.S. Immigration and Naturalization Service, *Statistical Yearbook of the Immigration and Naturalization Service, 1996* (U.S. Government Printing Office: Washington, D.C., 1997), p. 17.

levels during the 1930s. The immigration policies of the 1920s were maintained well into the 1960s, but World War II led to a temporary legislative initiative that sowed the seeds of an unintended and dramatic immigration harvest during the 1960s, 1970s, and 1980s—the 1942 bracero program, a wartime emergency measure that allowed American farmers in Texas and other Southwestern states to recruit temporary workers from Mexico to replace those drafted into wartime military service.

Changes in immigration laws during the 1950s incorporated the National Origins Quotas with little change. By the 1960s, however, their flagrant and substantially racist provisions (e.g., the exclusion of nearly all Asian immigrants and the numerical preferences for northern and western Europeans) became unsustainable in a nation with an unresolved history of racial segregation and discrimination. President Kennedy proposed major reforms to eliminate these offensive provisions, proposals that after his assassination were promoted by his brothers Robert and Edward and embraced by his successor, Lyndon Johnson.

The reforms eventually passed and signed by President Johnson in 1965 eliminated both the exclusion of Asian immigrants and the National Origins Quota System. At the same time, they embodied provisions intended to maintain a similar national-origins composition among immigrants: the method chosen gave a strong preference to immediate and extended family members of U.S. citizens. Proponents expected that future immigration streams would therefore be concentrated among the national origins of the 1965 population. A key goal was to make it easier for would-be immigrants from Italy, Greece, and Poland to come to the United States.

In response to questions about whether a repeal of the so-called Asia-Pacific Triangle provision that excluded most Asian immigration would produce a surge of Asian migration, Representative Emanuel Celler told his colleagues, "There will not be, comparatively, many Asians or Africans entering this country . . . Since the people of Africa and Asia have very few relatives here, comparatively few could immigrate from those countries because they have no family ties in the U.S." An advocacy group supporting increased access for Asian immigrants, the Japanese American Citizens League, agreed with this assessment: "Thus, it would seem that, although the immigration bill eliminated race as a matter of principle, in actual operation immigration will still be controlled by the now discredited national origins system and the general pattern of immigration which exists today will continue for many years to come." *Wall Street Journal* editorial writers summarized the shift from national origins to family ties: "This had more emotional appeal and, perhaps more to the point, insured that the new immigration would not stray radically from the old one."[10]

Everyone was wrong: the very opposite of what was predicted took place. This was a powerful example of the law of unintended consequences: "pioneer" immigrants from Asia, admitted under a labor certification system as nurses, doctors, engineers, and scientists, began to use the family-preference categories while they were still resident aliens to petition for admission of their spouses and children. The aliens recognized the advantages of expeditious naturalization, too, since it permitted unlimited admission of immediate family members and petitions for the admission of extended family, such as adult brothers and sisters. Family-based immigration from Asia grew, at first gradually and later rapidly.

In addition, a large-scale admission of Vietnamese began during the 1970s, along with smaller numbers of Laotians and Cambodians. Most were admitted under the President's "parole" authority or via special legislation. Overall immigration from Asia accelerated rapidly, especially after 1972: whereas it had been 5 percent of the total inflow at the time of the 1965 act, it exceeded 40 percent (of a much larger total) only fifteen years later.[11]

Meanwhile, the bracero program of 1942 had powerful and long-lived unintended consequences. By the end of World War II, farmers in Texas and elsewhere in the Southwest had become dependent on this hardworking, low-paid labor force and successfully lobbied for year-to-year continuation of the program. The braceros themselves, for their part, learned how to find employment at wages much higher than those in Mexico.

By the early 1950s, it became clear that the legal bracero migration stream was accompanied by a large and growing illegal stream of what were then known by the disparaging term "wetbacks"—people who swam across the Rio Grande to enter the United States. As the bracero program and the illegal migration began to attract opposition from organized labor, which worried about migrant competition for jobs, and from liberal church groups, concerned about exploitation, farming interests in Texas mobilized to protect the economic advantage they had gained from ready access to cheap, compliant labor, legal or illegal. Their most notable success was the so-called Texas Proviso, a brief clause that limited the force of the prohibition against the importation and harboring of illegal aliens.[12] The prohibition itself was clear: any person who

willfully or knowingly conceals, harbors, or shields from detection or attempts to conceal, harbor, or shield from detection, in any place . . . any alien . . . not duly admitted . . . shall be guilty of a felony, and upon conviction thereof shall be punished by a fine not exceeding $2,000 or by imprisonment for a term not exceeding five years, or both, for each alien in respect to whom any violation of this subsection occurs.

But the Texas Proviso effectively emasculated it: "Provided, however, that for the purposes of this section, employment (including the usual and normal practices incident to employment) shall not be deemed to constitute harboring." Texas farmers succeeded in preserving the bracero program much longer than they had perhaps expected; only more than a decade later, in 1964, were the forces aligned against the bracero program able to terminate it. But at this point, the Texas Proviso, buried quietly in the recesses of the Immigration and Nationality Act, kicked in.

Southwest growers who had lost their two-decade-long access to bracero labor learned quickly that there was real virtue in this provision. While harboring illegal aliens was a serious crime punishable by jail terms and hefty fines for each violation, to employ such persons knowingly—and provide housing as one of the "usual and normal practices incident to employment"—was deemed lawful. Moreover, the Texas Proviso codified a deep asymmetry in the relative power of employer and employee: unscrupulous employers understood that any workers who protested against wages or working conditions could be readily disposed of by alerting the Border Patrol about their unlawful residence, with no negative consequences for the employer.

Although measuring illegal immigration is almost impossible, given that these migrants naturally resist being counted, there is little doubt that such migrations grew rapidly during the late 1960s. By the early 1970s, liberal Democratic congressional leaders such as Peter Rodino, then chairman of the House Immigration Subcommittee, moved to expunge the Texas Proviso by making it unlawful for employers knowingly to employ illegal aliens—a provision that came to be called "employer sanctions." Similar provisions had long been components of labor law in most Western democracies. But in the United States, Rodino's proposal attracted strong opposition—from both obvious and surprising sources.

The obvious source of opposition were the groups that had promoted and benefited from the Texas Proviso—politically conservative Southwest agricultural interests (often large and highly capitalized, unlike the conventional American image of the Midwestern family farm). In many cases, these were expanding and profitable agribusinesses growing labor-intensive fruit and vegetable crops for an increasingly national market. For much of the 1970s, these interest groups blocked action in the Senate through their allies' control of key committee chairmanships.

More surprising was the later emergence of opposition to employer sanctions from organizations otherwise considered liberal. The most vocal of these were fairly new organizations such as the Mexican American Legal Defense and Education Fund, created during the 1960s civil-rights movement in emulation of successful black organizations such as the Legal Defense and Education Fund of the National Association for the Advancement of Colored People. These elite organizations were directed by well-educated, politically active Mexican Americans, but they lacked a mass membership base, deriving their support from liberal philanthropic foundations (Ford, Rockefeller, Carnegie) that supported political-legal movements to defend Mexican-American citizens against job and educational discrimination, especially in the Southwest. Although these groups described themselves as representing Mexican Americans, their positions were frequently in opposition to the views of most Mexican Americans, who on this subject did not differ greatly from other Americans.[13]

Still, it was strange that these liberal Mexican-American organizations formed coalitions with conservative Southwest growers to oppose any reversal of the Texas Proviso, by then under assault from liberals like Rodino. The growers appealed to conservatives by emphasizing the economic advantages and low costs to the regional or national economy of employing illegal immigrants and by tapping into their general distrust of governmental intervention in the labor market. Moreover, prosperous Southwest farming interests were able to mobilize, often at short notice, millions of dollars in political contributions that could be focused directly on wavering legislators. The Mexican-American political groups lacked these fund-raising capacities, but they brought to the table an argument that appealed to liberals—that employer sanctions would inevitably lead to increased racial and ethnic job discrimination, because employers would respond by not hiring people who looked or sounded foreign. Moreover, they formed alliances with liberal groups such as the

American Civil Liberties Union by arguing that any attempt to develop fraud-resistant methods to identify lawful workers would be an invasion of privacy.

On the basis of available survey data, it can be said that the lobbying activities of these groups operated in opposition to most public opinion on the matter, which consistently opposed illegal immigration by majorities of 70–90 percent. Moreover, smaller but still substantial majorities opposed expanded legal immigration.

Distribution of Responses about the Number of Immigrants That Should Be Permitted to Enter the United States
(in percentages of respondents)

Choices	1946	1953	1965	1977	1981	1982	1986	1988	1990
More/increase	5	13	8	7	5	4	7	6	9
Same/present level	32	37	39	37	22	23	35	34	29
Fewer/decrease	37 [14]*	39	33	42	65	66	49	53	48
No opinion/ don't know	12	11	20	14	8	7	9	7	14

In 1946, the question was phrased: "Should we permit more persons from Europe to come to this country each year than we did before the war, should we keep the number about the same, or should we reduce the number?" In subsequent polls the question was usually phrased: "Should immigration be kept at its present level, increased, or decreased?"

In 1990, the question was phrased: "Is it your impression that the current immigration laws allow too many immigrants, too few immigrants, or about the right number of immigrants into this country each year?"

*"None" was offered as a choice of response only in 1946.

Source: Rita J. Simon and Susan H. Alexander, *The Ambivalent Welcome: Print Media, Public Opinion, and Immigration* (Westport, Conn.: Praeger, 1993), p. 41.

As can be seen in the table, public opinion polls in the twenty-five years between the 1965 and 1990 immigration acts showed between 4 and 9 percent of the public preferring more immigrants, while between

33 and 66 percent desired fewer. After reviewing four decades of public-opinion polls on this topic, one supporter of expanded admissions reported, "Briefly, all of the data . . . indicated that most Americans say they would like to decrease the number of immigrants and refugees permitted to enter the United States. If public opinion polls dictated U.S. immigration policy, much of the restrictionist legislation of the 1920s would have remained in place, and refugee programs would probably never have been enacted."[14]

A cautionary note is in order here: American views on immigration are not so uniformly negative as such data suggest. It is well known, for example, that public opinion questions on whether certain categories of individuals should be admitted (e.g., close family members, refugees) elicit more favorable responses than do questions on aggregate numbers. This point is often made by those who advocate more open policies. In addition, Americans have more positive views of immigrants as individuals than they do of substantial flows of immigration. Finally, the United States is one of only three or four Western countries with long histories of acknowledged large-scale immigration (the others are Canada, Australia, New Zealand, and perhaps France).

One way of describing American attitudes toward immigration is to say that they demonstrate what may be termed "ambivalent romanticism."[15] While there is little or no public support for large or increased immigrant admissions, Americans romanticize past immigrants and view the country as a unique nation of immigrants. This is far from correct: only a small percentage of the U.S. population is foreign-born—smaller than many other countries, including Canada, Australia, Israel, Kuwait, even Germany and Switzerland—but the myth derives from the truth that the country was largely founded by immigrants and that substantial percentages of the U.S. population still, though themselves native-born, have parents or grandparents who were immigrants.

Even national icons such as the Statue of Liberty have been recast as symbols of immigration. The statue was conceived by French Republicans at the end of the Franco-Prussian War as a symbol of solidarity between the then-threatened French Republican tradition and that of the other great republic of the day. Only later—after the main immigrant-processing center was by the vagaries of geography built on Ellis Island in New York Harbor, a few hundred meters from Bedloe's Island, on which the statue had been erected; after a paean to immigration by the poet Emma Lazarus ("Give me your tired, your poor . . .") was placed on its pedestal; and after the promotion of World War I bonds had invoked its image in appeals to immigrants—did the immigration imagery of the statue become dominant.[16]

These ambivalent, romanticized elements of U.S. opinion about immigration give us one explanation for the peculiarities of contemporary debates, which so confound and bemuse observers from other liberal democracies. In most developed countries, nationalist sentiments lead conservatives to oppose large-scale immigration, with some espousing flagrantly xenophobic positions. Meanwhile, liberals and socialists, though often ambivalent, also tend to oppose large-scale immigration in the interest of protecting the poorer sectors of society from competition for scarce employment and housing. But in the United States, the positions are often reversed. The American New Right has taken up themes of what we might term "conservative libertarianism" and "cornucopianism," according to which governmental action to impede any of the forces of the free market (including migration) is suspect and there are no limits to the numbers of people that can be supported in ever-rising prosperity if only free rein is given to the genius of human creativity and the entrepreneurial spirit. The editorial page of *The Wall Street Journal* has twice advocated the adoption of a simple five-word constitutional amendment on immigration: "There shall be open borders."

American liberalism, on the other hand, with a weak democratic socialist tradition and a deep preoccupation with American racial conflicts, is heavily influenced by the ideologies of civil libertarianism and civil rights.[17] Civil libertarians are committed to preserving liberty by denying the state access to information that it might use to oppress its citizenry, while assuring to all persons (irrespective of their legal status) full constitutional guarantees and judicial due process. The civil-rights stream of American liberalism, though sometimes clashing with civil-liberties ideas about individual versus group rights of racial and ethnic minorities, either supports large-scale immigration of racial and ethnic brethren or maintains a sometimes uncomfortable silence out of solidarity with other advocacy groups.

Observers from other liberal democracies are also puzzled by American reactions to proposals for requiring better documentation for work authorization. Such measures have long been in place elsewhere and are not controversial. National insurance identification numbers are taken for granted and stored in national computers. These documents are not identity cards, which do elicit discomfort in some liberal European democracies (e.g., Great Britain) though not in others (e.g., France).

More important differences between the United States and western Europe are due to the unusual structure of the U.S. government. Of the three branches defined in the Constitution, the Congress (with occasional challenges from some members of the judiciary) has been most active on immigration and refugee matters and has, over the past decades, been increasingly dominated by interest groups, for some of which immigration policy is transcendentally important, worthy of nearly full-time attention and heavy financial investment.

In a system driven by interest-group politics, what really matters to a politician is the strongly held views of small constituencies; a single-issue bloc of less than 5 percent of the electorate can make the difference between re-election and defeat and can also represent lucrative sources of campaign finance. In the calculus of political judgment, an ambitious politician would be well advised to submerge the more broadly based but less committed views of the larger electorate and follow the advice of groups that can give him either substantial campaign funds or blocs of committed voters.

The outcome of the conflict over employer sanctions, between focused but narrow opposition and broad but diffuse support, was thus not surprising. From 1971 to 1986, the opposition was able to block efforts by the liberal Rodino and his supporters in Congress, as well as by the Nixon, Ford, and Carter Administrations; the scale of illegal immigration seemed, both at the time and more clearly in retrospect, to expand continuously, though the numbers of what is an inherently unmeasurable phenomenon were frequently exaggerated.

Then in 1986, after a decade and a half of contention, laws were enacted embracing employer sanctions for the first time but joined with a grand bargain: the millions of then-resident illegal aliens would be granted legal status. Also, strong opposition from employers of illegal aliens and from civil libertarians, ethnic lobby groups, and churches led to a compromise on the details of the new employer sanctions that in effect rendered them unenforceable. One example is the provision that up to twenty-nine different documents may be offered to employers to prove that workers are lawfully resident and entitled to work; in addition, employers are precluded from requesting any particular document they might consider less prone to fraud. The result: employer sanctions failed to do more than temporarily affect the flow of illegal immigrants, who took advantage of a surge of easily obtained and inexpensive fraudulent documents.

The deep chasm between public policy and public opinion on immigration issues reached its apparent nadir with the Immigration Act of 1990. The key premises were that illegal immigration had mostly been brought under control; that the economy had important labor shortages, especially among highly skilled workers such as engineers and scientists; and that additional admissions of such categories required no compensating reduction in admissions of those with family ties to U.S. citizens and resident aliens. It thus increased the numbers of legal immigrants admitted for permanent residence by 30–40 percent and favored skilled workers. In addition, it facilitated the admission for temporary residence of a category termed "priority workers"; the numbers involved each year were large (about sixty-five thousand), and the length of temporary residence was longer than might be supposed, typically three years, renewable for an additional three years.

As noted earlier, while Congress expanded the numbers of legal immigrants admitted annually by more than one-third with this law, only 9 percent of the public believed that then-current numbers were too few, while five times as many (48 percent) found immigrant admissions too many. The interest groups and politicians who pushed through the expansionary 1990 act were aware of public opinion but chose to act otherwise, and did so effectively.

Only three years later, a powerful anti-immigration backlash emerged, created by several relatively independent elements. First, it became clear that the numbers of illegal immigrants had not been declining, despite the assumptions of the 1990 act. Second, economic recession coupled with defense cutbacks following the collapse of the

Soviet Union produced surpluses, rather than shortages, of highly skilled engineers and scientists. Third, the state with the largest numbers of both legal and illegal immigrants, California, was suffering a severe economic recession and budgetary crisis. National public-opinion polls showed that, while the percentage favoring increased immigration remained below 10 percent, the percentage favoring reduced immigration rose to 61 percent in 1993.[18]

The backlash was most evident in California; the catalyst was a 1993 volunteer effort to put what came to be called Proposition 187 on the November 1994 election ballot; its purpose was to prohibit the state and local governments of California from giving illegal aliens free public education, nonemergency medical care, and local welfare or income-transfer benefits.*

Proposition 187 organizers wanted an endorsement from the Democratic and Republican nominees for the governorship, but both declined. Moreover, the proposition was opposed by nearly every elite entity, liberal and conservative alike, including most of the media and the leaders of religious, business, union, and professional organizations. At that time, polls uniformly showed that the Democratic nominee, State Treasurer Kathleen Brown, was well ahead of the incumbent Republican, Pete Wilson, who was widely blamed for the state's economic woes. During the spring of the election year, Brown held a twenty-percentage-point margin over Wilson. Then suddenly, Wilson reversed himself, endorsed Proposition 187, and made control of illegal immigration a central issue in his campaign. For him, this strategy had ironies, since as a U.S. senator he had promoted laws that constrained the ability of the federal government to regulate the employment of illegal immigrants by California agricultural interests.

The political payoff of Wilson's volte-face was dramatic. He rose rapidly in the public-opinion polls, and Brown's lead withered away. Within only a few months, polling data showed Wilson rising to fifteen

---

*The California Constitution states that such referenda may be placed on the ballot if they have the required substantial number of endorsing signatures from electors; if then supported by a majority of those voting, they become state law, bypassing the state legislature.

points ahead. The November election reinstalled Wilson for another term, and Proposition 187 was adopted by a margin of 59 to 41 percent, to the shock of the many groups that had opposed it.

Subsequently, Wilson announced that he would stand as a candidate for the Republican nomination for President in 1996 and that immigration issues would be central to his campaign. In 1995, however, he was forced to withdraw after medical problems affected his all-important speaking voice and he failed to raise the huge campaign funds necessary to be competitive in American Presidential campaigns. The Republican front-runner, Senator Bob Dole, later appointed Wilson his national campaign chairman, and Wilson continued to proclaim, with ever-increasing assertiveness, the damage done to California by the failure of federal immigration policy. As one commentator noted: "Nowhere has Wilson shown greater determination than in his attempts to curb illegal immigration and to confront Washington on what he perceives as inadequate federal funding to halt the flow of illegal immigrants into his state. And nowhere has Wilson had greater political success with an issue."[19]

Enforcement of Proposition 187 was quickly enjoined by a federal judge; its provisions continue to be moot, while the lengthy judicial process wends its way through motions, hearings, and appeals. Meanwhile, its proponents are trying to expand the grassroots campaign to other states that allow for citizen referenda.

Advocates of Proposition 187 had urged California voters to "send a message to Washington" by voting in its favor. Republicans and Democrats with little or no interest in immigration issues, having watched the astonishing reversal of fortunes between Kathleen Brown and Pete Wilson, apparently concluded that immigration was an issue of considerable interest to the voting public, not just to employers and ethnic or religious groups. In December 1995, a nationwide Roper poll reported that 70 percent of respondents endorsed limiting admissions to fewer than three hundred thousand per year (versus the eight hundred thousand–plus then current).[20]

A flurry of legislative proposals were introduced in the new Congress, some of which had their origins in recommendations from the Commission on Immigration Reform (of which one of the authors of this book—Teitelbaum—was a member and vice chair). Opposition arose from the same groups as in the past and from computer-software firms that wanted to be able to hire foreign engineers and programmers. Ultimately, three major laws were enacted in 1996: the Anti-Terrorism and Effective Death Penalty Act; the Personal Responsibility and Work Opportunity Reconciliation Act (known more generally as the welfare reform of 1996); and the Immigration Control and Financial Responsibility Act.

The Commission's recommendations were based on two principles. First, the United States should do more to reduce illegal immigration: managing the borders to prevent it, increasing penalties for smuggling, and testing systems to help employers determine quickly and reliably who is legally authorized to work in the United States. Second, the United States should strike two grand bargains to cope with the large and rising visa backlogs and immigrants' use of the U.S. welfare system: speed up the admission of immediate family members of resident aliens by allocating to this nuclear-family category the visas currently going to adult brothers and sisters of U.S. citizens; and permit legal immigrants access to welfare and other social safety-net programs but enforce the promises of financial support that are required of their sponsors.

Congress adopted much of the Commission's three-pronged package designed to reduce and deter illegal immigration: preventing unlawful entry and facilitating legal entry across borders; improving verification systems and enhancing labor-law enforcement to reduce access to jobs and income-transfer benefits for those who succeed in becoming unlawful immigrants, though in a considerably weakened form; and quickly removing illegal aliens when they are apprehended.

The Border Patrol was strengthened and other staff were augmented to expedite legal entries. A pilot program, voluntary for employers, to test a fraud-resistant verification system was authorized, but Congress refused to authorize more inspectors to enforce minimum-wage and other labor laws. Two of the bills made it easier to expel aliens convicted of felonies in the United States and to exclude foreigners who entered without valid documents. (If in the latter case an alien applies for asylum, a credible claim must be made promptly to the appropriate officer; if judged not credible, the rejected claim may be appealed to an asylum judge, who must make a decision within seven days.)

On legal immigration, the Commission concluded that the current system needs a major overhaul to establish clear priorities and to strengthen administrative credibility. At present, more than 1.1 million spouses and minor children of legal immigrants are in backlogs that require waits of up to ten years. In fact, many do not wait and jump the queue by entering illegally. Meanwhile, there are even larger backlogs, numbering 1.7 million, of adult siblings of U.S. citizens; those in the Philippines, Mexico, and other high-demand countries must sometimes wait for twenty to thirty years for permission to immigrate legally.

One of the grand bargains recommended by the Commission would eliminate immigration visas for brothers and sisters of U.S. citizens and use them to unite husbands and wives, parents and small children. But these provisions were energetically opposed by an unusual alliance of business, religious, and ethnic groups, which succeeded in blocking congressional action by bringing together opponents from the conservative and liberal wings of both parties. However, they could not prevent the adoption of congressional proposals for changes to the U.S. benefits system.

The Commission had argued for a second grand bargain on such benefits, guided by a clear line between illegal and legal immigrants. Those who lived in the United States in violation of immigration laws should be able to obtain only emergency, public health, and constitutionally protected services (under current judicial interpretation, the latter include free primary and secondary education). However, legal immigrants admitted in compliance with the law should continue to be eligible for all the same benefits available to U.S. citizens. The latter recommendation acknowledged that legal revisions were needed for affidavits of support, because U.S. residents often promised to support their immigrating parents but then refused to do so later and instead helped them to get public benefits such as Supplementary Security Income (SSI) and Medicaid. This behavior had been possible only because U.S. courts ruled that the affidavits were not legally binding. Hence, the Commission suggested that they be made so. The financial obligations would then be enforced unless the sponsor was unable to meet them because of unemployment, illness, or even death, in which event the immigrant parent would be eligible for public assistance. Instead, the new welfare law put a time limit of five years' access to such benefits for legal immigrants, although if they became citizens they would no longer be subject to this constraint. The Commission believed that this measure would give immigrants a perverse incentive to naturalize: apply for citizenship in order to get welfare. Subsequent amendments have relaxed some of those limits on benefits available to legal immigrants. The issues involved continue to be volatile and subject to change.

We can see, then, that the American political system has recently been more responsive to the preferences of ethnic and economic interest groups desiring increased immigration than to the wishes of broader, yet less organized groups of citizens who want to reduce it. Of one thing we can be sure: the conflict will go on, and given the volatility of migratory flows and the difficulty in measuring them, that conflict is bound to intensify.

These debates on fertility and migration have had demographic consequences in another sense, too. Fertility and immigration patterns clearly relate in complex, sometimes volatile ways to changing ethnic and racial identities, many of which both reflect and affect demographic categories incorporated in official censuses and statistics. How that process has shaped the U.S. Census is the subject of the next chapter.

chapter 8

AMERICAN POLITICAL INTERESTS AND POPULATION STATISTICS

The 1990 U.S. Census form contained a revised question about "race." This was to be answered in terms of one of sixteen categories, thirteen of which referred to different Native American and Asian and Pacific Islander groups, which together accounted for less than 10 percent of the population. Of those reporting themselves in one of these thirteen categories, that of American Indians, quite a few gave their tribal affiliations as Polish, Haitian, and Arab. Responses about ancestry on the 1980 and 1990 U.S. Censuses indicated, implausibly, that during this ten-year period the numbers reporting German, Italian, and Polish ancestry increased by 18, 21, and 14 percent, respectively, while those reporting French and English ancestry declined by 20 and 34 percent, respectively. Over the same decade, those reporting themselves as Cajun mysteriously increased sixty-seven-fold, while the numbers reporting Croatian ancestry increased by more than 100 percent.

How can we explain these and other baffling elements in the supposedly objective data of the census? The answer lies in the politics that have surrounded the collection and use of U.S. demographic data since the 1960s. Yet we must go much further back, indeed to the founding of the Republic, to identify the historical roots of the demographic politics that has flowered so profusely in our own time.

The idea of a comprehensive demographic census was critical in the political deliberations that created the U.S. Constitution. The census was a facet of the Great Compromise reached by the Constitutional Convention of 1787. Compromise was necessary on three contested issues: whether representation should be accorded to all "persons" or restricted to a limited number of categories;* how political power should be apportioned among large-population and small-population states; and what weighting should be given to slave populations.[1]

A decennial census was essential to the allocation and reallocation of political representation. The U.S. Constitution was not only the world's first written constitution but also the first to codify a regular census in such a way as to restrict or control later tampering by politicians seeking political advantage.[2] The question of who should be counted was answered in the following way, after much debate. It was agreed that the most inclusive concept—"persons" resident in the United States at the time—should be embraced for the purposes of the census rather than restricting the basic count to any of the more limited categories that had been proposed. (It is worth noting the deep paradoxes inherent in this decision: even with this expansive concept of "persons," a majority of those counted for purposes of representation—notably, all women and, of course, children—were at the same time excluded from voting, jury duty, and military duty.)

Having agreed on the fundamentals—a decennial count of all persons for purposes of allocating political representation—other compromises had to be reached. The first, a compromise between the big and small state representatives, led to the creation of a legislature consisting of two elected houses (a mutation of the British form, in which the Commons are elected and the Lords hereditary or appointed). In the House of Representatives, apportionment of seats to states would be done differentially by population as enumerated by the census, to protect the interests of the large-population states; in the Senate, each state would be given equal representation irrespective of its population, to protect the interests of the small-population states.

Delegates from slave states insisted that slaves would have to be counted, even if they were treated by their laws as legal chattel and precluded from voting. A different but in some sense related issue concerned how American Indians should be treated, given the ambiguity that those living on reservations held tribal nationality, which, among

---

*Alternative proposals would have limited representation to categories such as "adults," "voters," "men," "free men," "landowners."

other things, excused them from the obligation to pay taxes. On these matters, the Great Compromise was as follows: slaves and American Indians would be enumerated fully (or as fully as possible), but for purposes of calculating political apportionment, two-fifths of the enumerated slaves and all "Indians not taxed" would be excluded.

Adoption of the U.S. decennial census was a political decision, but it also aimed at limiting the political nature of the census. The original plan required that political considerations *not* be allowed to distort the basic data by which important components of political representation would be apportioned. At the same time, a number of political decisions were made during the constitutional debate as to how such census data would be treated. This push and pull between getting the basic facts and interpreting census categories politically has continued to affect U.S. population statistics in the more than two centuries since the Constitutional Convention of 1787.

For many decades, the most overtly political aspect of census data had to do with drawing the boundaries of electoral districts for federal representatives. Responsibility for redistricting lies with each state government. After certification by the federal government of the number of congressional seats to which it is entitled by the most recent census, each state must modify its district boundary lines to reflect any changes in the number of electoral districts and, in recent decades, to keep the number of persons in each district roughly comparable.

Given the decennial arrival of new census data and the need to redistrict, how might district boundaries best be drawn to the political advantage of those doing the drawing? An early Massachusetts governor, Elbridge Gerry, achieved immortality of a sort when in 1812 he engineered redistricting so as to distribute voters in a manner benefiting his party. A critical cartoon caricatured one of the more extreme state senate districts into the body shape of a salamander, thereby immortalizing the process of boundary drawing for partisan advantage as "gerrymandering." Elbridge Gerry went on to be elected Vice President under James Madison and died in office in 1814.[3]

Gerrymandering for partisan advantage was viewed with contempt and derision, and such opprobrium, along with several judicial reversals, caused the practice to wane. But it was far from dead and rose again during the 1970s and 1980s, in the service of what were seen by its proponents as the higher political goals of civil rights and minority representation. The Voting Rights Act of 1965 was adopted to end flagrantly discriminatory electoral practices in the Deep South through which the dominant white political class had minimized the numbers of black voters and black members of the U.S. House of Representatives. Among other provisions, the Voting Rights Act gave the Justice Department the right to review, and to reverse, redistricting decisions if they had the effect of scattering or otherwise minimizing the votes of minorities.[4]

As this and later laws and judicial interpretations were implemented, however, a new kind of creative boundary drawing arose. Congressional districts in shapes far odder than salamanders were devised and implemented, now with federal scrutiny and approval. The goal was, in a sense, one of political equity: to ensure that the number of black representatives was more in line with the proportion of black people in the electorate. Given the American system of single-representative constituencies (as compared to the proportional-representative systems of some other liberal democracies), it was inevitable that efforts would be made to concentrate minority voters into districts in which they represented the voting majority. If this required strange boundaries, so be it: the goal was high-minded.

The results became most apparent after redistricting based on the 1990 census. Given two facts—that residential segregation of minority groups (especially blacks) in some U.S. regions is substantial and that black American voters typically vote overwhelmingly for Democratic Party candidates—there was bound to be powerful political pressure applied. In general, black Democratic state politicians believed that creating "majority-minority" districts would increase the number of blacks (hence Democrats) elected. But Republican politicians also saw advantages: concentrating minority groups that voted for Democrats would solidify Republican holds on marginal districts that had previously contained some of these voters.

The outcome was the creation, frequently on a bipartisan basis, of new electoral districts with shapes that put Gerry's salamander to shame. The new Twelfth Congressional District of North Carolina was

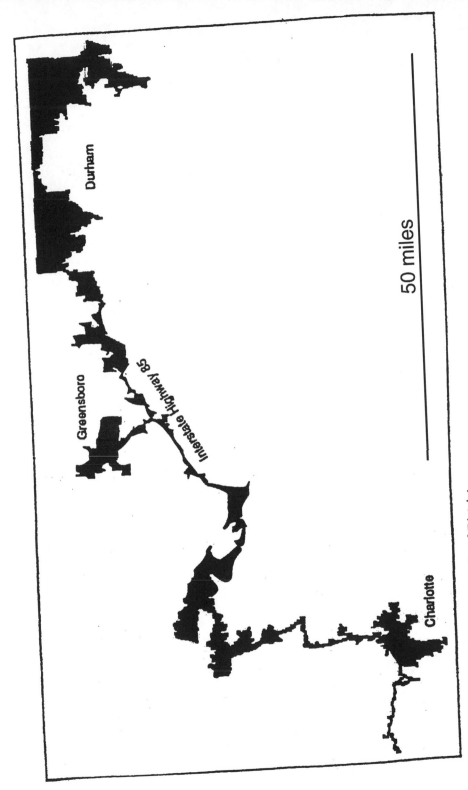

North Carolina's Twelfth Congressional District

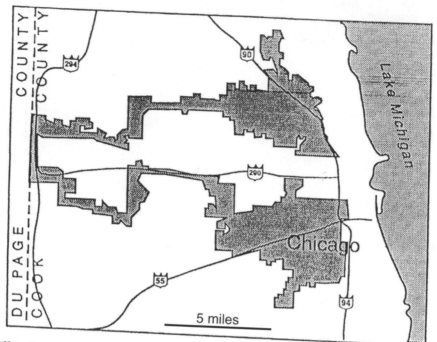

Illinois's Fourth Congressional District

configured in the shape of a snake. The goal was to create a majority-minority district by assembling predominantly black parts of cities, towns, and rural areas that stretched along an interstate highway for more than a hundred miles and that at some points was only a mile wide. A newly drawn Fourth Congressional District of Illinois, which zig-zagged for thirty miles in a tilted U-shaped pattern, was intended to maximize the concentration of Hispanic residents. In Texas, Louisiana, Georgia, and New York, several districts, such as the Thirtieth in Texas, were carved out for similar purposes.

In 1995, a new majority-minority district created in Georgia provoked a Supreme Court ruling challenging the fundamental concept of such boundary drawing.[5] In June 1996, the Court declared that legislative districts purposefully carved out to increase congressional representation of racial and ethnic minorities were unconstitutional if race was the predominant factor in their design. Such districts, including those in Georgia and North Carolina, were invalidated.[6]

The concepts of race, national origin, ethnic origin, ancestry, and nationality have a long and sometimes torturous history in the United States,* in many cases tied up with official census taking and other statistical activities. As we have seen, the Constitution created categorical distinctions that by modern standards are offensive and that were not expunged until after the Civil War. Given the political sensitivity of these categories in the United States, it is in some sense remarkable that any data have been collected consistently. Yet it is also true that the U.S. Census has not been permitted to include data about other sensitive categories of clear social relevance *and* of interest to political groups: in particular, data about religion.

Originally, racial categories in the census were simple: white, Negro, and Indian. From 1790 to 1860, enumerators (who during this period were federal marshals) were given no instructions as to how to define these categories; they were free to determine the race of each person in their enumeration districts. In five censuses between 1840 and 1910, enumerators were to subclassify Negroes by skin color, typically into blacks and mulattoes but in 1890 into blacks, mulattoes, quadroons, and octoroons, an effort generally agreed to have been a failure.[7]

Over time, these categories have been altered in the twenty-one rounds of the decennial census to reflect changes in political sensitivities or, in some cases, to develop information on subpopulations of interest to particular political groups. The 1990 census inquiry on race and ethnicity embodied three different (often overlapping) questions

*The word "nationality" itself has a more restricted meaning in American English than in other languages. Although some of the founders of the American Republic (such as Benjamin Franklin) and many at the turn of the twentieth century thought otherwise, the vision of America that has come to be dominant is universalistic: anyone, from any national, racial, religious, or ethnic origin, can become an American. "Nationality" in this context means, simply, citizenship, which after the abolition of slavery was available to anyone admitted for permanent residence after a waiting period of several years. The notion of groups of fellow citizens divided among different nationalities, as in the Soviet Union, therefore does not arise in the modern U.S. context.

and concepts: race, Hispanic origin, and ancestry. Until 1960, census in-
terviewers were empowered to code race of respondents based on their
own judgments at the time of the interviews. Since then, race has been
based on self-identification on a mailed questionnaire. The sixteen "race"
categories of the 1990 census represented one of the more elaborate
classifications.

The data about race gathered from such questions are inevitably
problematic. One respected researcher notes that more than nine million
people chose not to respond to these precoded categories;[8] most of the
nonrespondents were of Hispanic origin and wrote in "Mexican-
American," "Puerto Rican," and so on. These Hispanic respondents
were not re-coded in the race categories they had left blank, although
non-Hispanic nonrespondents were; for example, those who indicated
"German" were re-coded white; "Haitian" became black; "Syrian" was
re-coded to white; "Dominican" was re-coded to black. The researcher
notes that the "decision not to re-code the bulk of Hispanic responses
but to re-code virtually all others reflects political rather than demographic realities."

The 1990 census race question includes three categories of Native
Americans: Indian (Amer.), with the respondent requested to "print the
name of the enrolled or principal tribe"; Eskimo; and Aleut. To the discomfort of the Census Bureau, about 8 percent of persons responding as
"Indian (Amer.)" identified their tribes as Haitian, Polish, African-
American, Hispanic, Arab, or similar categories normally not considered
American Indian. There were also no fewer than 10 categories of Asian
or Pacific Islander in the 1990 census form (a consequence of pressure
from an Asian-American congressman holding a key committee position).

Serious problems of interpretation also afflicted the census question
about Spanish/Hispanic origin. This question, asked of all respondents,
was conceived during the 1970s by the Census Bureau and its advisory
committees as quite different from race; that is, a person could be of any
race and be either of Spanish/Hispanic origin or not. However, about 40
percent of respondents in both the 1980 and 1990 censuses who said
they were of Spanish/Hispanic origin specified no racial or other ethnic

1990 Race and Hispanic Origin Questions in U.S. Census

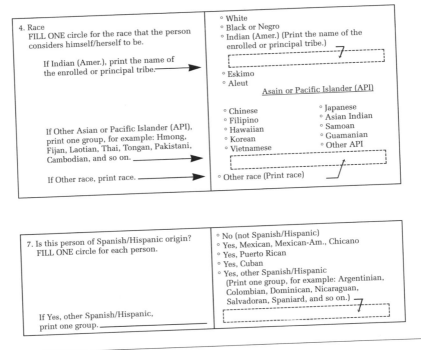

Source: 1990 Census.

identity. Furthermore, when Hispanic respondents were reinterviewed, about 10 percent of them did *not* identify themselves as Hispanic.

Finally, the ancestry question appearing on the long-form questionnaire sent to a 17 percent sample of households produced responses generally considered highly subjective and variable. Both the 1980 and 1990 census ancestry questions provided a "for example" list intended to illustrate what kind of information was being sought. But for some reason, the two lists differed. Now that we can compare responses in the 1980 and 1990 censuses, we can say with assurance that the choice of examples for the illustrative lists greatly affected the responses.

In the 1980 census, German and English were given as examples, and each elicited more than forty-nine million responses. In the 1990 census, however, German was again included but English was not: the

Ancestry Questions in 1980 and 1990 U.S. Censuses

14. What is this person's ancestry? *If uncertain about how to report ancestry, see instruction guide.*

(For example: Afro-Amer., English, French, German, Honduran, Hungarian, Irish, Italian, Jamaican, Korean, Lebanese, Mexican, Nigerian, Polish, Ukrainian, Venezuelan, etc.)

Source: 1980 Census.

13. What is this person's ancestry or ethnic origin?
   (See instruction guide for further information.)

(For example: German, Italian, Afro-Amer., Croatian, Cape Verdean, Dominican, Ecuadoran, Haitian, Cajun, French Canadian, Jamaican, Korean, Lebanese, Mexican, Nigerian, Irish, Polish, Slovak, Taiwanese, Thai, Ukrainian, etc.)

Source: 1990 Census.

numbers claiming German ancestry increased by 18 percent to fifty-eight million, while those claiming English declined by 34 percent to thirty-three million. Smaller groups (Italian, Polish, French) can also be compared, with equally disturbing conclusions: Italian and Polish, given as examples on both censuses, showed increases of 21 and 14 percent, respectively; meanwhile, French disappeared from the 1990 example list, and those reporting French ancestry declined by 20 percent.

Finally, there is the unexplained appearance on the 1990 "for example" list of the categories Cajun and Croatian, neither of which had been listed before. In 1980, fewer than 10,000 had described themselves as of Cajun ancestry, but when Cajun appeared as an example, more than 668,000 wrote it in as their ancestry. Similarly, between the 1980 and 1990 censuses, those indicating themselves to be of Croatian ancestry more than doubled, from 253,000 to 544,000. Suffice it to say that any census or survey question that is so sensitive to an arbitrary list of examples must be viewed as highly suspect.

The categories of race, ethnicity, and ancestry designated by the Census Bureau have always interested social scientists (among others), but their political importance increased dramatically only after these categories were used in awarding special protections or privileges.[9] The most dynamic period for the extension of allocations based on race, ethnicity, and ancestry occurred in the wake of the 1960s civil-rights struggle. During the late 1960s, some civil-rights leaders foresaw the day when such categories would become irrelevant, when a race- and ethnicity-blind society would be created out of the ashes of America's long-standing system of segregation and discrimination. Some went so far as to argue that information on racial and ethnic categories should be entirely eliminated from official statistics, on grounds that such categorizations perpetuated these un-American or increasingly irrelevant groupings.

The government did prohibit use of such categories in some spheres, principally when their use was hindering the reduction of discrimination. A clear example was the Equal Employment Opportunity Commission's (EEOC) prohibition on employers' obtaining data on certain subjects in job applications. First race, then sex, and ultimately age data were proscribed by the EEOC, and eventually photographs were eliminated as well.

But when it came to collecting official data through the census and on vital statistics, such restraint vanished. The government increasingly supported benefits and prerogatives that attended to the social and economic advancement of previously disadvantaged groups, programs known as affirmative action. Strong incentives thus arose for continuing to collect data about these groups, so as to be able to measure the extent to which the disadvantages were being corrected.

The affirmative-action initiatives of the 1970s began as mandates and incentives directing employers "affirmatively" to seek out and consider job applicants from underrepresented minority groups (and later women). The limited nature of affirmative action had been promised by civil-rights proponents such as then-Senator (and later Vice President) Hubert Humphrey, who in the debate on the Civil Rights Act of 1964 had assured concerned senators that if "any language [can be found] which provides that an employer will have to hire on the basis of percentage or quota related to color, . . . I will start eating the pages [of the bill] one after another."[10]

Yet such were the dynamics of this process that not many years had passed before affirmative action had been transformed by federal courts and agencies to mean "numerical goals and targets." Eventually, discriminatory behavior of employers could be judged not by the seriousness of their affirmative recruitment efforts but by the degree to which their actual hiring and promotion corresponded to the percentage of the disadvantaged minority group in the population. To apply this statistical test of outcomes, population data categorized by such groups were essential.[11]

In the case of one disadvantaged minority the Census Bureau itself produced a neologism, "Hispanic," that collapsed into a single category a number of otherwise distinct and socially recognizable groups. The boundaries of this new ethnic category were inevitably blurred, and, indeed, to the present day few who fit within the category consider themselves to belong there. Instead, they see themselves as Americans of Mexican ancestry, Mexican-American, or Chicano/Chicana;[12] Puerto Rican; Cuban-American; Dominican-American; Salvadoran; and so on. Moreover, the category is ambiguous for Brazilians and other Latin Americans who do not speak Spanish and for Spaniards who do.

Gradually, some advocates for minority groups realized that newly adopted affirmative-action protections and preferences made it advantageous to obtain the maximum possible count of their disadvantaged minority. Such data would help to increase the "numerical goals and targets" used for hiring and other protective and preferential measures and, thus, the group's political visibility and influence. It was no surprise, therefore, that they began to lobby to this end.

Initially these efforts concentrated upon wholly desirable efforts to minimize the undercount of such groups, which in some cases and locales could be substantial. Indeed, the Census Bureau had developed sophisticated statistical techniques for estimating undercounts and expressed great concern about those it estimated to have occurred during the 1970 census for certain minority groups (e.g., 7.7 percent of blacks were missed as against only 1.9 percent of whites).[13] To improve this situation, the bureau decided to convene advisory committees on three key under-enumerated minority groups: the Census Advisory Committee on the Black Population (1974); on the Spanish Origin Population (1975); and on the Asian and Pacific Americans Population (1976). These were conceived as technical advisory panels parallel to the bureau's long-standing advisory committees on census statistics in general. The point was to help the Census Bureau "improve communications with the affected communities and to help plan the 1980 Census" so as to minimize the undercount of these groups.

Early appointees to these panels consisted mainly of experts with technical knowledge about these populations. Gradually, however, political activists were appointed too, and when these advocates felt that the Census Bureau was not responsive to their concerns, they went directly to their supporters in Congress, the White House, and the media. One observer, Margo Conk, noted that, following the arrival of the Carter Administration in January 1977,

> the bureau "bowed" to the pressure of minorities and changed the race and ethnic questions for the 100 percent schedule. It expanded the list of possible responses to the race question and added a separate item on Spanish/Hispanic origin . . . Representatives of minority groups were pleased with these changes; demographers were not so sure of their wisdom.

Professional discomfort was especially apparent with respect to the Spanish/Hispanic question. Despite its focus on only a small percentage of the population, this question was placed on the 100 percent census form asked of all respondents—a victory for advocacy groups such as the Mexican American Legal Defense and Education Fund. But the appearance of Hispanic as a census category produced a political reaction among other ethnic groups not treated in the same manner, especially those from southern and eastern Europe. As special efforts to enumerate Hispanics became more widely known, organizations claiming to represent white ethnics (i.e., native-born Americans whose ancestors had emigrated from southern and eastern European countries during the nineteenth and early twentieth centuries) complained to their political representatives that the census did not accurately count their numbers. The failure, in their view, was in the long-standing question about "place of birth of parents." Since there had been little emigration from these countries since the 1920s, their parents were typically U.S.-born, even though many increasingly viewed themselves as Polish-American, Irish-American, Italian-American, and so on. To rectify this failing, they argued for the addition of a new question on self-reported ancestry, national origin, or ethnicity.

Census Bureau professionals opposed this on technical grounds. The place-of-birth-of-parents question had been collected on all U.S. Censuses since 1890 and was a valuable source of information about social mobility and the economic and social integration of the children of immigrants. Moreover, because of limits on the length of the census form, there was no way that the full diversity of ancestry could be listed, and hence an open-ended fill-in-the-blank question would be necessary. Given that millions of census forms are processed, the question (even if restricted to the 17 percent sample who receive a longer census form) would present formidable problems of individual coding of responses. Yet as Conk observed, "Once again, political pressures prevailed over professional judgment . . . and the 'ancestry' question was adopted for the . . . sample form."

Interpreting data from the ancestry questions on the 1980 and 1990 censuses did indeed prove highly problematic. Meanwhile, space limitations and other considerations led the place-of-birth-of-parents question to be dropped entirely. As a result, census-based analyses of the progress of second-generation offspring of recent immigrants became difficult if not impossible.

The other major debate about the 1980 and 1990 censuses concerned whether the bureau should adjust the enumeration to correct for the undercount. For several decades, demographers and statisticians had been worried about this undercount and undertaken expensive measures to reduce it. However, by the 1970s the undercount had become a hot political issue.

First, the Supreme Court during the 1960s had begun to render judgments that forced states to reapportion their legislatures and congressional districts on the basis of the census. These mandates followed forty years of refusal by the Court to intervene on these matters. In 1946, for example, Justice Felix Frankfurter had ruled that congressional reapportionment was a "political thicket" that the courts had no right to enter. (This ruling upheld the constitutionality of the Illinois congressional delegation, the largest district of which represented 915,000 persons while the smallest had only 112,000.) A more activist Court now moved to mandate the principle of "one man, one vote," ruling in 1962 that the Tennessee legislature had to be reapportioned for the first time since 1901. This meant, of course, that demographic data derived from the census, long ignored in reapportioning political power within states, was suddenly salient.

The second reason for the rising political importance of the census was the growth during the 1950s and 1960s of federal grants-in-aid to state and local governments, apportioned on the basis of formulas derived from census data. Conk's summary is illuminating:

> By the late 1970s, 146 categorical grant programs supplied funds to state and local governments. The amount of money distributed jumped from $10 billion in 1964 to almost $35 billion in 1972 and then to $80 billion in 1980. In percentage terms such outlays accounted for almost a quarter of the federal budget in the early 1970s; they made up a fifth of the revenues of state and local governments.

It was hardly surprising, then, that in the buildup to the 1980 census, officials of cities with large minority populations, which the Census Bureau had acknowledged were subject to substantial undercounting in 1970, began to demand that the numbers obtained from the 1980 census be retrospectively adjusted. These proposals raised extraordinarily difficult technical and legal issues, and they deeply divided the professionals working on the census.[14]

The political and economic stakes were seen as so high that even before the census went to the field a flurry of lawsuits were filed, notably by Detroit and New York City. In late 1980, after much internal debate, the director of the Census Bureau announced that the bureau would not "adjust the 1980 Census population to compensate for undercount unless directed by the courts."[15] There ensued a long series of court cases,

rulings, and reversals that demonstrated well the ambiguities of the issues involved. Indeed, the court cases included expert testimony from
prominent statisticians and demographers on both sides of the dispute.
Ultimately, more than two years after the 1980 census numbers had been
released unadjusted, the Supreme Court upheld the Census Bureau.

Undeterred by this ruling, New York City (joined by Los Angeles,
Chicago, other cities, and the National Association for the Advancement
of Colored People) refiled its suit after the Secretary of Commerce decided not to adjust the 1990 census figures. The Secretary acknowledged
that despite its best efforts the bureau had failed to count 1.6 percent of
the population, including about 4.8 percent of blacks and 5.2 percent
of Hispanics, but concluded that adjusted figures would be less accurate
than the original count. This case wended its way through the federal
judicial system and reached the Supreme Court in January 1995. In
March 1996, the Court issued an unusual unanimous ruling in which it
rejected the claims of New York City, finding that the Census Bureau had
undertaken "extraordinary efforts to include traditionally undercounted
minorities in the 1990 Census" and that the Secretary of Commerce "was
well within the constitutional bounds of discretion over the conduct of
the Census provided to the federal government . . . In 1990, the Census
Bureau made an extraordinary effort to conduct an accurate enumeration, and was successful in counting 98.4% of the population."[16]

The political controversies surrounding the census did not end here,
however. Active disputes continue over the design of the year 2000 census, driven in part by increasing disagreements about how best to deal
with the undercount and by concerns about the high costs projected by
the bureau. With congressional reapportionment and some $150 billion
in federal transfers now affected by census data, regional and partisan
concerns have risen.

Following the contentions surrounding the 1990 census, the Census
Bureau proposed that a complete enumeration be attempted, with estimates then made by sampling procedures for no more than 10 percent
of the population who would not be contacted. Opponents, mostly
Republican, fear that such procedures might be subject to political
tampering, thereby tainting the whole census with constitutional

uncertainties. "Let us not allow them to develop Censusgate," said Representative Bob Barr of Georgia.

Moreover, demands are being made for a multiracial category to deal with people born of increasingly common mixed-race unions. The Office of Management and Budget led a comprehensive review by some thirty federal agencies of the race and ethnicity categories that it had mandated in 1977 with its Directive No. 15. The conclusion, announced in late 1997, was that Americans would for the first time be allowed to choose more than one racial category when describing themselves on the census and other federal forms. The decision rejected the alternative of a separate "multiracial" category, urged by some but opposed by many major civil-rights organizations concerned about possible reductions in the numbers identifying themselves in particular minority groups. Notwithstanding this decision, disagreements seemed likely to emerge as to how those describing themselves in multiple racial categories would be classified and tabulated. Such disputes virtually assured that controversy about the U.S. Census would be perennial.

The intense politics and litigation that have surrounded the U.S. Census since the 1960s illustrate well that what social scientists, demographers, and statisticians consider technical matters of objective data collection can, and perhaps always will, become heavily politicized. Interest in such issues among politicians and activists is greatly magnified when the official data are deployed in the allocation of political power, economic benefits, employment, and educational opportunities. Once again, we see abundant evidence of demographic and political issues mingling.

The United States has moved increasingly toward using allocation mechanisms as tools of redistributive justice. It is a fair prediction that whenever industrial democracies embrace similar public policies there will be highly charged debates about censuses and other official data. In demography, all numbers count; but in politics, some numbers count more than others.

chapter 9

CANADA: CIVIL FISSURES

"French-speaking Quebeckers have one of the lowest birthrates among 'the white races.'" So said Lucien Bouchard, leader of the Quebec separatist opposition in the Canadian federal Parliament in Ottawa, during his passionate October 1995 campaign to promote a yes vote on sovereignty for Quebec.

"We're beaten, it's true. But by what? By money and by the ethnic vote. That's it." Thus spoke a bitter Quebec Premier Jacques Parizeau after the sovereignty referendum failed by a razor-thin margin of 50.6 percent against to 49.4 percent for. (The absolute margin of defeat was 53,000 votes out of 4.8 million cast, the latter representing a remarkable 94 percent voter turnout.)

Parizeau's argument, apparently, was that a large majority of the province's *pure laine Québecois* (literally, "pure wool Québecois," meaning those derived from the province's eighteenth-century French settlers) had supported sovereignty for the province (60 percent of Francophone voters, or about 82 percent of the province's population, voted yes) but that their wishes were frustrated by the near-monolithic opposition (more than 90 percent) of *les autres,* non-Francophone minorities consisting of Anglophones (about 9 percent) and "allophones" (mostly immigrants whose native language is neither French nor English, about 8 percent of the population). In Parizeau's words, such divisions offered "temptations for revenge."[1]

Parizeau's statement provoked passionate criticism not only from opponents of sovereignty for Quebec and from immigrant groups but also from some of his fellow "sovereigntists." He refused to apologize but acknowledged that he had used "terms that could have been better chosen."[2] Bouchard, soon to succeed him as Quebec's Premier, publicly repudiated the remark, notwithstanding his own comment about low fertility among Québecois, which had also elicited strong criticism.

Rarely have the concerns arising from low fertility and rapid immigration been so passionately expressed as in these recent debates in Canada. During its history, parts of Canada initially registered fertility levels that were at the high extreme of recorded human experience; today, fertility in these same regions is near the low extreme. Canada is also one of only three or four nations that consider themselves traditional countries of immigration, and Canadian immigration levels in recent years have been exceptionally high relative to the country's modest population base. Moreover, Canadian politics has long been transfixed by a struggle of nationalisms, represented as a linguistic divide between Francophone Quebec and the other nine English-speaking provinces and two territories (though several provinces, such as New Brunswick and Nova Scotia, have substantial French-speaking minorities).

To evaluate these political disputes, some reference to underlying demographic trends may be helpful. Canada's earliest recorded fertility rates were high by the standards of western Europe. Around 1870, total fertility still exceeded six children per woman. From then on, Canadian fertility declined rapidly, to around five in 1891 and just more than three by 1921. Following a nadir of roughly three during the Great Depression, Canada (like the United States, Australia, New Zealand, and not many others) experienced a large and sustained postwar baby boom, with fertility rates rising to more than four children per woman during the 1950s.[3]

By 1960, when our story begins, the Canadian total fertility rate was still high at 3.89, a level not seen since before World War I. There ensued a rapid and largely unanticipated decline (paralleling that of the United States) by 40 percent during the 1960s, to 2.33 in 1970. The decline continued during the 1980s; in 1990, fertility was recorded at 1.75 and in 1995 at 1.64.[4]

The fertility history of Quebec alone has also tended toward both high and low extremes. In his classic article on the level of human fertility in the absence of conscious control of family size, the late French demographer Louis Henry described the fertility levels of eighteenth-century Quebecois as the second-highest ever recorded (exceeded only by the Hutterites, an Anabaptist sect whose religious commitments favored exceptionally high fertility).[5] Yet by the 1980s, fertility in Quebec had declined to a level that ranked (along with West Germany, Italy, and Hong Kong) among the lowest in the modern world.

Like that of its North American neighbor to the south, Canada's demography has been affected heavily by international migration ever since European settlement began. However, Canada has also experienced high levels of emigration by immigrants, much of it to the United States. Since increases in immigration have usually been followed by rises in emigration, the percentage of foreign-born has increased less than the gross levels of immigration. For example, during the second and third decades of the twentieth century, more than three million immigrants came to Canada, which at the time of the World War I had a total population of only eight million. Yet the 22 percent of the population that was foreign-born, already high because of heavy immigration during the preceding decade, did not increase.[6]

In general, Canada has long registered a high percentage of foreign-born compared to most other industrial countries. The current level of roughly 15 to 16 percent is considerably higher than that of the United States, for example, though lower than Switzerland (18 percent) and Luxembourg (30 percent),[7] but Canada makes it easy for foreigners to become permanent residents and to naturalize, while foreigners in Switzerland and Luxembourg are temporary and unlikely to be allowed to naturalize. As in the past, there appears to be substantial emigration from Canada by both immigrants and native-born (the former are about eight times more likely to depart than the latter). In contrast, most legal immigrants to the United States since World War II have become permanent residents. And of emigrants from Canada, about 40 percent are destined for the United States.[8]

Again like the United States, the national origins of immigrants to Canada have changed dramatically since the 1960s. As recently as 1966, more than three-quarters of immigrants to Canada came from Europe and the United States. By 1986, the overwhelming majority came from developing countries of Asia, Latin America, and the Caribbean.[9]

Trends in both fertility and immigration have exacerbated the underlying tensions between Quebec and the rest of Canada. While fertility in Quebec declined to near global lows during the 1980s, that in the rest of Canada remained much higher, and the resulting differentials seriously concerned Quebec nationalists as to the long-term future of the province's French-speaking population. Such concerns, while exaggerated, were not wholly unfounded. Whereas demographic projections made fifty years ago suggested that Quebec's population would exceed Ontario's by the 1970s, in 1995 Quebec's population was only 65 percent of Ontario's; indeed, the percentage of Canadians living in Quebec declined from twenty-nine in 1961 to twenty-five in 1994.[10]

Meanwhile, the high immigration levels became another source of friction. During the late 1980s and early 1990s, the Canadian federal government of the Progressive Conservative Party had raised overall admission levels for immigrants and refugees. The largest number took up residence in Ontario, thereby further increasing its demographic weight relative to Quebec's. Moreover, of the substantial fraction of immigrants who settled in Quebec (mostly in Montreal), a majority were either Anglophones or allophones, who preferred to speak English rather than French. Hence, low fertility among Francophones was accompanied by the rapid growth of immigrants speaking or learning English.

A further complication is that Canada was an early adherent to policies now generally described as multicultural. As early as 1971, the Canadian government under former Prime Minister Pierre Trudeau proclaimed the promotion of multiculturalism as official policy, a position in which Canada (joined later by Australia) is still virtually alone among industrial countries.[11] One explanation for the positive disposition toward such a policy among Canadian leadership groups is the country's unique experience both as a traditional promoter of immigration and as bilingual—no other officially bilingual or multilingual industrialized country (e.g., Belgium) is also a traditional country of immigration, and no other traditional immigration country (e.g., the United States) is officially bilingual. Indeed, the 1971 policy embrace of multiculturalism was explicitly directed toward Canada's new, diverse immigrants. In the analysis of one observer, it was intended

> to inculcate among Canadians greater sensitivity and under-
> standing toward so-called "New Canadians," to make it easier
> for newcomers to integrate by softening the cultural shock they
> all underwent . . . At its inception, multiculturalism was as-
> sumed by the public to be intended to mean legitimating cultural
> differences, as of folklore, of music and dance and song, and
> even, if only temporarily, of language.[12]

Others saw a more Machiavellian intention. Trudeau aimed, they asserted, at "muting Quebec's French-speaking minority by making it one
in a sea of ethnic voices . . . [or] luring immigrant voters with federal
dollars."[13]

In addition to liberal immigration policies, Canada's refugee and humanitarian admissions policies are among the most open of industrial
countries'. In 1989, faced with an enormous backlog of unadjudicated
claims for refugee status at Canadian ports of entry, the Progressive Conservative government of Prime Minister Brian Mulroney delegated adjudication of such claims to a new and independent Immigration and
Refugee Board. This board has been both lauded and vilified for the high
rate at which it has approved claims for refugee status: in 1993, 55 percent of the claims that were pursued were approved; in 1994, 70 percent.[14]

In 1992, approximately 52,000 refugee and humanitarian admissions
were granted permanent residence in Canada, whose total population is
27 million. (For comparison, during that same year, the United States
admitted 117,000 refugees—more than twice as many, but with a population nearly ten times larger, at 256 million.) Of those admitted, 29,000
met the UN Convention definition of a refugee; most of these were "re-
cognised" as refugees after arriving in Canada and claiming asylum, with
only a minority selected directly from abroad.[15]

The combination of low fertility and high immigration has produced
unusually complex and heated debates in Canada. Though Canadian fer-

tility since the 1970s has been below the replacement level, and hence the long-term size of the indigenous population is on a trajectory of decline, the same is true for virtually all industrialized countries, and Canadian levels have been much higher than those of many western European countries, a fact of which many Canadian leaders have been fully aware. Nonetheless, expressions of concern about low fertility have been more regular and forceful in Canada than in Germany or the United Kingdom, though perhaps less strident than in France. In 1984, an expert group convened in Montreal by the Canadian government evoked imagery of population decline in a style more typically heard in Paris, describing continuing population increase as "one of the major factors contributing toward a dynamic society." They recommended financial incentives to raise fertility, acknowledging that these would be costly, but asked rhetorically "whether the goal of maintaining the population was not as important as that of national defence. Perhaps as much could be spent for the first as for the second; in the long term, there is no point in 'defending' a population that is disappearing!"[16]

In 1988, an analyst at the Institut National de la Recherche Scientifique in Quebec reviewed with approval the pro-natalist policies then being pursued by the governments of France and East Germany. Following what he described as the success of these policies, he recommended: paid maternity leave up to at least thirty-two weeks; tax credits for child care; primary-school education beginning at age five instead of six; and a Can$200 per month government-paid child allowance for parents of third children for the five or six years of the preschool period. Also in 1988, the Quebec provincial government in its May budget provided a Can$3,000 child allowance for a family's third child, spread over the first two years of the child's life.[17]

Others in Canada believe that large-scale immigration is an alternative means to increase the population so as to meet a widely proclaimed national demographic target of thirty million. Although the origin of this target is uncertain, it has taken on a kind of mystical significance in Canadian politics. (Earlier in this century, the commonly cited target was twice as high; in 1904, Prime Minister Wilfrid Laurier enthusiastically predicted that there would be sixty million Canadians— a tenfold increase—within the lifetimes of those in his audience.[18]) In any event, Statistics Canada, the government's statistical office, estimated that the target of thirty million was reached in 1996.

In 1990, the Mulroney government announced that it would increase immigrant and refugee admissions by about 25 percent, aiming at 220,000 in 1991 and 250,000 per year thereafter. The 250,000 target was described as representing annual admissions equal to 1 percent of the population base, and part of the rationale for the policy was the need to maintain population growth.[19] In 1993, an official of Statistics Canada stated, "At this time we're in a situation where the birth rate is below the replacement level. It's inevitable that if you prolong this trend very far into the future, you wind up with the extinction of the population . . . Either the birth rate must rise or we must open our doors very wide to people who want to live here."[20]

During the parliamentary election campaign that year, both mainstream opposition parties (the Liberals and the New Democrats) indicated their support for this policy.

The Mulroney government's annual targets were exceeded—immigration numbers in 1992 and 1993 were 252,000 and 254,000, respectively.[21] One enthusiastic journalist commented on the 1994 report released by Statistics Canada: In 1992 and 1993,

> immigration had contributed more to Canada's growth than the natural increase in the population, the first time that has happened since the opening of the Prairies before the First World War.
>
> Net immigration—the difference between immigrants and emigrants—boosted Canada's population by 206,900, while the excess of births over deaths added 193,100.
>
> As a result, Canada's population rose 1.3 per cent to 29 million last year [1993], outpacing the 1.1 per cent growth in the U.S., 0.9 per cent in Australia, and a marginal 0.3 in Europe.[22]

The point had been made earlier by the Minister of Citizenship and Immigration under the newly elected Liberal government, who stated explicitly that his government's 250,000 per year "help us to sustain an annual population growth rate of about 1.5 percent—higher than any other industrialized nation."[23] However, later in 1994, the same Minister announced a reversal of policy, declaring the desirability of reducing admissions of immigrants and refugees. Supporters of the earlier policy denounced the shift as a purely political reaction to the growing strength of the Reform Party.

How can we explain the high levels of support among Canadian leaders for substantial population growth, compared with the sangfroid of their peers in Britain and most other western European countries? At least four issues are relevant.

First, Canada has a very low population density, which is why its leaders agree that the country needs demographic growth to reach necessary economies of scale, fully populate its territory, and exploit its rich natural resources. (That much of Canadian territory is located within the Arctic Circle is sometimes not taken into account in these density calculations.)

Second, Canadian fertility has declined rapidly, especially in Quebec. That Canada was one of only three or four countries to experience a big, sustained postwar baby boom meant that the sudden appearance of low fertility profoundly shocked people and called into question their assumptions about what level of fertility should be considered "normal."

Third, the Francophone intellectual tradition at the center of Canadian society may offer a cultural explanation of the high profile of demographic issues. In France, as we have seen, elite and intellectual interest in demographic matters is much higher than in any other Western country. Only in France could a debate about which demographic rate better reflects underlying fertility behavior be conducted, with passion, in the mass media. The ties between French and Québecois elites and intellectuals are numerous and sometimes close, and many Québecois economists and demographers have either studied or worked in France. It would be surprising, therefore, if concerns so prominent in Paris did not resonate to some degree in Montreal, Quebec, and Ottawa.

Finally, the cultural and linguistic divisions of Canada add another layer of anxiety about numbers, relative power, and cultural hegemony that is not experienced in most other Western countries.

The political salience of the language question in Canada has meant that both fertility and immigration rates have been scrutinized to determine their effects on the balance of English- and French-speaking populations. That fertility in Quebec declined during the 1980s to much lower levels than those of other provinces and territories generated anxiety among Quebec political elites. Québecois demographers, some of whom were educated in France, contributed to the debate, producing long-term projections to illustrate the potential decline of the French-speaking population.

By 1994 (the latest year for which complete data are available), however, the gap had closed, as Québecois fertility rose from its record lows and fertility in the rest of Canada declined. Statistics Canada reported that Québecois fertility increased substantially between 1986 and 1994, from 1.37 to 1.61 children per woman. As a result, Québecois fertility approached that of the rest of the country, as overall national fertility rose only slightly during the same period, from 1.59 to 1.66.[24]

When differentially low fertility rates occur at the same time as major migration trends, it is no surprise to find contentious legislative and judicial dispute. When fertility rates in Quebec fell rapidly during the 1960s and 1970s, the language choice of immigrants with mother tongues other than English or French (allophones) became increasingly important vis-à-vis those who spoke the two national languages. To the dismay of Québecois leaders, allophone immigrant students, an increasing percentage of all students in Quebec, were showing a strong tendency to become Anglophone.

This issue figured in some of the most influential writings of Québecois separatists, such as the late René Levesque and Jacques Parizeau. The former founded the separatist Parti Québecois in 1968 and served as Premier of Quebec in 1976–85; the latter was leader of that party and Premier until he stepped down following the narrow failure of the 1995 referendum. Levesque's *An Option for Quebec,* which was described in his preface as "this little book" but on the back cover as "the book that took Quebec by storm . . . forced the Quiet Revolution into a new and dynamic phase," was written only six months after he had left the Liberal Party in 1967 to establish the Sovereignty Association Movement, which developed into the Parti Québecois. In this book, Levesque confronts—directly and at considerable length—the peril he perceives for French Quebec posed by low fertility coupled with English-speaking immigration:

French Quebec itself is, literally, in danger of death. Several factors . . . emphasize the deterioration of our relative population strength. First of all the birth rate has decreased at a dizzying rate . . . Emigration, for its part, acts against us . . . Finally, there is immigration!

From 1945 to 1967 inclusive, Canada accepted some three million immigrants. More than 35 percent, on the average, were of Anglo-Saxon origin. As for the French, there were 4,408 of them out of 146,758 immigrants in 1965, or 3 per cent . . . Nothing could be less surprising, for of thirty-five immigration offices six are in the United Kingdom and Ireland, five in Germany, and four in the United States . . .

We know the results of this policy for the rest of Canada. It has become a unilingual country where, in eight provinces at least, the French minorities are irreparably submerged.

As for Quebec, this policy combined with the falling birth rate is leading straight to a demographic catastrophe.

Levesque included in his book an earlier essay by Parizeau, described as a "remarkable study," in which he argued that the priorities shared by French-speaking Canadians differed from those of other Canadians. Of all the examples he could have cited, Parizeau chose the conjunction of low fertility and immigration:

> In Quebec, it is now understood by an increasing number of people that the combination of a rapidly declining birth rate and the failure to assimilate immigrants into the French stream present dreadful dangers for the French community in North America. The reorganization of family allowances, facilities for working mothers, and new immigration policies became objectives of far greater significance than in the rest of Canada.[25]

Eventually, the provincial government in Quebec City intervened, seeking to raise Quebec's fertility rate, demanding control over immigration admissions to the province, and requiring allophone immigrant children to be educated in French schools only.

Control over the entry of nonnationals is, universally, one of three core elements of national sovereignty, along with the right of the sovereign power to raise taxes and provide for national defense.[26] In an exceptional departure from this view and from the policies of nearly all other states, the Canadian government acceded to demands from Quebec officials, who demanded provincial autonomy in determining the composition of immigrants to Quebec. One analyst summarized the situation as follows:

> The strong tendency for allophones to adopt English as the language customarily used can be seen as a logical result of the policy that prevailed in the education system prior to 1974, a policy which allowed freedom of choice in the language of instruction. Greek and Italian children therefore found themselves in schools which favored their social integration into the English language group. Still . . . French is slightly ahead of English among other [immigrant] groups (combined), and its lead is even more pronounced among the children of the new wave of immigrants (Haitian, Latin American, and Sino-Vietnamese). This is an obvious consequence of Bill 22 and Bill 101. Since language legislation makes it obligatory for these children to be taught in French, they come into contact with Francophone pupils and are francized [adopt French culture and language]. The study reveals that allophone students attending French schools with a Francophone or allophone majority are for the most part francized, while those registered in schools with a significant Anglophone element are usually anglicized.[27]

In February 1991, the federal government of Canada signed a comprehensive agreement, the Canada-Quebec Accord, with the provincial government of Quebec. The accord gave Quebec sole responsibility for selecting those independent immigrants and overseas refugees destined for Quebec, in effect delegating at least this element of national sovereignty to the province. In addition, the federal government agreed that the provincial government would design and deliver its own reception and integration services (linguistic, cultural, and economic) for immigrants, financed by substantial funds (on the order of Can$90 million per year) that would be transferred from the federal to the provincial government for this purpose.

The Canadian government's support for multiculturalism is another important aspect of this debate. The policy was first implemented with financial support to ethnic and cultural organizations, which caused few ripples, but subsequent policy proposals and actions were more controversial. Advocacy by affected groups has been strong. Religious organizations have demanded that the government support their schools and that public schools close on their religious holidays. A black community group has proposed that the legal system treat black people who commit minor crimes differently from other groups. In response, the Canadian Minister of Justice suggested in 1994 that a "cultural defence" be available to certain minorities for some violations of Canadian law, such as polygamy and the wearing of ceremonial weapons, but withdrew the proposal quickly after a firestorm of public criticism.[28]

While the multiculturalist policies generally have been supported, then, there is growing opposition to them. One recent book argued, "Depending on stereotype, ensuring that ethnic groups will preserve their distinctiveness in a gentle and insidious form of cultural apartheid, multiculturalism has done little more than lead an already divided land down the path of further social divisiveness." A prominent Toronto columnist wrote in late 1994 that Canadian multiculturalist policy "is the principal reason why there are no Canadians in Canada, only hyphenated ones, the single exception, ironically, being Quebecers."[29]

In 1993, a political earthquake struck the then-ruling Progressive Conservative Party, led by Mulroney's successor, Prime Minister Kim Campbell. Her party, which in 1988 had won 169 of 295 seats in Parliament, won only 2 seats nationwide in the elections and not only lost its parliamentary majority but failed to qualify as "an official party" (meaning its M.P.s could not ask questions in parliamentary committees on their own initiative). Its popular vote fell from 43 to 17 percent.[30] This ignominious defeat was unprecedented in Canadian history. In part, it was due to economic woes and the unpopularity of the Mulroney government's tax and other policies, but fundamental to the Progressive Conservative collapse was the rise of the Reform Party.

The Reform Party, established only in 1987, is led by Preston Manning, an evangelical Christian and son of a former premier of Alberta; at the time of the 1993 campaign, the party held one seat in Parliament. Its electoral platform included the following items: (1) eliminate the Canadian government's Can$35 billion fiscal deficit over a three-year period; (2) make the criminal-justice system more accountable to victims of crime; apply stricter criteria for granting parole; reform Young Offenders Act; (3) promote constitutional reform to provide that the Canadian Senate be elected (rather than appointed); (4) ensure that immigration meets economic needs and scale it back to 150,000 per year; and (5) foster a commitment to "one nation," meaning no special status for Quebec; provinces to have exclusive jurisdiction over their culture and language; Quebec cannot assume a special economic relationship with the rest of Canada as it considers a sovereignty referendum; and opposition to official multiculturalism.

The electoral effects of the Reform Party and the Bloc Québecois (the Quebec separatist party at the federal level) were dramatic. In the largest province, Ontario, Reform split the weakened Conservatives to give the opposition Liberals an unprecedented sweep of 98 of 99 seats; the one non-Liberal seat went to the Reform Party; the Progressive Conservatives lost all 42 of their parliamentary seats in Ontario, while the moderate-left New Democratic Party lost all 10 of theirs. (The Progressive Conservatives regained control of the Ontario parliament in June 1995.) In Manitoba and Saskatchewan, the Liberals also gained seats.

Farther west, however, the situation was dramatically different. In Alberta, Manning's redoubt, his party won 22 seats to only 4 for the Liberals. In British Columbia, Reform captured 24 seats to the Liberals' 6, while the Progressive Conservatives lost 11 seats (including that held by Prime Minister Campbell).

Nationwide, the Liberals won 177 of 295 seats; the Bloc Québecois won 54 and became the official opposition; and the Reform Party won 52. The Progressive Conservatives and New Democrats both failed to elect even the minimum twelve M.P.s needed to qualify for official party status in the Commons, meaning its M.P.s could no longer ask questions in the House of Commons, had no right to speak as part of the regular rotation, were allocated no seats on Parliamentary committees, and received no research funds—in short, the former governing party fell to the status of a small independent grouping in a parliamentary system in which everything is divided by party. Of course, the Canadian winner-take-all electoral system amplified the Progressive Conservatives' disaster—they received 17 percent of the popular vote nationwide but less than 1 percent of the parliamentary seats, while the New Democrats got 7 percent of the total vote but 3 percent of the Commons. In contrast, the Reform Party got 20 percent of the popular vote and 17 percent of the Commons.[31]

The underlying forces that produced this debacle were the same that have bedeviled all recent Canadian governments—the fissiparous pressures created by the language issue, the place of Quebec in the federation, and the sharply different political outlooks of voters in the western provinces. Separately and from divergent perspectives, the Reform Party and the Bloc Québecois challenged the electoral strategy that had worked so well for Mulroney in 1988. Mulroney, a bilingual Québecois of Irish stock, had combined policies that appealed to the traditional prairie conservatism that prevails in western Canada with accommodation to French separatists. But by 1993, this strategy had collapsed completely: after a series of lively nationwide debates, two constitutional reform plans for the status of Quebec had failed to win approval, and western conservatives had wearied of the separatist demands and of Mulroney's efforts to meet them; Quebec separatists in turn decided they had to eschew accommodation and move toward separation.[32] Reform in the west and Bloc Québecois in the east mounted effective challenges to the long-dominant national parties.

In the national Parliament, the effect of these regional changes was markedly different. The Reform challenge essentially demolished the Progressive Conservatives in the west and at the same time divided the Conservative vote in the largest province, Ontario, thereby clearing the way for the Liberal sweep. Meanwhile, the Bloc Québecois generated enough support to prevent the Progressive Conservatives from gaining many seats in Quebec. The result was a kind of electoral pincer movement—unintended and uncoordinated, to be sure—that made for a national disaster for the Progressive Conservatives.

No one knows to what degree the Reform Party's support increased because it was challenging the mainstream consensus for high levels of immigration and refugee admission. In March 1995, a national poll (excluding Quebec, where immigration policy is controlled by the provincial government) reported that 59 percent of respondents favored and 31 percent opposed a five-year suspension of all immigration, to give Canada time to integrate its many new immigrants. This poll, conducted by a professional firm, was commissioned by the Immigration Association of Canada, a group that lobbies for reduction of Canadian immigrant admissions; hence its results may have been subtly tilted. Nonetheless, they suggested a surprisingly high level of support for what would be a draconian shift in long-standing Canadian policy.

The Reform Party's immigration spokesman, Art Hanger, M.P., immediately cited the poll results as evidence of public support for its position.[33] And the Liberal government, led by Prime Minister Jean Chrétien, announced a series of changes in immigration and refugee policies. These included applying a Can$975 right-of-landing fee per adult immigrant to cover part of the costs of the immigration system (zero-interest loans to be made available to those who qualified); requiring that some sponsors of would-be immigrants post bonds, to assure that those whom they sponsor would not depend on welfare; and various changes in the Immigration and Refugee Board (eliminate patronage appointments by having an independent advisory panel review nominations, and reduce the number of board members by allowing each case to be heard by one member rather than two).[34]

The reaction to these new measures was passionate. Officials of the Canadian Council on Refugees termed the right-of-landing fee a "head tax," recalling the "blatantly racist" nineteenth-century policy of heavily taxing Chinese immigrants to deter their entry. (The nineteenth-century tax of Can$500 was sufficient to buy a house under then-current prices.)[35] They argued, "In the face of right-wing pressures, the government has adopted a hostile attitude towards refugees and towards their international obligations to protect those who flee war, human rights violations and persecution."[36] Meanwhile, the Chrétien government announced that it intended to admit about 220,000 immigrants in 1996 and between 195,000 and 220,000 in 1997. The Liberal Party election platform ("Redbook") had embodied a commitment to raising annual immigration numbers to 1 percent of the Canadian population (i.e., about 300,000), depending on absorptive capacity, and there was strong advocacy for this, but it appears that the post-election program review undertaken by the new government led to lower levels.[37] It should be noted, however, that even this reduced number is a much higher rate than the American one. (Of course, the United States experiences higher levels of illegal immigration and lower levels of emigration by immigrants.)

Though some might wish to discount the angry words of refugee advocates, many observers agreed that the strong Reform showing in the 1993 election had led the Liberal government to co-opt much of Reform's political agenda: "Much of what was Reform's radically conservative message—deficit fighting, tighter immigration policies, and a harder line against Quebec nationalism—had become Chrétien Liberal policy. (All Canadian governments are now, to some extent, Reform governments.)"[38]

From our perspective, the 1993 election was a unique moment in Canadian history that suddenly opened a political space—some would say a threatening political chasm—for public expression of anxieties about balance among linguistic groups, ethnic groups, native- and foreign-born, bilingualism and multiculturalism, and so on. Strident electoral politics and harsh political rhetoric revealed the sharp departure from Canadian political discourse based "on civility and compromise rather than, as south of the border, upon the free market virtues of competitiveness and the quest for victory."[39]

The 1995 referendum on sovereignty for Quebec was one of many expressions of this new tone. During December 1995, the leading proponent of sovereignty, Lucien Bouchard, and its leading opponent, the Quebec Liberal Party leader, Daniel Johnson, received death threats from shadowy groups calling themselves the Anglophone Assault Group and the True Quebecois Sovereignty group, respectively. The Quebec police clearly took the threats "very seriously."[40] Meanwhile, in Ottawa, Preston Manning declared that any separation of Quebec would require negotiating a legal, constitutional amendment with the rest of Canada, without which Quebec's separatist leadership would "illegally impose its own laws in place of the laws of Canada, and punish any of its citizens who choose to honor Canada's laws . . . If a state like Quebec itself defies the Canadian Constitution" by unilaterally declaring independence, he said, the government should use military force to protect Canadian citizens still living in Quebec from such illegal actions. Regions within Quebec that might vote against independence, he continued, should be allowed to remain in Canada. An unnamed source within Quebec's government called Manning's declaration an exercise in "fear-mongering. Do you think international opinion will let this happen? France is a friend of Quebec, and you might see the French air force over the skies of Quebec."[41]

The post-referendum political rhetoric also took on a strongly ad hominem character, aimed principally at Chrétien and Manning. Manning suggested that Chrétien might be impeachable "if it becomes evident that there is a screw loose." Chrétien responded that Manning might have had "too much rum in his eggnog" at a Christmas party, to which Manning retorted that he is a teetotaler. Then Deputy Prime Minister Sheila Copps stated that Manning "is obviously operating about five bricks short of a load" and should "stop smoking what he's been smoking and take a vacation."[42]

A 1996 campaign for a Montreal parliamentary seat offered yet more evidence of the political centrality of multicultural and immigration themes. The economically depressed Papineau-St. Michel district in Montreal, with one-third of its residents unemployed or dependent on income transfers, contains the largest concentration of the sixty thousand Haitians living in Canada. Following the January announcement of an election in Papineau-St. Michel, the welfare of Haiti assumed "overarching importance in Canadian foreign policy."[43] The Liberal Party candidate, Pierre S. Pettigrew, federal Minister of International Cooperation, announced two new foreign-assistance programs for Haiti, and on the weekend before the election, he hosted Haiti's new President, René Préval, in Papineau-St. Michel. The Chrétien government described the timing of the visit as a "coincidence" related to a trip Préval took to the United States, but Minister of Foreign Affairs Lloyd Axworthy noted wryly, "It's amazing how these things work out." A few weeks before the election, the government agreed to take over the lead role in the UN peacekeeping mission in Haiti, replacing a force led by the United States with seven hundred Canadian troops (at a cost of Can$22 million) for four months. In the view of Alain Gagnon, a political scientist at McGill University, "If we didn't have such a major Haitian community, Canada would be much more discreet and much less forthcoming in its support to Haiti."[44]

In the increasingly tense Canadian politics surrounding language, ethnicity, and immigration, even the Canadian Census came under fire, as its parallel in the United States had over similar issues. The census's ethnic-origin question requires respondents

to say which of ten groups—from white through Arab to Filipino and Korean—he or she belongs to, and more than one "if applicable." Why? For the administration of equal-opportunity programmes under the Employment Equity Act and other laws, say officials. The hell with that, say some members of the right-wing Reform Party, who think "affirmative action" has gone far enough; one Reform MP has called this question "garbage," inviting everyone to answer it with "Martian." Others complain that, at a time when national unity is needed, the census is creating even more hyphenated Canadians.[45]

It is too early to say whether the election of 1993 was a political watershed or a temporary aberration. Within several years, pundits were describing Canada's four parties other than the governing Liberals as "fighting for their lives." The Chrétien government's strategic move to embrace parts of the Reform Party agenda on immigration, Quebec nationalism, and budget deficits forced Manning's party further to the right. Reform's credibility was tarnished by intemperate statements about homosexuality and corporal punishment by several of its M.P.s. Manning tried to interest the decimated Progressive Conservatives in a full or partial merger, arguing that this was the only way conservatives could hope to challenge the Liberals. But the Progressive Conservative leader, Jean Charest, rebuffed the suggestion, believing that a revival of his party was likely by the time of the next election.[46]

Meanwhile, the Bloc Québecois in the federal Parliament was weakened by the departure of its charismatic leader, Lucien Bouchard, to become Premier of Quebec, in which position he had to defer his nationalist agenda and face a program of needed deficit cutting to revive Quebec's flagging economy. His budget measures have been politically unpopular, and the Liberal Party in Quebec has begun to close the sovereigntists' lead.

The federal parliamentary elections of June 1997 hardly clarified the situation. The Liberals won 155 of 301 Commons seats, down from 177 out of 295 seats won in 1993. The Reform Party gained clear status as the Official Opposition, winning 60 seats versus the 52 it won in 1993. The Bloc Québecois declined to 44 seats from its 1993 total of 54, while the Progressive Conservatives recovered somewhat, to 20 seats, and the New Democrats to 21. All five parties thereby exceeded the 12 seats needed for status as official parties. For the first time in Canadian history, there are five such official parties in the House of Commons.

However, the most striking outcome of the 1997 election is the evidence it provides of what the weekly Canadian news magazine *Maclean's* called "a fractured country." The governing Liberals gained nearly two-thirds of their seats (101 of 155) in the single province of Ontario, although even there they failed to achieve a majority of the total votes cast. An additional 26 Liberals were elected from Quebec, and some additional seats from all of Canada's other regions. Meanwhile, Reform won almost all of its 60 seats from the two western provinces of Alberta and British Columbia, while the New Democrats achieved something of a breakthrough by winning eight seats in the Atlantic provinces. The Progressive Conservatives, who almost disappeared in the 1993 election, achieved some modest successes in eastern Canada, but failed to recover any seats in their onetime strongholds of Alberta and British Columbia and won only a single seat in Ontario.

With five official parties and increasing divisions among regions, Canadian political commentary has taken on a distinctly gloomy tone. In the words of *Maclean's*, "The election leaves the nation splintered as never before." There is widespread anticipation of increasing political conflict over the status of Quebec: Reform's 1997 electoral campaign lagged in the West until it was revived by its claims that the Liberals and

Progressive Conservatives were "soft" on Quebec sovereignty, and the status of Reform as the official Opposition party in Parliament may increase electoral support for sovereignty within Quebec.

Even in Canada, then, a country proud of its traditions of "civility and compromise," worrying echoes can be heard of the clashes occasioned elsewhere by the convergence of nationalism, low fertility, and high immigration.

PART FOUR

TRANSNATIONAL ISSUES

chapter 10

DEVELOPMENT, MIGRATION, AND FERTILITY

In previous sections, we have examined population issues in national contexts. But there are more general international themes: the process of social and economic development and its relation to fertility and migration; asylum, refugee status, and immigration; and the demographic and political repercussions in Europe and North America of the rise of Islamic fundamentalism.

No one can seriously doubt that, over the past two centuries, the economic and social transformations of development in the now industrialized world were closely related to equally profound transformations in that world's demographic characteristics. The nature of the connection is disputed; its significance is not. Between 1800 and the present, mortality and fertility rates in Europe and North America declined sharply; internal migration transferred populations from primarily rural to primarily urban settings; and international migrations surged outward from Europe, then slowed, then surged toward Europe. In the macrohistorical perspective, one can readily see, and appreciate, the links of such changes to development.[1]

What is less well understood is the problematic connection between economic and social development and demographic trends over shorter periods, for example, a few decades. While this may appear to be a technical matter appropriate to scientific interpretation, it has in one form or another attracted political and intellectual attention for at least two centuries, and because of the continuing ambiguities of available evidence, the subject is still debated today. A brief glance at some of the terms of the argument may help illuminate the dilemmas.

The intellectual ancestry of today's debates may be traced at least to the late-eighteenth-century writings of the Marquis de Condorcet,[2] who described in detail the danger of excess population, a phenomenon he was one of the first to analyze. In concert with his fellow *philosophes*, he was, however, confident that rapid population growth could be managed by the "natural" processes of economic growth and human progress. Fertility rates would inevitably decline as economic productivity improved and natural resources were used more efficiently. A better educated populace would understand that voluntary control of fertility was both prudent and beneficial.

Thomas Malthus's *Essay on the Principle of Population*, first published in 1798, was a polemical riposte to these optimistic arguments (he mentioned Condorcet, as well as his own father, in the full title). For Malthus, an economist and contemporary of David Ricardo, Condorcet's optimism flew in the face of economic realities. Unless certain prescriptions were followed, there was no reason to expect such enlightened behavior among the masses.

Thus was the battle joined. Condorcet's arguments were echoed and later amplified by a diverse array of social thinkers (most energetically by Marx and his followers). A properly organized society would make individuals (especially women) and families behave in ways that would lead to population growth rates low enough to pose none of the threats foreseen by Malthus. Any apparent population problem was in reality a problem of social organization that could be (and in their view had to be) rectified. Of course, there was no consensus as to what a properly organized society would be. Prescriptions ranged from the triumph of socialism to the elimination of statist interventions, from transforming traditional gender relations into full equality for women to reinforcing the patriarchal family structure, seen as God's will.

Malthus's arguments, too, were echoed and amplified. Aggregate fertility was likely to exceed sustainable levels unless societies and governments made a real effort to encourage fertility reduction. Malthus's prescription was to encourage deferring marriage until couples could support a family, and hence eliminate what he considered the incentives to fecklessness embodied in the English Poor Laws. Many who shared Malthus's belief that affirmative measures were needed to lower fertility differed as to the actions required. Some advocated the dissemination of knowledge and means for effective contraception; though some of these considered themselves Malthusians, in fact they were advocating an approach strongly opposed by Malthus himself.[3] Others (including, in the twentieth century, many ecologists as well as many politicians in India under Indira Gandhi and in the People's Republic of China) believed that dissemination of knowledge and means for fertility control was not sufficient. They proposed varied disincentives to large families, ranging from economic penalties affecting taxes and employment to coercive sterilization or abortion. Proponents of such disincentives have ranged across a wide ideological spectrum—from the Communist leadership of China, to the free-market leadership of Singapore, to some elements of Western environmentalist groups. Thus do older intellectual currents take on forms that would make their authors turn in their graves; such ideas are likely to go on changing indefinitely, since the data and analytic tools required for a definitive assessment do not exist. Instead of adding to the debate, it may be more useful to consider what empirical research has uncovered about fertility and development.

The total fertility rate in Europe in the nineteenth century varied considerably, but in most regions it fell within the range of 4 to 6.5 children per woman. Then, led by a remarkably early (and still poorly understood) fertility decline in France, European fertility dropped at least 50 percent by the 1930s, which as we have seen raised concern. Biological decadence, genetic senescence, even race suicide were mentioned as reasons for this drastic change.

Partly in response to such explanations, economists and other social scientists developed alternative, wholly socioeconomic hypotheses embodied in what came to be known as the theory of the demographic transition. This theory—more a historical generalization than a set of empirically testable propositions—posited that the convergence of industrialization, urbanization, rising literacy, and the decay of extended-family networks led first to a drop in mortality rates and then to the adoption of voluntary controls of fertility within marriage.[4] During the transition period between these two trends, which might last many decades, rapid and substantial population growth took place. As a grand generalization referring to a two-century-long period, this idea had some merit.

Outside demography and history, however, it is not widely understood that the European fertility decline occurred in most cases only after many decades of economic development and that the timing and pace of the declines in different countries were not directly related to the level or pace of economic development there. To give one example, France's early fertility decline occurred in a largely rural, agrarian, and weakly industrialized society, while in England, the crucible of the Industrial Revolution, fertility declines "began perhaps a century later than France's and the onset of British industrialization."[5] Evidently, declines in fertility can lag many decades behind the breakthrough to sustained rates of rapid economic growth or (as in France) can precede it. Successful economic development leading to high living standards, urbanization, and mass compulsory education has been shown to be sufficient, but not necessary, to bring about fertility declines of 50 percent or more. Nor are the timing and pace of fertility change easily explained. We now have numerous cases from contemporary developing countries that are consistent with the pattern derived from the earlier European experience, although the speed of economic and demographic changes has been more rapid during the twentieth century than during the nineteenth.[6]

The link between development and international migrations in the past is also evident but opaque. Massive emigration accompanied the rapid industrialization of northern and western Europe in the nineteenth century: between 1850 and 1914, some fifty million Europeans left for other regions, most of them for the Americas and Antipodes. Until just before World War I, European emigration was still heavy, although it had begun to moderate in northern and western Europe and mostly came from the less developed regions to the east and south.[7] Subsequent trends were greatly affected by dramatic shifts in immigration policy (especially in the United States), by the Great Depression, and by World War II. It is impossible to say what might have happened to them had these earthquakes not occurred. But by the 1950s, the pressures that had impelled tens of millions to leave Europe over the preceding century had eased.[8]

Beginning in the 1960s, the trajectory was reversed: large and increasing numbers of migrants began to move *into* western and northern Europe. Initially, these were "demand-pull" migrations, with governments and employers actively recruiting workers during an extended economic boom.[9] Later, the immigration continued but became more "supply-push," with rapidly rising claims for political asylum and movements associated with the fall of Communism.

In short, the international migration experiences of western and northern Europe can be divided into four phases: decades of large-scale emigration prior to 1914 at a time of rapid industrialization; a waning of this emigration during times of economic instability, war, and depression in 1914–45; two decades of rapid economic growth in the 1950s and 1960s, accompanied by immigration to western and northern Europe from other world regions; and since 1970, during renewed economic instability, a rising trend of immigration to Europe and North America.

Ample evidence from the twentieth century confirms the convergence of accelerating economic growth and accelerating emigration.[10] In general, during the first several decades of accelerating economic growth in a poor country, the development itself creates increasing pressures that favor accelerated emigration:

- Rapid industrialization and economic growth are profoundly destabilizing to established economic and social relations; the wage disparities between urban and rural areas, accompanied by increasing agricultural productivity, usually stimulate rural-to-urban migration.
- Rapid urbanization saturates labor markets and increases income inequalities.
- Economic and urban growth produces what has been called a revolution of rising expectations; literacy increases, and along with it the knowledge and financial resources people need to undertake international migration, especially those at the lower end of income distribution.
- Though income inequalities may be increasing, so too is the level of household income for nearly everyone, income that can be invested in international migration.
- Finally, improved transportation and telecommunications facilities (especially in towns and cities involved in interna-

tional markets) make the attractiveness of international migration known and available to more people while reducing its cost.[11]

Recent experience indicates that even very rapid economic growth does not quickly narrow the large wage differentials that typically prevail between a developing country's workforce and those in already industrialized countries. This is in part because the labor forces in developing countries continue to grow rapidly for decades. Also, even very rapid economic growth rates cannot narrow tenfold wage differentials in less than several decades. Only after long periods of sustained change does industrial growth moderate the economic and demographic pressures favoring emigration. High levels of economic development generally produce moderate or low levels of fertility and emigration—eventually. But in the transitional decades of economic growth, fertility declines can be very slow in coming, and meanwhile emigration pressures increase.

The study of the effects of fertility rates on economic growth and prosperity has a long and tendentious history, as our brief remarks on the Condorcet-Malthus dispute suggest. Strong differences of opinion persist even within disciplines, particularly in economics, since many economists consider demographic change either peripheral or "exogenous." Statistical assessments of relationships between rates of economic and population growth (not fertility) have been popular, but they almost always produce ambiguous conclusions. This is not surprising, since slow population growth rates have occurred both in very poor, stagnant economies, which typically combine high fertility with high mortality, and in prosperous, rapidly advancing societies, where both fertility and mortality rates are low. Moreover, high population growth rates (due to sustained high fertility rates and declining mortality levels) can result both from the mortality-reducing effects of economic development and from sanitation and health improvements due to imported technologies in a setting of slow economic advance.

These analyses, therefore, are unlikely to be fruitful and predictably yield conflicting, ambiguous findings. The central question to ask is whether statistical associations can be made between rates of economic growth and fertility levels.[12] A related, more difficult but still important, question is whether the historical rates of economic advance would have been greater had fertility been moderate rather than high.

Overall, economists who responsibly appraise the economic effects of high fertility range from those who believe those effects are negative to those who believe that no such firm conclusion can be substantiated by the available evidence. But these latter, inconclusive findings are often filtered through ideological lenses, with advocates claiming that economic research demonstrates that high fertility is a "neutral" or even "positive" factor in economic growth.[13] Such pronouncements clearly exaggerate the findings of often flawed economic analyses.

Demographic analyses seem somewhat more reliable. Many demographers have concluded that, in most developing countries (excluding those such as Kuwait or Saudi Arabia, with large natural resources and small populations) where mortality has already declined to low or moderate levels, sustained high fertility does not preclude economic advance and political stability but makes them more difficult and problematic. The reasons are straightforward. High-fertility populations, whether with low or high mortality rates, have high proportions of children; 45–50 percent of the population will be fifteen and under. Assuming that education is encouraged or required and child labor prohibited, this near majority of the population cannot produce much of economic value, conventionally measured; rather, its education and training require heavy expenditures of public and private resources. If a high-fertility population also has low-to-moderate mortality among infants and children, then the number of dependent children increases rapidly, requiring equally rapid expansion of facilities for education and child health— and this in a still-poor economy with severe constraints on resources. Predictably, some fifteen or twenty years later, the size of the labor force will also increase rapidly, even though the country may suffer from unemployment and underemployment, producing an additional stress on an already fragile economic and political system.

In this view, high fertility is not necessarily the primary developmental problem, and economic development can be achieved without fertility decline. The conclusion is more modest: economic develop-ment, other things being equal, would be faster and easier if the fertility rate was moderate rather than high.

Because of the complexities and debates over economic development, it is not surprising that there is deep disagreement about the effects of in-ternational migration trends on it. This is a contentious subject, which can be discussed here only briefly.[14]

Everyone agrees that most migrants are individually seeking to im-prove their economic and/or social conditions. Similarly, many devel-oping countries accept without argument that the emigration of their citizens promotes their national economic development in at least three ways: by serving as a source of foreign exchange sent home by workers abroad (remittances); by reducing unemployment in their saturated labor markets; and by alleviating overcrowding and other aspects of domestic poverty. A number of nations—South Korea, Bangladesh, Jordan, Bar-bados, and Mexico, to name only a few—have promoted or welcomed emigration for these reasons. Nonetheless, in the aggregate, the effects are poorly understood and appear to be at best mixed.

As to the first argument, about official remittance flows, there is agreement that the volume of money is sizable, second in value only to crude oil. For developing countries, this may equal or surpass half the value of official development assistance. In some countries, the remit-tances are an important element of gross national product, sometimes equivalent in value to half of merchandise exports.[15] Also, substantial fractions of these remittances flow through informal channels, and the official figures may well be underestimates. Alas, here the consensus ends.

For some analysts, the remittances distort the economy and fuel in-flation in land, housing, and construction materials; for others, they in-crease domestic production by facilitating the import of needed goods. Some believe the money is squandered on consumption rather than in-vested in production, while others believe that even consumption ex-penditures stimulate the economy and reduce the need for government subsidies. Equally contradictory interpretations are made about other possible effects. Some believe that emigration reduces unemployment in the nations of origin, but others worry that unemployment is increased by the departure of key workers and resultant bottlenecks in productive economic sectors. Emigration may also have contradictory effects on the skilled labor available: needed skills may be lost to migration; or migrants may return with skills acquired abroad or with resources to invest in improved education for their children. As we have pointed out, some see emigration as a valuable mechanism that reduces poverty, but others note that the poorest seldom have the means to migrate. There is some evidence that migration may exacerbate existing income inequalities, though other findings suggest that the effects are neutral.

These difficult issues became matters of international politics at the three population conferences we have already considered—in 1974 in Bucharest, in 1984 in Mexico City, and in 1994 in Cairo. Our claim that this period is one of increasingly vociferous argument about these issues may be substantiated by a brief survey of the twists and turns of these meetings.

The organizing principles and dominant perspectives of international debate on population and development shifted noticeably between each of these meetings. Given that these were *intergovernmental* conferences, the contrasts were due to changes not only in the realm of ideas but also in the shifting fortunes of the main world powers and power blocs.

The 1974 World Population Conference in Bucharest was organized at a time of great alarm about the "population bomb," and the notion that such a meeting would benefit both developing and developed nations had been promoted by some influential Americans. One of the most prominent was General William Draper, who had been a strong proponent of activist population policies in Asia in the 1950s, after his service in World War II and as an administrator of Marshall Plan reconstruction initiatives. For Draper and his associates, the then very rapid population growth under way in Asia, Africa, and Latin America presented a profound barrier to economic development; they thought the world needed international agreements that included demographic targets for reducing population growth, targets to be achieved with vigorous governmental promotion of voluntary family-planning practice, assisted financially by bilateral and multilateral agencies.

But these views were not shared by the governments of developing countries. Their highest priority in 1974 was to adopt what they termed the New International Economic Order (NIEO), a transformation in international economic relations that would transfer wealth and income from the rich countries of the Northern Hemisphere to the poorer countries of the Southern one. These poorer countries, organized as the Group of 77, were diplomatically and financially supported in their initiative by the industrialized countries of the Soviet bloc as well as by the oil-exporting countries, which had just engineered a fourfold increase in world oil prices. The Bucharest conference was characterized by contentious claims from both "North" and "South."

By the time the 1984 conference convened in Mexico City, many leading delegations had changed their positions in striking ways. As we have seen in chapter 7, the U.S. delegation no longer led the charge for energetic population policies. Instead, it argued that poverty in the developing world arose from an excess of government intervention in the market and that economies freed of statist shackles could support any number of people. At the conference, the U.S. delegation was marginalized, since both developing-nation delegates and those from its Western allies agreed that population trends were hardly neutral forces in development. The developing countries, in particular, had shifted dramatically since 1974 toward the earlier American position, and active government efforts to encourage voluntary family planning had become common.

The most extreme shift was the Chinese one. In 1974, the chief delegate of China had minimized the importance of population trends for development as follows:

Of all things in the world, people are the most precious . . . Man is in the first place a producer and only in the second place a consumer . . . The population [of Asia, Africa, and Latin America] has grown rather quickly. This is not at all a bad thing but a very good thing . . . The large population of the Third World constitutes an important condition for strengthening the struggle against imperialism and hegemonism and accelerating social and economic development.[16]

Ironically, the revisionists who produced the White House policy statement of 1984 had unwittingly embraced these core arguments of the Chinese Communists, who in 1974 were still committed to the Marxist view that population surplus cannot occur under "correct" economic policies. But the Chinese official views had moved to the opposite extreme, such that by the 1980s the very future of socialism in China was seen as fundamentally depending on draconian state action to bring about sharp fertility declines. The Chinese government abruptly adopted stern fertility-reduction policies, sometimes crossing the line from voluntary action into coercion.

In the decade after the 1984 Mexico City meeting, positions shifted yet again, and in three dramatic and revealing ways. First, the public positions of the Clinton Administration converged dramatically with those of the western European delegations. Second, Marxist positions on population questions faded away, along with the regimes and supporters officially committed to them. Third, international migration was now a central element in the debate.

The convergence of official U.S. government positions and those of European governments was one outcome of the demise of the Reagan-Bush Administrations and the 1992 election of Bill Clinton as President. As we have seen, Reagan and Bush had allowed the population views of the pro-life and New Right movements to dominate American policy. Clinton had campaigned against these positions, as had Vice President Albert Gore, a prominent leader of the U.S. environmental movement.

The Clinton Administration's position, combining the perspectives of those concerned about population, environment, and women's rights, was compatible with views long espoused by European, especially Scandinavian, governments: that rapid population growth is not neutral (as claimed during the Reagan-Bush period); that women should be able to have safe abortions; and that women's education and economic well-being are essential to efforts to restrain rapid population growth. So the empowerment of women was the conference's dominant theme, and the population question was defined so as to emphasize its broad sociological, rather than its purely demographic, character. This meant that although demography was central, demographers were not.

Nothing is stable in the field of demography. As soon as the 1994 Cairo conference had been adjourned, political conditions significantly changed again, especially in the United States. In the congressional elections of 1994, the Republican Party captured leadership of both houses of Congress, and the stage was set for persisting political controversy about population, family planning, abortion, and foreign assistance. These points of friction remained after Clinton's re-election in 1996 alongside a Republican-controlled Congress.

The second point, concerning the Marxian arguments so visible at the 1974 and 1984 conferences, is self-evident. The dissolution of the U.S.S.R., the political transformation of eastern Europe that eliminated a voting bloc of states supporting the traditional Marxian position, and the profound change in Chinese public policy on population meant that no bloc of votes promoted the Marxian approach.

The third point, the salience of international migration issues by the 1990s, requires further elaboration. For one thing, it is important to remember how recently international migration had become an issue of high politics. Concern is not surprising when we recollect that the number of officially recognized refugees, mostly from developing countries neighboring Europe, had escalated from about eight million to nearly twenty million.[17] Simultaneously, international migration had come to be seen as a safety valve for the surplus labor supply in those nations, whose emigrants were an important export generating valuable hard-currency remittances to their families at home.

As a result, the Cairo population conference showed a dramatic increase in the number of recommendations concerning international migration.[18] Several themes stand out. First, the right of sovereign states to regulate access across their borders was strongly affirmed, subject only to certain provisions in the refugee conventions and to the exhortation that national admission policies be nondiscriminatory. Second, efforts by some nations to assert that reunification of migrants' families is a right were rejected, but governments were urged to recognize its "vital importance." Third, it was strongly asserted that all people should have a right to stay in, and return to, their country of birth, and the rights of minorities also to stay put was emphasized, partly in response to the terrible bouts of ethnic cleansing and genocide that had occurred in Bosnia and Rwanda. Fourth, encouragement was given to efforts to foster the positive effects of international migration—the flow of remittances and the transfer of technologies. Fifth, efforts were endorsed to control the people and organizations trafficking in undocumented migrants, women, children, and coercive adoption. Sixth, there was a call to give special attention to protecting women and children migrants. These recommendations had varying weight in the domestic politics of nations with diverse attitudes toward international migration.

In general, the international conferences on population and development offered useful texts for the study of attitudes about fertility, migration, and nationality. They show a deeper understanding of population and development issues over the past three decades, and a greater tendency to embed political and cultural values in discussions of demographic issues. To explore this pattern of change, we examine the following questions:

1. Have demography and ideology become more or less entangled? The shifting currents of policy and rhetoric from the mid-1960s onward have mixed demography and ideology in increasingly powerful ways. Debates about population trends have been entwined with alternative views of development; with ideological commitments such as those to Marxism or to free-market economics; with religious faith and practices; with the contested issues of the Cold War; and with conflicting ideas as to the proper roles and status of women. These mixtures are at the very core of international debates about fertility, migration, and nationality, and any efforts to disengage them are likely to be hopeless.

2. Has the significance of demographers in policy debates increased or diminished? Here, too, there is little doubt. The role of demographic analysis has diminished, as the boundaries of the population debate have widened and come to include those committed to one or another nondemographic concern. It was inevitable that less attention would be paid to scientific evidence and more to the passions and rhetoric of groups organized toward political ends. In short, population debates entered the political mainstream, with all the accompanying positive and negative

implications. In the United States, technically competent demographers were marginalized in the Reagan and Bush Administrations, which found their assessments incompatible with political commitments to the pro-life and New Right movements, but even since 1992 demographic expertise has remained peripheral. Apparently, activists influential in both the Reagan-Bush and Clinton Administrations—despite their differences—have believed that demographic work on population issues is less important than in the past. Some have objected to demography as ideologically awkward; others find it too technical, too narrow, or insufficiently responsive to the issues that animated them. One result has been that the category "population" has become progressively broader and more inclusive.

3. Has international migration become a central issue in population and development discussions? The subject is a latecomer to international debates, as we have seen, partly because until recently demographers, economists, and other social scientists gave it little analytic attention. The 1994 UN conference changed all that, and given the ideological positions, political movements, and cultural trends of our times, it is likely that it will continue to be at the heart of international discussions of population questions.

Many current discussions about fertility, migration, and development use, implicitly or explicitly, a model of change that places social and economic causes on one side and demographic outcomes on the other. But the world is not so simple. It would be unwise to conclude that economic growth always produces rapid fertility decline or discourages emigration from developing countries. Some alarmists anticipate that hordes of starving immigrants will appear on the shores of Europe, desperate to gain entry.[19] (This is, as we have said, the nightmare of the French novelist Jean Raspail in his horrifying dystopia *The Camp of the Saints*.[20]) This metaphor of immigration as plague is a classic example of complicated economic and demographic processes being oversimplified by fevered imaginations. Migration to Europe and the United States is indeed related in complex ways to the economic development of Asia, Africa, and Latin America. But no one should minimize the noneconomic, political factors that force people to leave their homes to seek safety abroad. It is to this subject that we next turn.

chapter 11

REFUGEES, ASYLUM SEEKERS, AND
IMMIGRANTS

Out of the disaster of World War II came one of the humanitarian achievements of modern history: an international system that protects refugees. Before the war, there had been some ad hoc arrangements, organizations, and international laws dealing with this issue, but in 1951 the still-young United Nations adopted a formal Convention Relating to the Status of Refugees.

The convention recognized that the upheavals of the 1930s and 1940s had exposed a fundamental problem in international law and civilized behavior. In law, each individual was a national of some state upon which he or she could call for protection and succor. Yet certain states had flagrantly—indeed, monstrously—persecuted their own citizens. So long as those people remained within their states' boundaries, the principles of state sovereignty and nonintervention prohibited other nations from humanitarian intervention. No one had the stomach to confront this dilemma of jurisdiction and persecution. But what of those who managed to escape by crossing borders into another state? Under pre-1945 international law, no state had any responsibility to admit those in flight from such persecution.

The solution embodied in the 1951 UN Convention was to define a special category of persecuted people who had departed their own states and could not call on them for protection. Under such exceptional circumstances, said the Convention, other states agreed to accept certain obligations to admit and protect such people. The Convention definition of a refugee is a person who, "owing to a well-founded fear of being persecuted for reasons of race, religion, nationality, membership in a particular social group, or political opinion is outside the country of his nationality, and is unable or . . . unwilling to avail himself of the protection of that country."[1]

This internationally accepted legal definition of "refugee" differs markedly from the journalistic and common usage of the same English word. For example, any person fleeing civil war, generalized violence, environmental catastrophe, famine, epidemic, poverty, or any other circumstances not characterized by persecution on the five specified grounds does not qualify as a Convention refugee. Signatory states thus did not accept responsibility for protecting other states' citizens, however desperate they might be, except in cases where other states were the persecutors.

The protections of the Convention were also limited geographically. Naturally enough, the focus was on Europe, which had produced millions of refugees and displaced persons over the preceding two decades.[2] During the 1950s and 1960s, human-rights groups, churches, and political and ethnic activists found the substantive and geographical restrictions unacceptable and urged that they be relaxed.

In 1967, the geographical limitation to Europe was eliminated when the UN Convention was revised as the Protocol Relating to the Status of Refugees. In 1969, the Organization of African Unity (OAU) adopted its own convention, embracing the UN Convention definition but adding that, in Africa, "The term refugee shall also apply to every person who, owing to external aggression, occupation, foreign domination or events seriously disturbing the public order . . . is compelled to leave . . . to seek refuge in another place."[3] Similar language was used in the Cartagena Declaration of 1984, relating to strife-torn Central America. Despite the persistent pleas of human-rights and refugee groups, the OAU and Cartagena language is the only expansion of the UN Convention and Protocol definitions with formal multilateral support. Most other nations, notably those in the industrial world, have resisted additional categories.

There is a final set of provisions and distinctions that must be appreciated: this relates to those seeking asylum, who are distinguished from refugees mainly by their geographical location. In order to qualify as a Convention refugee, a person must be "outside the country of his nationality," while asylum seekers are granted refugee status not from a place of temporary refuge in a third country but at or within the borders of the country where they seek to settle. In such cases, the *non-refoulement* provision of the UN Convention and Protocol comes into operation, the clause that prohibits signatory states from returning bona fide applicants to their native lands if they would be subjected to persecution there; but, at the same time, no signatory state is obliged to admit bona fide refugees who apply for admission from a third country. This narrow and abstruse provision posed vexing problems for liberal democracies such as Germany and the United States in the 1980s and soon brought the international refugee system to a crisis point.

Sorting international migrants into categories is a legalistic process with significant consequences. Refugees and asylum seekers are only two of the categories, and no matter how desperate their circumstances, most would-be migrants cannot qualify as either. At the same time, the liberal democracies have been conscious of the terrible consequences that may result if they incorrectly return (*refoule*) a bona fide refugee claiming asylum. At the strong urging of human-rights groups and the United Nations High Commissioner for Refugees, they have agreed to administrative and judicial procedures that are meant to ensure a careful assessment of asylum claims.

Until recently, perhaps the most elaborate procedure was that of the Federal Republic of Germany, based on Article 16 of its Basic Law, or constitution, which reads: "The politically persecuted shall be granted asylum." This brief statement, as German judges liberally interpreted it, led to two surges of claims for asylum and ultimately to traumatic political debate, prompted by vicious and repeated incidents of violence by Germans against foreigners.[4]

The first phase began a few years after the termination of the *Gastarbeiter* (guest worker) program in 1973, more than a decade after its inception. More and more people, especially Turks (the West German government's asylum form was reprinted in Turkish newspapers), who might previously have sought *Gastarbeiter* status began to appear at West German borders and in West German cities to claim political asylum. The extended adjudication process required by court interpretations of Article 16 meant, as we have seen, that merely filing such a claim would guarantee years of residence, during which a work permit and access to

212

government benefits, such as child allowances and payments to low-income persons, were available. While fewer than 5 percent of such claims ultimately were deemed valid, the practice was to "tolerate" the continued residence of those whose claims were denied.

For would-be workers from poor countries who knew of this system, it was an offer too good to refuse. Asylum claims rose rapidly from about 16,000 in 1977 to 33,000 in 1978 to 51,000 in 1979.[5] When the number reached 108,000 in 1980, there was political consensus that the system had broken down but no agreement on how to fix it. The opposition Christian Democrats and their allies urged that Article 16 of the Basic Law be amended, but the governing Social Democrats were strongly opposed and opted instead for legal and administrative changes that were meant to reduce the incentives that encouraged questionable asylum claims. These changes seemed to work well for several years. Claims for asylum declined to fewer than 20,000 in 1983. But then the claims again increased, and the source countries now included nations with few prior connections to Germany (e.g., Pakistan, Sri Lanka, Somalia).

By 1989, the earlier peak of 108,000 had been exceeded, and the numbers continued to rise rapidly. Once again, the Christian Democrats (by then the governing party) sought to amend the Basic Law, but the Social Democrats successfully opposed such changes by denying the government the necessary two-thirds majority in parliament. By 1991, the number of asylum claims had reached 256,000.[6] In addition, many "ethnic Germans" from eastern Europe were admitted, though many were descendants of sixteenth- and seventeenth-century migrants, had little in common with Germans in Germany, and spoke no German. With the Berlin Wall gone, many people also left East Germany, with expectations about finding employment and housing in the western provinces that provoked what one observer has called "a German-German cultural shock."[7]

Since the government did not count asylum claimants and German migrants as foreign immigrants, a large gap grew between official immigration totals and the numbers of newcomers the public perceived as foreigners. One example: in 1989, more than a million people coming from other countries settled in West Germany; nearly 345,000 of these were from East Germany, but even so, the government reported only 211,000 foreign migrants, classifying the rest as Germans or asylum seekers.[8]

To the deep shock of Germany and much of the rest of the world, random acts of unprovoked assault on those believed to be foreigners began to disrupt German life. Peaceful residents were assaulted on the streets and in their homes, and this of course evoked ghosts of a German past still hardly forgotten in Germany or the rest of Europe. Most of the violence appears to have been local and spontaneous, though undoubtedly there was some loose coordination among the neo-Nazis and skinheads. For whatever reason, the authorities were unable to prevent the assaults, which by 1991 numbered well over a hundred a month.

The debate in the German parliament about both the mass migrations and the violence against foreigners was extraordinarily angry. Accusations of cynical political expediency, organized terrorism, and Nazi atrocities flew wildly in all directions; "the insults and accusations that echoed through the chamber reflected the frustration of many Germans in the face of surging immigration and daily attacks on foreigners," as *The New York Times* put it. The first Social Democratic speaker referred to the Christian Democrats' leader as a *Schreibtischtäter*, a word normally used to describe the Nazi bureaucrats who administered mass extermination policies. The Christian Democrats responded by comparing the Social Democrats' proposals for temporary camps for asylum claimants to Nazi concentration camps. In the despairing words of one Social Democrat, "They're trying to corner us on an issue for which we don't have any good solution. I'm afraid it may work."[9]

Meanwhile, public opinion polls showed some sympathy for those engaged in violence. But in November 1992, a Turkish home was firebombed and three residents burned to death. There was mass revulsion against the perpetrators, with a grassroots campaign stimulating hundreds of thousands of Germans to march in candlelight demonstrations opposing the violence against foreigners.

In December 1992, as the number of asylum claims moved toward that year's total of 438,000, the parliamentary stalemate was broken by a compromise under which the Social Democrats agreed to drop their opposition to a constitutional amendment to Article 16: applicants from countries determined by the government to be free of persecution (known in refugee-policy jargon as safe countries) could be turned away at borders and airports, with no review of their asylum claims; those from other countries would be admitted as before while their claims were reviewed. A second key provision allowed for the rejection of asylum claims from those seeking to enter Germany by way of a third "safe" country. In effect, this shifted the responsibility of asylum adjudication to such countries as Poland, the Czech and Slovak Republics, and Austria, which had been major transit points for people intending to claim asylum in Germany, and the compromise provided for "administrative and financial help" for such countries as needed. The compromise also, for the first time, put numerical limits on the admission of foreign-born ethnic Germans.

As the new procedures began to take effect and to be understood abroad, the number of asylum seekers filing claims in Germany declined rapidly and by 1995 had fallen to 136,000, a 69 percent drop from the 1992 total.[10] The number of violent attacks on foreigners waned, as did support for right-wing political parties such as the Republikaners. Politicians of mainstream parties breathed sighs of relief. But the compromise did not impress some advocacy groups, especially with respect to its safe-country provisions. Herbert Leuninger, spokesman for the German refugee support group Pro Asyl, commented, "There are practically no countries that are free of persecution. I would say that even Germany doesn't qualify any more."[11] These groups are likely to contest determinations about safe countries both politically and judicially. In any case, experience suggests the wisdom of caution in interpreting recent declines as indicative of longer-term trends.

Whatever the future may bring, Germany has been at the core of recent trends in asylum claims across Europe. As may be seen in the chart, the number of such claims in Europe in 1987–92 quadrupled, in tandem with German trends, then, as the revised German policies took hold, the number of claims filed in Europe as a whole declined rapidly, to a level more than 50 percent lower by 1995.

In many respects, the German experience with asylum claims has been shared in muted form by other industrialized countries in Europe and North America.[12] Sweden, with a population one-tenth that of Germany, registered eighty-three thousand asylum claims in 1992, twice as

Asylum Applications and Geneva Convention Status Decisions in Participating European States, 1983–95

Year	1983	1984	1985	1986	1987	1988	1989	1990	1991	1992	1993	1994	1995
Asylum Applications	65,400	98,600	165,100	195,100	172,950	221,050	313,700	434,300	560,000	692,685	549,655	320,017	283,423
Geneva Convention	19,868	21,164	23,397	20,425	20,494	22,554	22,848	26,284	32,544	29,262	46,767	46,093	43,100

Estimates for 1995 based on data for most IGC participating states

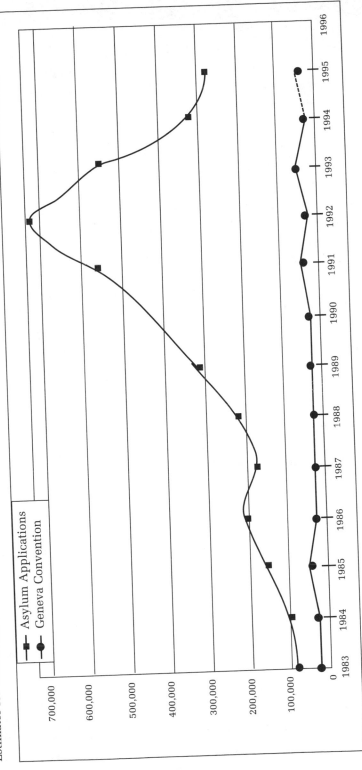

Source: Inter-governmental Consultations on Asylum, Refugee, and Migration Policies, Vienna, Austria.

many as in Germany on a per capita basis. France had twenty-nine thousand, notwithstanding prevalent anti-immigration sentiments—ranging across the political spectrum—that helped to defeat the Socialist government in the 1993 elections. The Italian government reported only twenty-five hundred asylum claimants that same year, but given the weakness of Italian controls on unlawful immigration, the most likely explanation is not low numbers but fewer needing to claim asylum in order to live there.

In the United States, backlogs of asylum claims reached into the hundreds of thousands by 1993, notwithstanding deployment of Coast Guard vessels to deter and intercept would-be claimants from Haiti. One new source of asylum claimants was Fujian Province, in China. Several incidents, including the fatal grounding of a tramp steamer (the *Golden Venture*) full of Chinese migrants off a Long Island beach near New York City, made it clear that networks of Chinese and American facilitators were generating large profits by charging upward of $30,000 per person to smuggle people into the United States, where they could file claims for asylum. The Chinese cases showed how fertility and asylum policies interact in wholly unexpected ways: most of the claimants who had paid so much to the smuggling networks obviously had been told about a regulation, promulgated only a year or two earlier by a pro-life Bush Administration official, certifying that fear of the Chinese government's "one-child family" policy was enough to demonstrate persecution under the terms of U.S. and international law. What these Chinese migrants may not have anticipated is that, once in the United States, they and their families could be coerced by the smugglers into indentured servitude verging on slavery, others into prostitution, to repay the money they owed.

Reactions to these incidents have varied greatly, ranging from political stalemate and street violence in Germany, to political firestorms in France, to disorganized temporizing in the United States. Yet although governments are often rightly criticized for failing to think beyond the short term, it cannot be said that they failed to anticipate the asylum problem.

In the mid-1980s, a number of Western governments concluded that they were all dealing with an unprecedented situation. As early as 1985, a Swedish initiative led to a series of unusual, informal meetings among seven European countries (Denmark, France, Germany, Netherlands, Sweden, Switzerland, the United Kingdom) under the awkward rubric "Inter-Governmental Consultations on Asylum, Refugee and Migration Policies" (hereinafter referred to as the IGC). A small secretariat in Geneva was created to operate jointly with the office of the UN High Commissioner for Refugees (UNHCR). Within a few years, the IGC had generated considerable dynamism. However, the ambiguous relationship between the two was problematic, especially since many UNHCR staff saw themselves as advocates for the people contesting the failure of nations to respect the treaty obligations under the UN Convention and Protocol. The number of governments participating in the IGC grew to fourteen, then sixteen. Ultimately, the IGC's coordinator was forced by the UNHCR to resign, and he moved his office to Vienna with the financial support of several IGC governments.[13]

The convulsive events in Germany and elsewhere, and the acrimonious political debates that have surrounded them, inevitably brought the international refugee system to its deepest crisis since its inception in 1951. That system showed, in a sense, the triumph of universal values of international human rights over the customary concerns of national sovereignty and domestic politics. Yet its origins lay in the postwar plight of European refugees within Europe and had very little to do with the needs of African or Asian refugees and others who began to claim the rights it offered. Moreover, some important elements of official and public support for it arose distinctly out of the Cold War. For four decades, Western governments had been able routinely to denounce Warsaw Pact nations for prohibiting the free departure of their peoples, a position that was politically plausible only so long as the numbers of people actually able to leave and claim refugee status were minuscule. But when the Berlin Wall and the Iron Curtain came down, the West was hoist on its own petard.

The future course of refugee and asylum policies is impossible to anticipate. Collectively, the sixteen states participating in the IGC estimate that the cost for processing and assisting asylum claimants reached nearly $10 billion in 1992, having quadrupled from the estimated $2.4

billion only seven years earlier.* Though data are not available, the expenditures have, presumably, declined since 1992 along with the reduction in the numbers of asylum claims. To put these sums into a comparative framework: The Organization for Economic Cooperation and Development (OECD) reports that total flows of overseas development assistance from the twenty-one industrialized members of OECD's Development Advisory Committee totaled about $61 billion in 1992.[14] The 1992 budget for the UN High Commissioner for Refugees in 1992 exceeded $1 billion, a record.

It should come as no surprise that there is increasing support for tightening the restrictions on the entry of refugees in Europe. The French parliamentary elections of 1993 produced dramatic political shifts away from the then-governing Socialists toward the two main parties of the center-right, both of them more hostile to refugees. The success of the Socialists in the parliamentary elections of 1997 represented at least a partial reversal of that shift. The German parliamentary compromise of 1992 has been too recently implemented to allow a firm assessment, but it may ultimately prove significant. The refugee policies of Sweden and other countries have shifted, with not inconsiderable pain, from more to less open.

There are countervailing trends in North America, although to some degree these are reflections of policies adopted many years ago rather than affirmative choices about the present. In a confused legislative process during 1989 and 1990, at a time of robust economic growth when some employers were claiming labor shortages, the U.S. Congress raised the number of legal immigrants to be admitted each year by 35–40 percent. Around the same time, the asylum adjudication system was reformed to eliminate the Cold War criteria of earlier years, although the new system had barely gained its footing before it was swamped by the Haitian boat-people crisis and by a rapid acceleration in the number of

---

*The estimated annual costs of asylum processing and assistance in the sixteen states (in billions of U.S. dollars) were as follows:

1985	1987	1989	1990	1991	1992
$2.4	2.9	4.8	6.0	7.2	9.9

Source: Inter-Governmental Consultations, Annex A to 3 February 1993 Overview.

asylum claimants from other countries. Asylum claims by boat people from Haiti (and, more recently, China) have become particularly vexing for President Clinton, who during his first Presidential campaign had been critical of the Bush Administration's policies but once in office found himself forced to continue them. In 1995, the Administration instituted substantial reforms to U.S. asylum procedures aimed at avoiding the lengthy delays in adjudication and hence reducing the unacceptable growth in backlogs.

There are other ways in which refugee politics has developed in recent years. In 1994, the Clinton Administration decided that only direct military intervention could remove the military junta in Haiti that was contributing to continuing emigration of Haitian boat people. A democratically elected government was reestablished in Haiti, though a foreign military presence seems necessary to sustain it.

In Canada, reform of asylum procedures preceded those in the United States. Whether or not the new system will work depends on the number of questionable claims it receives. U.S. and Canadian officials have encouraged western European governments such as Germany's to accept that their nations have become countries of immigration. They urge these governments to establish numbers and procedures for legal immigration and refugee resettlement and to facilitate naturalization of long-resident foreign nationals. German policy makers have noted these suggestions without so far acting on them. Overall, the pattern is one in which immigration and refugee issues are decided at the highest political level. The issues raised by refugees, asylum seekers, and immigrants are—like these unfortunate people themselves—here to stay.

chapter 12

ISLAMIC FUNDAMENTALISM AND THE WEST

Population politics in Europe and North America has been profoundly affected by two major features of life in the Middle East. The first is the continuing Arab-Israeli conflict. The second is the rise of radical Islam, in the form of both the Shi'ite revolution in Iran and Sunni fundamentalism. Here, as elsewhere, the period from the 1960s to the 1990s is marked by profound social and political discontinuities. The upheavals have spilled over into European and North American affairs in ways that no study dealing with international migration can afford to ignore.

The first development was to a degree an outcome of earlier European influence and domination of the Arab world. The four Arab-Israeli wars—1948, 1956, 1967, and 1973—were a direct result of the decolonization of lands in the Middle East that had previously been parts of the French or British empires. They also arose out of the consequences of the Nazi plan to exterminate European Jewry, without which the political impetus behind the movement to create the state of Israel would have been much weaker. After each conflict, major population transfers occurred: of Jews to Israel from many countries all over the world, of Palestinian Arabs either to refugee camps or to new homes in the Middle East, Europe, and America. As the Jewish diaspora came into Israel, a new diaspora of Palestinians was born.[1]

The 1967 war and its catastrophic conclusion for the Arab world sent shock waves throughout Islamic society, exposing a dangerous fault line. The rift was between the Arab, Asian, and North African governments of largely Muslim states and a new Islamic opposition whose hostility to the corruption and Western character of their leaders attracted mass support—from Pakistan to Morocco. The geopolitical landscape of the Middle East also changed after the massive defeat of 1967 and the more mixed outcome of 1973. Syria retained its military and political ties to the Soviet bloc, but Egypt under Anwar el-Sadat shifted from an alliance with the Soviets to one with the United States. Massive American aid to Egypt and Iran helped in the industrialization of their economies, but at the price of producing an anti-Western and anti-modern fundamentalist movement. A popular uprising of Shi'ites swept aside the Shah of Iran in 1979. Remarkably similar movements of Sunni fundamentalists emerged as well, and still threaten a number of regimes, including those of Egypt and Algeria.[2]

There were both "push" and "pull" factors in the trajectory of radical Islam. Its adherents reacted against contemporary trends and were pushed into action, but they also were pulled into groups that offered essential services as well as a sense of hope for the future. The massive programs of industrial and social change that many Muslim countries went through were conventionally grouped under the term "modernization." If the 1960s saw modernization triumphant, the 1970s witnessed its spectacular failure. To be sure, some groups benefited from Western aid and development projects, but for the masses modernization meant upheaval and little more. They were better educated than in the past, but when they moved to towns and cities they faced chaos and mass unemployment. The only people offering them help were radical Muslims. When natural disasters occurred in Egypt, it was the Muslim Brotherhood, not the Egyptian state, that lifted the wounded and the dazed out of the ruins of their homes.

The radical Muslims went further. They taught their fellow citizens to see the bankruptcy of postcolonial society and of the leaders who, they believed, had been co-opted by the West. To them, Islam Westernized was Islam destroyed. Their very religion was, they believed, in danger of disappearing. In this difficult phase in the history of the faithful, a new approach had to be found.

By now, radical Islam has grown into a powerful political force. Its structure is decentralized and it is difficult to destroy, since new cells spring up almost immediately. It has demonstrated real organizational power and has offered a host of services otherwise unavailable to millions of Muslims. To understand the attraction of these groups, we must recognize that they have helped to make a kind of civil society in the midst of poor, deeply inegalitarian states. To this task, they have brought that sense of persecuted fraternity that gives underground movements remarkable tenacity and solidarity.

Almost always, these groups are out of power, so it is wrong to generalize from the Iranian case to radical Islam as a whole. Many radical Muslims, for instance in Algeria and Egypt, believe in seizing political power—through the ballot box where possible, through violence where necessary. Yet most have recognized that they cannot take power by force and have renounced violence, setting their hopes on the long-term spread of political and social influence. In this way, they have set the agenda of political debate about issues they consider essential, such as the segregated education of girls and boys. Their presence in the giant arc from Morocco to Pakistan is a constant signal that Islam is alive and must be reckoned with.

Fundamentalism describes more a temperament than specific convictions. It may be useful, though, to summarize a set of beliefs common to many (though by no means all) of the Muslims loosely referred to as fundamentalist. Their first notion is that Islam is a religion of totality: there is no divorce between politics and theology. A second is specific to Shi'a, and not Sunni, Muslims: the Shi'a hold that there was a time in the past when Islamic law governed society and when justice reigned; Islamic law is therefore a potential source of future political authority. A third belief, common to both Sunni and Shi'a radicals who see the world in black-and-white Manichaean terms, is that the Muslim world is riddled with corruption, some of it derived from infection with Western values, some of it homegrown. The disease must be purged; only then can *Shari'a,* or Islamic law, return peacefully to rule the Muslim world.[3]

The implications of this social force for migration, fertility, and national identity in both the Islamic world and neighboring regions are widespread and serious. Muslim migrants are numerous in every major European country. Fundamentalists are among them, and whenever the migrants think of themselves as mistreated by their European or American hosts, fundamentalism tends to grow. Many do not subscribe to Western views on assimilation and citizenship, preferring to tolerate the rule of infidels so long as they can practice Islam. Though tens of thousands live in the West, their hearts are not in it.[4]

Perhaps most important, their views about women and the family are classically reactionary. Many want to set the clock back to a time when Islamic values were taught primarily within the family and when women were treated in the manner of early Islam. To be sure, many Western Muslim men and women accept women's rights as consistent with Islam. Fundamentalists disagree. Western notions of gender equality are, therefore, anathema to most of them. Many oppose sterilization and contraception, though when population growth has threatened the future of the Islamic state, as in contemporary Iran, they have decided that family planning is justifiable.[5]

Any account of migration in the period since the 1960s, therefore, must take account of this remarkable social phenomenon. The integration of Muslims into Europe is made significantly more complicated when some of them profess beliefs incompatible with Western definitions of citizenship, equal rights for all, and the sovereignty of the nation.[6] And the fraction that subscribes to extreme fundamentalist views has helped to transform the atmosphere in which population politics, both in the Middle East and in the developed world, is debated.

Israel is an immigrant state. Its Law of Return gives immediate citizenship to any Jewish person, as defined by traditional Jewish law, who requests it. Israel is also an ethno-religious state, defined by its commitment to the renaissance of the Jewish people in its biblical homeland in Palestine. The minority Christians and Muslims living in Israel as Israeli citizens number just over a million, about 25 percent of the total. They are accorded full rights of religious expression (though not of missionary activity, which is deemed offensive to the Jewish faith) but do not have the right to purchase land and do not serve in the Israeli army, the central socializing institution of the state. They are represented in the Israeli parliament, but the per capita investment in urban and rural infrastructure in areas inhabited by Israeli Arabs is substantially lower than in predominantly Jewish areas. Israeli Arabs live in the only democracy in the Middle East, but they are decidedly second-class citizens there.[7]

Their situation took its current form when the Gaza Strip and the West Bank of the river Jordan were occupied by Israel after the 1967 war. One million Arabs were added to the population under Israeli authority, including the residents of Arab Jerusalem, annexed to Israel and made part of a unified Jerusalem in 1968. Arab Jerusalemites henceforth lived in Israel, though (to our knowledge) virtually none took up Israeli citizenship.

To make the demographic mix even more complex, Israeli settlers returned to parts of Jerusalem and the West Bank in which Jewish settlements had existed before the 1947–48 civil war. Land and property were expropriated for them, and despite complex litigation over the next three decades, large tracts of Arab land were transferred to Israeli control. On this land, more than 150 settlements were constructed, drawing in young couples happy to exploit generous state financial help in housing, as well as religious people who believed they were walking in the footsteps of the prophets. By 1995, a hundred thousand people lived in these new townships and farms. To most Arabs on the West Bank, these new settlers were classic colonizers. Many of the newcomers were Americans; then came South Africans, Russians, and Georgians. Arabs rejected their claim that they had a right to the land through ethnic and historic ties linking them to the people of Israel who had lived in the Holy Land before the time of Jesus. Why should they, the Arabs, pay the price for European crimes against the Jews?

Since 1967, both Israeli and Arab propagandists adopted pronatalism as a strategic weapon. For Israelis, a high birthrate and a high immigration rate were essential for the survival of the state. Israeli society is fundamentally secular, and female participation in the paid labor force is the norm. Family allowances reward large families, though high inflation minimizes these benefits. There is as well in Israel a vocal and politically powerful community of Orthodox Jews, who encourage large families and oppose the principle of sexual equality and women's liberation.[8] An increasing proportion of the Jewish population of Jerusalem is Orthodox; their aim is to form a majority of the city's inhabitants by the year 2010. Palestinian propaganda also exalts the virtues of large families and traditional values. Women's rights come after the national struggle, if they are considered at all.[9]

During the long Israeli occupation of the West Bank, it was inevitable that opposition groups would proliferate. Among them was Law in the Service of Man, established by English- and American-educated Arab lawyers dedicated to monitoring human-rights abuses. More radical elements followed different paths set by factions affiliated with the Palestine Liberation Organization (PLO). Effective intelligence and ruthless countermeasures kept the opposition strictly within bounds until 1982.

Then, when Israel invaded Lebanon, the political balance in the Middle East changed. Israel succeeded in dislodging the military forces the PLO had ensconced in Lebanon but at the price of splitting its own society (and army) down the middle—unhappy at fighting a war not of necessity but of choice. Worse, from the Israeli point of view, was that the invasion of Lebanon sucked the combustible material of fundamentalist Islam into the Arab-Israeli cauldron.[10] Perhaps it would have arrived sooner or later, but in any case the war in Lebanon, like most wars, took a course no one could have foreseen.

Mass opposition to Israeli occupation on the West Bank and in the Gaza Strip was touched off in the late 1980s by a relatively minor incident—a nasty traffic accident in which Arab workers waiting for transport to Israeli towns were killed. But it was merely the spark: the tinder had been there for years, made up of the countless indignities and humiliations inevitable in an extended occupation. The uprising was called the Intifada, or "shrugging off" the occupation.[11] It substantially raised the price Israel had to pay for continuing to occupy the West Bank and Gaza, and many Israelis began to question the utility of this policy. By a narrow margin, the Labor Party was returned to power in 1991; it started serious negotiations with Palestinians to establish self-rule on the West Bank and in Gaza.

But the injection of fundamentalism into the conflict had made it even harder to secure a way out. Instead of PLO-sponsored antagonists, the Israelis had to cope with Hamas, fundamentalists of both Shi'a and Sunni Islam supported by Iran, whose aim was to bring to the downtrodden Arabs of Palestine the same message of hope and salvation that the imams had brought to those who suffered under the Shah. After terrorist incidents in 1992, the Israeli government, led by Yitzhak Rabin, who had been commander in chief of the Israeli army in 1967, decided to expel four hundred activists and leaders of Hamas. They pushed these men across the border to Lebanon, where, to the Israelis' surprise and consternation, their entry was blocked by Lebanese troops. These men, stranded in a no-man's-land, vividly illustrated the plight of displaced Arabs and the willingness of fundamentalists to suffer for their beliefs.

The increasing strength of Hamas led the Labor Party and the PLO to find common cause through a peace settlement in 1993. The final disposition of territories and questions of sovereignty are still unclear, but this mutual recognition of Israel and the PLO transformed Middle Eastern politics.

Fundamentalists in Gaza and on the West Bank have conducted a protracted war against this new phase of negotiation. Arab suicide bombings within Israel led to a swing of support in public opinion strong enough to unseat the Labor Party and in 1996 to bring to power a hard-line Likud government under Benjamin Netanyahu. An Israeli hard-liner's assassination of Prime Minister Yitzhak Rabin had also contributed to this ascendency of the Right. Rabin's successor, Shimon Peres, was politically less powerful and less popular than Rabin, and his Labor coalition was voted out of power by a narrow margin. Subsequent suicide bombings in Jerusalem and Tel Aviv continued to threaten the hard-won gains of the peace process.

For our purposes, the most important feature of the new situation has been its placing radical Islam on the front line of the struggle between Arabs and Israelis. Here, the older conflicts become entangled with the global presence of Islamic fundamentalism.[12]

The Iranian revolution of Ayatollah Khomeini was the culmination of tremendous shifts in the Islamic world. In reaction to the corruption, brutality, and Western bias of the Shah's regime, religious leaders in Iran began to formulate an Islamic position that ultimately destroyed the Pahlavi dynasty. It arose in the Iranian countryside, where impoverishment in the 1960s showed how little benefit had come from the Shah's highly publicized projects to modernize Iran. Young people who migrated from villages to towns and from towns to cities had, whatever their level of education, pitifully few jobs to go to. They heard the imams' message that the world of the Shah was corrupt and had to be overthrown.[13]

And so it was, but in a way no other twentieth-century revolution had done. The Shi'a revolt was a re-creation of early medieval Persia in the setting of a twentieth-century state. The core of the Shi'a faith (shared by perhaps seventy million people, or 10 percent of the Islamic world) was the story of Ali, cousin and brother-in-law of Muhammad and the fourth caliph following the prophet. Ali's grandson Hussein was killed by corrupt tribesmen at the Battle of Kerbala (in present-day Iraq) in 680. His martyrdom and the fall of the House of Ali are relived every year by the faithful in the ritual of the Ashura, on the tenth day of Muharram, when zealots whip themselves and shed their blood as Hussein shed his in the seventh century. This ritual, which was enacted sporadically over the centuries in Shi'a populations, began to recur in Iranian towns and villages in the 1960s.

Shi'a fundamentalism contends that the Islamic faith is a guide to social organization and political life; that, for the brief period between the death of Muhammad in 632 and the end of the fourth caliphate in 661, there was a generation of justice, a reign of true Islamic law; and that this code of practice can be restored, so long as the West and its proxy rulers in the Muslim world are resisted, rejected, and deposed.

Shi'a fundamentalists, like many dedicated fundamentalist religious people, live a political myth. They subscribe to a story about the past that explains the world and galvanizes the faithful for action today. They infused this myth into the Iran-Iraq war, and a variant on it was added to the Arab-Israeli conflict at the time of the invasion of Lebanon. Iranian funds and training came to the aid of Palestinians, as they had to Afghans, and created armed groups, including Hezbollah, or the Army of God. When the PLO was expelled from Beirut, the United States sent in troops to try to fill the power vacuum. The Americans were evicted by Hezbollah, whose suicide bombing there killed hundreds of American troops and convinced the Reagan Administration to withdraw from Lebanon. These Islamic militants then engaged the Israelis and their proxy Christian Lebanese forces. The result was a bloody stalemate, with kidnappings and killings on both sides. Fundamentalism began to spread within the territories occupied by Israel, and now the Israelis confronted a new, more dangerous enemy than the one they had aimed to destroy by invading Lebanon in 1982.[14]

But we need to go well beyond the Iranian revolution and its aftershocks to account for the upsurge of fundamentalism among the Sunni peoples, the perhaps 600 million Muslim inhabitants of states from Morocco to the Philippines. Muslim migration to Europe and North America is primarily from these Sunni communities.

Emmanuel Sivan has termed Islamic fundamentalism "a world view harking back to essential verities of the Faith,"[15] a view shared by hundreds of millions of Muslim believers, Sunni and Shi'ite alike. We have noted fundamentalism's profound cultural pessimism, its sense of imminent doom, of the drowning of Islam's message in a sea of imported Western ideas. We have noted too its indictment of religious and political leaders who failed to confront or reverse what it considers the modern assault on Islam.

Of equal importance is a sense of urgency, of alarm, of the need for immediate action. Fundamentalists are in a hurry. They cannot wait for the long term, because the ogre of modernity is not at the gates but long ago entered the citadel and corrupted the state itself. The age of barbarism is not tomorrow, it is today. To fundamentalists, "Westoxicated" leaders in command of ruthless security services and armies and with plenty of lackeys in the religious academies and institutions pose perhaps the greatest danger Islam has ever faced. That is why fundamentalists believe in mobilizing the masses, especially young men, to undermine and ultimately transform or (in extremis) overthrow these diseased regimes.

How many people are prepared for political action on behalf of fundamentalism is difficult to determine. The hatred of modernity is commonplace, and cynicism about political corruption in Islamic states is widespread. But even if only a small proportion—perhaps 10 percent of university students in Egypt, according to one study—is fundamentalist in the full sense of arriving at a justification of revolt, this radical strain has nonetheless set the terms of the debate within Islam about the kind of state in which it is possible to live an authentically religious life. The radicals are the bad conscience of the religious conservatives, reminding them of their multiple compromises with state authorities. In this environment, numbers and influence are not coterminous. A determined 10 percent minority of activists presents a clear and present danger to many Arab regimes. And there is a much larger group of potential supporters and fellow travelers of fundamentalism than may appear at first sight. Sunni fundamentalism has achieved success in mass mobilization movements in Sudan (where the President is a fundamentalist), Algeria, and Egypt; in the latter two cases, fundamentalists threaten to overthrow the state.[16]

The iconography of martyrdom, the nurturing of a sense of injustice, and the need to right a terrible wrong are more intrinsic to Shi'ite than to Sunni political culture, and the roots of revolt among Sunni Muslims are not so deeply embedded in their history. Also, Sunni Islam is more hesitant when confronting the sins of regimes in the Arab world.

In Egypt, the fundamentalist writer Sayyid Qutb borrowed creatively from a fourteenth-century theologian, Ibn Taymiyya, to create a theory of revolt consistent with mainstream Sunni thought. The men who assassinated Sadat subscribed to a theory of tyrannicide elucidated in an influential tract titled *The Absent Precept*, which also revived a number of Ibn Taymiyya's ideas. Both Qutb and the author of this tract were executed, as were those who shared their views.[17]

There is no indication that Sadat's assassins were imitating in any way Shi'a notions of revolution. Sunni fundamentalists came to similar conclusions but through a different path, railing against the eclipse of the *Shari'a*. They hold that a Muslim becomes an infidel when he fails to keep or apply the *Shari'a*. The only recourse for true believers at a time of barbarism is to create small cells of the faithful, who must act quickly in whatever way they can. For some, that includes violence; for almost all, it means ill-treatment in Egyptian, Syrian, or Algerian prisons, where torturers instill in the survivors an even greater determination to continue the struggle.

Another aspect of Islamic fundamentalism is its transnationalism. Most fundamentalists subscribe neither to Pan-Arabism nor to nationalist movements. Their vision is theologically and geographically transcendent. This makes them a particular threat to the military powers that control many states with large Islamic populations. From his prison cell,

Sayyid Qutb laid down this challenge to those who took seriously the duty of the Muslim as a citizen of a state:

> The homeland a Muslim should cherish and defend is not a mere piece of land; the collective identity he is known by is not that of a regime . . . Neither is the banner he should glory in and die for that of a nation . . . His jihad is solely geared to protect the religion of Allah and His Shari‘a and to save the Abode of Islam and no other territory . . . Any land that combats the Faith, hampers Muslims from practicing their religion, or does not apply the Shari‘a, becomes ipso facto part of the Abode of War. It should be combated even if one's own kith and kin, national group, capital and commerce are to be found there . . . A Muslim's homeland is any land governed by the laws of Islam. Islam is the only identity worthy of man . . . Any other group identity . . . is a jahili [barbaric] identity of the type humanity has known during its period of spiritual decadence.[18]

It is not surprising that Qutb's ideas brought him to the gallows, but there are many links between activists like him and fundamentalists elsewhere in the Islamic world. With mass media that know no frontiers, with the experience of an armed conflict in Afghanistan that attracted Muslims from all over the Arab world, and with the existence of sympathetic regimes such as those of Iran and Sudan, one cannot say that fundamentalism is limited to a few isolated localities.

With these political developments in mind, it should be apparent why demographic issues are of such significance in the conflict between Westernizing regimes in the Muslim world and their fundamentalist opponents. Since fundamentalism focuses on the family as the pivotal social unit through which Islamic values are lived and carried on, anything perceived as subverting family life, as it operates within patriarchal authority structures, is anathema.

Gender equality is a case in point. Any move toward improving the legal and social status of women is likely to incur the wrath of fundamentalists for many reasons. It would take authority away from the

Shariʻa. It mattered little that acts such as the Egyptian Personal Status Law of 1979 were mild; this law enabled women to initiate divorce if their husbands took a second wife against their wishes; it allowed for divorce hearings before a judge and gave women greater rights with respect to alimony, custody, and domicile. For fundamentalists, women's work is legitimate but not if it occurs at the expense of child care, and the choice of profession ought to be consistent with women's maternal instincts. Above all, the imagined vulnerability of women to the suggestiveness of the mass media needs to be countered by true Islamic teaching. For this reason, audiocassettes are sold all over Europe and the Middle East with sermons on Islam for women to listen to while they do housework.

On the subjects of family planning and contraception, the fundamentalist message has been mixed and ambivalent. The state authorities' acceptance of family planning made it suspect to fundamentalists; the location of this measure within a strategy of economic growth with an inevitably Western goal made it the devil's work.

Yet, in postrevolutionary Iran, a contrasting perspective emerged. *Raison d'état* now strengthened the case for family planning. The Tehran journal *Ettelaat* published a series of articles in October 1991 describing the deleterious social effects of rapid population growth in Iran. The demographic and economic distance between Iran and other, more developed countries, the authors noted, pointed to a "catastrophe lurking ahead if no immediate and drastic measures are taken." Then, in 1992, the survival of the Islamic regime itself was posited on reducing the birthrate, in an article titled "Reversing Population Growth Rate," in the Tehran journal *Keyhan* on 8 December:

> The vital importance of population control is now recognized by the Islamic Republic of Iran from the highest officials to the rank and file . . . The government should continue its campaign until the average Iranian in cities and in rural areas understands that a large family will not but bring despair, misery, indignity, a lower standard of living, and deprivation.
>
> The Islamic Republic should face the population explosion in Iran as the moral equivalent of war. Let's face it, population

growth such as we have in Iran, if not more destructive to the country than war, would certainly not be any less so. The difference is that the destructive impact of a war is more immediate and observable . . . Unless the government regards population growth as one of the important, if not the most important, tasks facing it requiring emergency mobilization of its means, the problem will continue to get worse . . . There is no doubt that the population growth rate as it is in Iran should stop, and stop now, or else its consequences will overwhelm everyone, man or woman, young or old, and rich or poor.[19]

There is a deep irony in this volte-face (which parallels a similar reversal of policy in China in the 1980s). What was once anathema on ideological grounds becomes defensible when the needs of the revolution coincide with the needs of the state to feed its citizens. The success of fundamentalism in stopping the fertility decline or actually raising fertility levels made the job of feeding a growing population both urgent and increasingly difficult.

Egyptian data indicate how fundamentalism and fertility may be positively correlated. Despite faulty data, it is clear that the Egyptian birthrate was in substantial decline from the 1952 revolution to the early 1970s: from 45.2 births per 1,000 in 1952 to 35.1 births per 1,000 in 1970. But then—at roughly the moment when Islamic fundamentalism began to spread, especially in Upper Egypt—the reported Egyptian birthrate rose, reaching 38 in 1978 and staying around that level ever since. It is possible that improved registration has inflated the birthrate figures in recent years, but this is not sufficient to undermine the weight of evidence that the decline in the Egyptian birthrate has stalled.

Given that the death rate declined continuously and sharply in the 1970s and 1980s, this stabilization or rise in fertility was bound to push the rate of natural increase upward in Egypt. In 1952, it was 2.74 percent a year; in 1978, it rose to 2.80 percent, and in 1991 to 2.90 percent. Sudan registered the same rate as Egypt in 1991. In Iran, the rate of natural increase is 3.3 percent.[20]

Of course, there are many other reasons for fertility decline leveling off in countries with large Islamic populations, but it may not be too rash to conclude that since 1970 the Islamic revival has impeded efforts to reduce fertility and may even have produced an upsurge in births. It is this harsh reality that the Iranian regime has recognized, albeit belatedly; whether it can reverse a trend that its own teaching set in motion is yet to be seen.

There is some evidence in Algeria and elsewhere that travel between North Africa and Europe has spread the notion that contraception is one way to achieve a higher standard of living. When part of a Muslim family lives fairly well in Paris with a few children, relatives with many children seem to find their model of prosperity attractive. All may be devout Muslims, but the lower fertility of European Muslims provides a model for family formation among non-European Muslims: migration produces an imitation effect, which may help to account for fertility declines among some non-European Muslims.[21]

Adding to the volatility of the situation in the Middle East and elsewhere is the complicated overlap between the ways that fundamentalism and migration respond to the rapid economic changes of modernization on the Western model.

The shift of labor from rural villages to towns and from towns to cities has made for vast numbers of migrants within developing countries. As we have noted, many arrive in suburban or urban areas disoriented and unfamiliar with ways to find shelter and employment. Given the chaotic bureaucratic structure of states like Egypt, it is usually futile to expect help from local or state officials. Fundamentalist groups like the Muslim Brotherhood fill this vacuum left by indifference, corruption, and inefficiency, especially in times of extreme need, such as during the 1992 earthquake in Cairo. The Egyptian state was nowhere to be seen in the early stages of helping the survivors and coping with the aftermath of the disaster. Islamic fundamentalist organizations, in contrast, were out on the streets, where their credentials as defenders of the poor and disinherited were both valid and attractive to urban immigrants.

The chaos of economic development also turns newcomers to fundamentalism in other ways. Many highly educated men and women in engineering or the sciences have wound up with virtually no hope of finding jobs. Their expectations of the benefits and fulfillments of their professions have been raised and then lowered, and they are deeply frustrated by the inability of the economy to provide them with useful careers. It is not surprising, therefore, that many recruits to fundamentalist groups are what, in another context, are called "reactionary modernists"—people familiar with science and technology who want to use them to facilitate a return to the true faith.[22]

The volatility of economic life in developing societies impels many people to look for jobs in other countries. But, as we have seen, foreign aid and trade will not immediately lessen this emigration of men and women; on the contrary, at certain stages of economic development internal economic growth stimulates migratory movements of many kinds. And the destination of such migrants depends on labor policies and growth trajectories in other states. Where migrants go is also a function of existing networks of ethnic minorities elsewhere. Two examples may suffice to show the complexity of this process and its ramifications for wider political conflicts.

Consider the case of Kuwait. Its independent existence was an imperial afterthought, in line with decisions about borders in the Middle East that were either arbitrary or expressed subtle and unsubtle strategies of divide and rule. It has a small native population—perhaps one-third of the 1.4 million residents in 1991 were born there—with a high level of education, high per capita income, and high fertility. In 1991, Kuwait's total fertility rate was 4.7 children per woman, and with a relatively low infant-mortality rate (16 per 1,000 births), it had a high level of natural increase: 3 percent per year.[23] Oil wealth and its favorable trading position have given immigrant labor many opportunities in Kuwait, where high wages and adequate social services have drawn in many workers, particularly Palestinians, some 250,000 of whom were resident in Kuwait in 1990. Given the proximity to both Iran and Saudi Arabia, wider Islamic currents were bound to affect Islam in Kuwait; and given the proximity to Iraq, which contested the location of its border with Kuwait (or even its existence), it was only a matter of time until this powder keg blew up.

The first pressures came from Shi'a fundamentalists, whose violence was countered by tough action on the part of Kuwaiti security forces. The second pressures were of another order entirely, resulting in Iraq's brief invasion in 1991 and the subsequent expulsion of the Iraqi army and many of its alleged sympathizers, especially Palestinians, after the war. If there is a classic case of how fertility, migration, national identity, and religious and ethnic quarrels intersect, it is in Kuwait.

The second case is Algeria. With a population of twenty-six million in 1991, Algeria's fertility is even higher than Kuwait's. The total fertility rate in Algeria in 1991 was 5.4 children per woman, but a high infant-mortality rate, and consequently a high death rate, keep Algeria's rate of natural increase to a still considerable 2.7 percent a year.

Here, too, rapid economic growth has been destabilizing. At first, it raised expectations, but then economic stagnation frustrated them. Highly educated Algerians have seen the decline in the price of oil wipe out their hopes for a comfortable and fulfilling professional life. Fundamentalist Islam offered an answer for these alienated people, and they organized a popular political movement which in 1992 seemed on the verge of a decisive electoral victory. A massive crackdown on the part of the security forces put an end to this challenge for power, at least for the moment.

Europeans still feel the shock waves of the conflict, some directly. In 1996, a series of bombings on the rapid-transit system in Paris was apparently the work of Algerian militants opposed to what they believed was French collusion with the Algerian government in suppressing Islamic fundamentalism. The fundamentalist aim to establish an Islamic state in Algeria may succeed. If it does, the implications for western Europe are far-reaching. Algeria was a French *département* until 1964; after independence, one million residents of Algeria fled to France and settled there. Would an Islamic revolution in Algeria produce another tidal wave of immigrants? No one can know; credible predictions in this field are impossible. Fewer migrants fled Iran after the revolution of 1979 than anticipated, but the analogy is somewhat forced, since Iran was not tied culturally or linked directly with any Western country.

Similarly, fundamentalist currents run deep in Morocco. Should they surface after a change in the monarchy, the temptation to move across the narrow strip of water to Spain would be hard for many to resist. And from there, all Europe beckons. Once more, this is not an immediate threat but a real contingency.

Images and perceptions matter as much as documented trends. The fear of a wave of Islamic immigrants coming to Europe and taking jobs at a time of mass unemployment is bad enough. When it is coupled with a fear of fundamentalism, understood as fire-breathing ayatollahs and mullahs sending suicide bombers to their deaths, the atmosphere in European cities with large Muslim populations can hardly be tranquil.

The torching of the home of Turkish immigrants in Germany, or the desecration of Muslim and Jewish cemeteries in France, shows that there are those in Europe ready to target all "foreigners" as the enemy. When more combustible material is added in the form of fundamentalist Islam, the likelihood of further trouble in Europe becomes a certainty. And each outbreak of European nativism provides fundamentalists with new Muslim recruits in Europe. So the spiral of fanaticism and hatred grows.

Accusations about Islamic fundamentalism entered the bloody civil war in Yugoslavia, too. Serb propagandists have distributed an English version of a document, *The Islamic Declaration: A Programme for the Islamization of Muslims and the Muslim People*, written in the 1970s by the current President of Bosnia, Alija Izetbegovic, who was imprisoned for his political views. Its discussion of women's rights gives some notion of its point of view:

No one has the right to refer to Islam as a reason to keep women disenfranchised; abuses of this kind must be brought to an end. Such attitudes do not represent a Western feminism, which has displayed a tendency to impose the measures, whims and mastery of a depraved element among the female sex. Neither is this equality in the European sense. It is an underlining of the equal values of men and women, together with the underlining of the differences between them, which should be preserved . . .

In these times, when the family is in serious crisis and the values are being questioned, Islam reaffirms its allegiance to this form of human life. By contributing to the security of the family nest and excluding external and internal factors which destroy it (alcohol, immorality, irresponsibility), Islam protects in a practical way the real interests of the normal, healthy woman.

Instead of an abstract equality, it ensures women love, marriage and children, with all that these three things mean to a woman.

To Izetbegovic, Islamic ideas must first be realized through education, then through taking power. The coup d'état is not the right way: "We must therefore be first preachers and then soldiers." But power is the destination:

> The Islamic movement should and can start to take over power as soon as it is morally and numerically strong enough to be able to overturn not only the existing non-Islamic government, but also to build up a new Islamic one.[24]

Some scholars vigorously contest the view that Izetbegovic is a fundamentalist. "None of his actions have given credence to this charge," notes Ivo Banac. Despite such rebuttals, repeated accusations tend to turn into political "facts" in the Balkans as elsewhere.

Islamic fundamentalism has reached North America, too. Sheikh Omar Abdel-Rahman, a blind Sunni cleric from Egypt who resided in the United States, is the theological leader and inspiration of an Egyptian fundamentalist group, the Gama'a el-Islamiya, or Islamic Group. This group is waging a shadowy guerrilla war against the Egyptian government. Followers of Sheikh Omar assassinated Sadat; others have been tortured and killed by the authorities in Egyptian prisons. How Sheikh Omar got to America is a matter of some dispute.[25] Either through an error by consular and immigration authorities or through discreet representations of the Central Intelligence Agency, with whom he and his allies had worked in Afghanistan, Sheikh Omar managed to get a visitor's visa in Khartoum, though his position in Egyptian politics had put him on the "watch list" of undesirable potential visitors.

Following years of massive American financial and political support for both Israel and Egypt, some of those who attended Sheikh Omar's mosque in Jersey City, New Jersey, apparently decided to teach the United States a lesson. In 1992, they bombed the World Trade Center in Manhattan, killing six people and injuring hundreds. This was the nightmare of Middle Eastern terrorism in the midst of Manhattan. In 1990, another follower of Sheikh Omar had assassinated the extremist Israeli leader Rabbi Meir Kahane in New York. The conviction of Sheikh Omar and some of his followers of conspiring to cause explosions has not ended the story.

Where this matter will ultimately rest is unclear. We have raised it simply to illustrate how events in the Middle East have a ripple effect in Europe and North America. Migration, fertility, national identity, and fundamentalism are so tied together that understanding each component is essential for an informed discussion of their repercussions in population politics.

CONCLUSION

In the introduction, we advanced several claims that the three decades from the mid-1960s to the mid-1990s constitute a coherent period in both demographic and political history. Beginning in the 1960s a profound shift in fertility patterns took place throughout the developed world. The baby boom was over; a new period of declining and unprecedentedly low fertility had begun, and at the same time, mortality levels were continuing to fall to historically low levels. Meanwhile, international migration as a dynamic force in population movements grew rapidly. In 1960, natural increase and migration each accounted for about half of the total population increase in the Federal Republic of Germany, for example, while in 1990 migration accounted for virtually all of it. Between 1960 and 1990, Italy shifted from being a country of emigration and relatively high fertility to being a country of substantial immigration and very low fertility. On the other side of the Atlantic, the same changes could be observed. In the United States in 1960, only one-eighth of the population increase was due to immigration; in 1990, one-third of it. Canada registered a similar trend: from less than one-tenth of the population increase in 1960, immigration accounted for almost half in 1990.

The reasons for this profound shift in the balance of demographic factors in overall population growth are clear. There was a massive and ubiquitous decline in domestic fertility and a large (though uneven) increase in immigration throughout the developed world. This new fertility-migration nexus characterizes what could be called the "migration generation" and has been the central subject of this book. We have tried to show that the balance of demographic forces had distinctive features in different countries, reflecting past developments and traditions, but that the underlying influences were roughly similar.

We have also argued that this demographic shift was particularly troublesome because it coincided with momentous changes in the nature of the international political system. During the same period, the Cold War waned and ultimately ended. From the ugly confrontation of the

Cuban Missile Crisis in 1962 through the disastrous wars in Vietnam and Afghanistan, an equation of power based on the nuclear weapons controlled by the United States and the Soviet Union had dominated the international order. By 1990, that conflict had effectively ended. And when the Soviet system collapsed, powerful centrifugal forces were released, as civil wars spread from Azerbaijan to Bosnia. At the same time, centripetal forces in western Europe created their own problems. In both western and central Europe, moves toward international integration have also reawakened nativist and nationalist currents. And the question of what constitutes a nation in this federative age naturally focuses on border controls and immigration. These issues were already sensitive in the 1960s, but, as we have shown, they have become explosive. Ugly scenes of anti-immigrant violence recall past chapters in the all-too-voluminous history of European racism and xenophobia.

Anti-immigrant sentiment in the United States is nothing new either, but the form it has taken over the last thirty years shows the new prominence of immigration in overall demographic growth. And in Canada, worries about immigrants have coincided with the centuries-old quarrel between French-speaking Québecois and their English-speaking neighbors, a quarrel exacerbated by immigration. Newcomers of whatever language group are much more likely to become English speakers than French speakers.

In other cases, it is not the language of immigrants but their religion that excites controversy and at times open opposition from native-born citizens. Once again, we hear echoes of the past in these confrontations. But since the 1960s, a new element has entered the equation of assimilation. Though Muslims have lived in Europe peaceably for centuries, and Islamic immigrants are scattered throughout the Continent as they are in North America, the character of their faith has become a public issue because of the new prominence of a very small number of fundamentalists within their community. The trajectory of fundamentalism can be traced to reactions in Iran, Egypt, Pakistan, and elsewhere to the mixed record of these states' efforts at industrialization and urbanization in the 1950s and 1960s. Whatever its sources, the power of fundamentalist ideas to mobilize millions cannot be denied.

Muslim immigrants in Europe and North America now bear an additional burden: the fear that their attitudes are incompatible with integration into their host cultures and countries—and worse, that they have large families. The specter of a demographic tide of Muslims sweeping across Europe, all carrying the Koran and wearing the *chador*, is nonsense, but powerful nonsense nonetheless. Some in the press or in power cultivate such fears: after the Cold War, another evil empire is just the thing they are looking for. The problem remains, though, that some Muslims do not want to integrate into Western society. They want to live in the West among the infidels but not join them. Here, too, precedents abound. Hasidic Jews are in the same position; so are Mennonites and other Protestant sects. However, these latter groups are numerically insignificant and have little to do with international political conflicts. Fundamentalist Islam is both demographically substantial and very political.

It is unrealistic to assume that debates in Europe and North America about immigrants from North Africa, the Middle East, Iran, or Pakistan can be conducted without reference to this fundamentalist phenomenon, another instance of the overlap of demographic and political issues that characterizes the period under discussion.

How can demographic knowledge help us to navigate these new and troubled waters? Here we confront another set of problems related to the nature of demographic science itself.

In discussions of population issues, rhetoric has always expanded more rapidly than scientific knowledge. This is because not only does good science take time, but its tools develop unevenly. The scientific study of migration has not kept pace with parallel advances in other parts of the discipline of demography.

By the 1960s, demographers had developed powerful tools for analyzing and projecting population trends. These were constructed on a sophisticated understanding of two of the three major forces of demographic change—mortality and fertility. During the eighteenth and nineteenth centuries, with the important insight that death could be viewed

244

as a statistical phenomenon of aggregates rather than as only an individual calamity, analysis of "bills of mortality" and ultimately the creation of life tables became possible. Such mortality studies formed the early core of the discipline, as well as the basis of a new and profitable business sector, life insurance. The 1930s were an equally creative period, this time for understanding fertility as an aggregate phenomenon. The realization (and, frequently, resulting alarm) that European and American fertility had declined substantially to below-replacement levels— itself a concept developed then—led demographers to explore the forces behind such dramatic changes. The first academic centers of demographic research were established in Princeton and London in 1936, in Paris in 1946. There was a great intellectual flowering in demographic analysis that produced much of the mathematics underlying formal demography as well as historical generalizations of the so-called theory of the demographic transition, aimed at accounting for fertility decline without using the biological explanations popular among eugenicists (declining vitality of the species, etc.).

Meanwhile, in Germany and Italy some academics with demographic expertise were participating in tendentious analyses emphasizing differential fertility between the Aryan and "inferior" races.[1] These activities had long-term intellectual and political consequences for German demography, which became suspect after World War II and remains problematic in some circles even to the present—one reason German demographers are less active in their country's affairs than those in France or the United States.

Following World War II, Western schools of demography diverged. French demographers did innovative work in technical analysis, while some expressed their fears about the dangers of low fertility. British demography in the 1950s and 1960s remained concentrated in London, while a strong school of historical demography developed at Cambridge. American demography led in the study of high-fertility countries in the developing world and (along with American higher education in general) expanded rapidly. Programs in population studies were developed at Princeton and Brown Universities and the Universities of Michigan, Chicago, Pennsylvania, California (Berkeley), and Wisconsin. A generation of demographic scholars from all over the world were trained at these European and American research centers.

During this time, the third primary demographic force—migration—attracted only limited attention. A few demographers studied the large international migrations earlier in the century; others focused on internal migration, especially rural-to-urban. Yet international migration was never addressed intensively and systematically, as first mortality and then fertility had been.

By the 1960s, demography as a science had reached the height of its analytic power, and demographers had become influential in framing public policies to deal with the high fertility registered in much of the developing world. In their analyses and policy prescriptions, a sophisticated understanding of trends and patterns in mortality and fertility gave them real insights. Demographers were prominent at the 1974 World Population Conference in Bucharest, but their influence waned as the issues became politicized; by the time of the 1984 conference in Mexico City, their role was much diminished. At the 1994 conference in Cairo, demography was central but not demographers; instead, pride of place was held by activists concerned about women's rights.

There were many reasons, some of them purely political, for this waning of professional demographers in policy discourse, but one explanation is related to migration, a subject on which they could not speak with the same authority and precision as they did on mortality and fertility.

By the 1980s, mortality in industrial countries had declined to very low levels, and fertility, too, was falling sharply (often to below-replacement level); meanwhile, the magnitude of international migrations to these same countries increased. Thus, as this third force of demographic change rose to prominence at a time of declining rates of natural increase, the question arose as to what demographers could say that would help policy makers and the public come to informed conclusions about this volatile issue.

Few of the well-established centers of demographic research were active in this area. In part, this was due to the intractable and unreliable nature of statistical evidence on immigration. In part, it showed the lack of adequate governmental funds for research; immigration fell outside the interest of most funding agencies. In part, it arose from an understandable tendency among some scholars to avoid emotional political controversies.

The weakness of insight into the underlying forces and likely futures of international migration has seriously limited demographic knowledge. Long-held demographic premises proved vulnerable, because the intersection of fertility and migration was insufficiently understood. One such error was the presumption that U.S. fertility rates would continue to move downward as women's educational levels rose and more women joined the paid labor force. To the contrary, American fertility increased around 1990, driven in part by higher fertility rates among recent immigrants. Demographically based projections of declining enrollments in big-city schools proved disastrously wrongheaded, as influxes of immigrant children swelled enrollments in New York and Los Angeles. Similar projections in Europe were confounded by the appearance of asylum seekers and refugees from the Balkans and elsewhere. In sum, demographers' capacity to speculate sensibly about demographic futures has deteriorated as the demographic wild card, international migration, has been played.

One implication of the political-demographic issues discussed in this book is that confusion and inaccuracy are bound to persist unless international agencies and national governments commit to building up the scientific study of an issue so vital to our future. To prevent rhetoric from overwhelming reason, objective and dispassionate research on migration must develop rapidly. It is alarming that the power of demographic paradigms to guide our understanding of population change has decreased in direct proportion to the increasing prominence of migration as a demographic force. Remedying that situation is in the interests of policy makers, demographers, and the public.

Until we have a better understanding of the forces underlying migratory movements and their consequences, we must make do with what we have. Is there any way to project some of the findings we have sketched in this book into the not-too-distant future?

First, we must make distinction between projections and predictions. A *projection* is simply the playing out of assumptions about future fertility, mortality, and migration, and there is an almost infinite array of such assumptions. To put the matter starkly, all projections (assuming accurate calculation) are "correct" in the sense that the output is always determined by the input assumptions, which may be plausible or wildly implausible; the resulting projection itself is "correct" even if the assumptions are bizarre. A *prediction* is a statement about what the future is likely to be, for example, a statement that the population is likely to grow to X million by year Y. Such predictions can, of course, be supported by projections. In other words, a demographic prediction is a projection which asserts that certain assumptions about the future are highly plausible.

Typically, those who make demographic projections offer several alternative calculations based on a range of assumptions about future fertility, mortality, and migration. For example, the U.S. Census Bureau's latest demographic projection report includes ten alternates. But users of projections usually prefer a single set of numbers to plug into their econometric models or political forecasts. Hence, they often use the medium or average projection, the middle of the range between extreme assumptions.

Given this cautionary note, can anything sensible be said about likely future trends in fertility levels and international migration in the nations we have discussed? The short answer is that future fertility levels are unpredictable and international migration even more so. The likelihood that demographic projections provide accurate forecasts of the long-term future—never strong—is sharply reduced by our inability to make plausible assumptions.

Still, some useful negative predictions can be made. Few demographers expect a repeat of the post–World War II baby boom, though it is sobering to note that no demographers in the 1940s anticipated it. At present, the fertility of almost every industrial country is at or below the replacement level of 2.1 children per woman, and in some countries (e.g., Germany, Italy, Spain, Russia, Hong Kong) it is far below that level. The most plausible future level of fertility in industrial countries is moderately below replacement, that is, lower than the current levels in the

United States and Sweden but well above those in Germany and Italy. However, no one should be astonished to see fertility rise; there is nothing magical about the 2.1 figure. The extraordinarily low recent levels in Italy and Spain seem unlikely to persist. Overall, then, a fertility range from nearly 50 percent below replacement (as in Germany) to just above replacement seems plausible.

While we can predict that international migration will increase, we cannot guess the actual magnitude of it. Enormous and rising differences in prosperity among nations in a world that is increasingly connected by modern communications and transportation suggest that the *potential* levels of international migration, already very high, are likely to rise; the *actual* flow of international migration is only a small fraction of this potential, mostly because of national controls over the entry of foreigners. There can be no doubt that, were this a world truly without borders, levels of international migration would rise far higher than they are today. A decision to increase or decrease admission of legal immigrants or refugees, to strengthen or weaken controls over illegal immigration, or to loosen or tighten criteria for granting political asylum can dramatically affect numbers. This in turn implies that predictions about future international migration can be only as good as predictions about political developments and decisions in a given country.

The available evidence contradicts the confident predictions of some free-trade proponents that international migration will decrease with the recent trade liberalization (such as the North American Free Trade Agreement) or other strategies designed to accelerate economic development. To the contrary, the evidence suggests that accelerated economic development may *increase* emigration over the next two to three decades, before the predicted migration-moderating influence of increased domestic prosperity is felt.[2] All projections of demographic increase among population groups with substantial foreign-born components (e.g., Hispanics and Asians in the United States, Muslims in France) depend heavily on assumptions about the nature and effectiveness of policies on immigration. Given the political volatility of the issue, long-term projections about the future ethnic or linguistic composition of national populations are conjectural at best. Commentators need to exercise more than the usual reserve (even humility) in this difficult, politically explosive area of speculation.

What are the options open to politicians and administrators? Here, too, caution is in order. Demographic behavior is both social and biological, and frequently very slow to change in response to governmental policies. There are exceptions—such as the soaring fertility of Ceausescu's Romania in the mid-1960s—but the general rule is that demographic outcomes of population policies are rarely predictable.

This is the case in each geographic region discussed in this book, where demographic change has been remarkably stubborn or unresponsive to legislation. This is especially true of fertility. Some developing countries have succeeded in lowering birthrates, with family-planning and educational programs contributing to an environment conducive to fertility reduction. But governments trying to increase the birthrate have had a much harder time, whatever their ideological character, since they have rarely had the resources or power to reverse declining marital fertility. To be sure, coercive measures can work, though it is some comfort to know that most politicians shun them. As we have noted, it took a dictator to double Romania's birthrate, and even Ceausescu had to desist from his pro-natalist project, whereupon the Romanian birthrate returned to a very low level. And once punitive measures to outlaw or control contraception or abortion are ruled out, the instruments available to governments that want to raise fertility seem ineffectual. Hitler, Stalin, and Mussolini wanted to increase birthrates. So did de Gaulle. Their efforts produced minimal results at best. Modest-to-generous family allowances of the kind introduced in France just before World War II were continued in the Fourth and Fifth Republics, but these measures failed to produce a major change in fertility levels. Massive increases in family-allowance payments might do the job, but virtually no political party in France (or elsewhere in Europe or North America) is prepared to enact the tax increases needed to pay for them.

Fertility behavior is normative, a product of subtle and enduring material and cultural forces. How a couple wants to spend their lives is not simply a function of direct expenditures or indirect opportunity costs. Childbearing in industrialized countries is not a rational economic enterprise; hence, the fiscal or budgetary measures a state introduces are unlikely to reach deeply enough within society to effect a change in the values that surround family life. This is the primary reason why most programs aimed at increasing the birthrate have failed.

With immigration, states can act with more authority and force. National sovereignty includes the power to bar immigrants, even when that power is not exercised. Well before World War II, the American government drastically affected European migratory movements by progressively closing its doors to newcomers in 1921 and 1924. After 1945, the German-speaking populations of Poland, Czechoslovakia, and other parts of Europe that had been occupied by the Nazis had no choice but to move west. The German government still operates under a definition of German nationality that is racial-ethnic in character; meanwhile, French nationality is defined not by bloodlines but by residence. These political decisions, codified in law, profoundly affect the choices made by people who want to live in these countries.

As we have noted throughout this study, the intersection of low fertility levels and volatile international migratory flows is the new and powerful feature in demographic trends. It is not at all surprising, therefore, that state action is most visible and controversial on migration issues. And given the relative paucity of demographic tools to measure and predict migratory movements, it is less demographic thinking than political and ideological commitments that govern state action here. It is no longer possible to separate population policies from much wider considerations of national identity and international affairs.

By far the most important of these considerations is the political significance of nationalism. Since the collapse of the Soviet empire, older nationalisms have re-emerged: a united Germany now encounters a fragmented former Soviet Union and a shattered Yugoslavia, and, farther west, the strengthened institutions of the European Community have been resisted by those unprepared to pass on to Brussels certain elements of national sovereignty that have been theirs for centuries. A common European currency generates nostalgia for the good old pound sterling or the French franc, and contempt for the unelected bureaucrats in Brussels reminds many Europeans that their capacity to vote their displeasure about national life may be slipping away.

In North America, the very concept of a united Canada is under siege by Québecois separatists, and American nationalists have trouble with the increasing number of residents whose first language is Spanish. To some, immigrants are a threatening rather than invigorating force in national life, a drain on national resources or even a fifth column within the nation. Everywhere in the developed world, national forms and customs are in the crucible.

These instabilities have had a direct bearing on how the issues of fertility and international immigration are perceived and evaluated, both by demographers and by the public. The politicians who seek partisan advantage from these crucial matters are playing with fire. Others are responsibly and cautiously seeking to understand these powerful forces and the profound implications for the future of their nations. If they and we can distinguish between what is description and what is belief, and accept that both elements are unavoidable in these discussions, the public may become better informed about issues of fundamental importance to their lives and those of their children. Only then may it be possible to defuse at least some of the explosive material embedded in population debates today.

BIBLIOGRAPHY

I. ARTICLES

Acheson, Donald. "Health, Humanitarian Relief, and Survival in Former Yugoslavia." *British Medical Journal* 307 (3 July 1993), p. 44.

Banac, Ivo. "Bosnian Muslims: From Religious Community to Socialist Nationhood and Post-Communist Statehood, 1918–1992." In Mark Pinson, ed., *The Muslims of Bosnia-Herzegovina*. Cambridge, Mass.: Harvard University Press, 1994, pp. 129–53.

———. "The Fearful Asymmetry of War: The Causes and Consequences of Yugoslavia's Demise." *Daedalus* (Spring 1992).

Bell-Fialkoff, Andrew. "A Brief History of Ethnic Cleansing." *Foreign Affairs* (June 1993).

Boban, Ljubo. "Jasenovac and the Manipulation of History." *East European Politics and Societies* 4, no. 3 (1990), pp. 580–92.

Bodansky, Yossef. "Islamist Leaders 'Legalize' War on Infidels and Accommodating Muslims." *Defence and Foreign Affairs* (July–August 1995).

Calot, Gérard. "Fécondité du moment, fécondité des générations: Comparaisons franco-suédoises." *Population & Sociétés*, no. 245 (April 1990).

Connelly, Matthew, and Paul Kennedy. "Must It Be the Rest Against the West?" *Atlantic Monthly*, December 1994, pp. 61–84.

Crane-Engel, Melinda. "Germany vs. Genocide." *The New York Times Magazine*, 30 October 1994, pp. 56–59.

David, Henry P., and Nicholas H. Wright. "Abortion Legislation: The Romanian Experience." *Studies in Family Planning* 2 (1971), pp. 205–10.

Eckart, O. "Effets et limites des aides financières aux familles: Une expérience et un modèle." *Population* 2 (1986).

Field, Mark G. "The Re-legalization of Abortion in Soviet Russia." *New England Journal of Medicine* 255, no. 9 (1956), pp. 421–27.

Gedmin, Jeffrey. "Comrade Slobo." *American Spectator*, April 1993.

Gottlieb, Gidon. "Nations without States." *Foreign Affairs*, May–June 1994.

Hamilton, Ian. "Salman Rushdie's First Life." *The New Yorker*, 26 December 1995.

Henry, Louis. "Some Data on Natural Fertility." *Eugenics Quarterly* 8, no. 2 (1961), pp. 81–91.

Hollander, Samuel. "Marx and Malthusianism." *American Economic Review* 74 (1984), pp. 139–51.

Illsley, Raymond. "Occupation Class, Selection, and the Production of Inequalities in Health." *Quarterly Journal of Social Affairs* 2 (1986), pp. 151–65.

254

Keyfitz, Nathan. "The Limits of Population Forecasting." *Population and Development Review* 7 (December 1981), pp. 579–93.

Laber, Jeri. "Bosnia: Questions about Rape." *The New York Review of Books*, 25 March 1993, pp. 3–6.

Lapidus, Gail. "Ethnonationalism and Political Stability: The Soviet Case." *World Politics* (July 1984).

———. "Gorbachev and the National Question." *Soviet Economy* (1989).

McIntyre, R. J. "On Demographic Policy Debates in the USSR." *Population and Development Review* 8 (June 1982).

Marmot, M. G. "Social Differentials in Health within and between Populations." *Daedalus* 123, no. 4 (1994), pp. 197–223.

Meron, Theodor. "The Case for War Crimes Trials in Yugoslavia." *Foreign Affairs* (1993).

Moeller, Robert G. "Women and the State in the *Wirtschaftswünder*: Protecting Mothers and the Family in Post–World War II West Germany." *Feminist Review* (1990).

Morrison, Peter A. "Demographic Perspectives on the Voting Rights Act." Working paper P-7905, revised text of briefing co-hosted by the U.S. House of Representatives, Subcommittee on Census, Statistics, and Postal Personnel and the Population Resource Center, Washington, D.C., 19 October 1994.

Penalosa, Fernando. "Toward an Operational Definition of the Mexican American." *Atzlan* 1 (1970), pp. 1–11.

Rabia, Ali, and Lawrence Lifschultz. "Why Bosnia?" *Monthly Review* 45, no. 10 (1994).

Reimers, David M. "An Unintended Reform: The 1965 Immigration Act and Third World Immigration to the United States." *Journal of American Ethnic History* 2 (Fall 1983), pp. 9–26.

Ronge, V. "Öst-West-Wanderung nach Deutschland." *Aus Politik und Zeitgeschichte: Beilage zur Wochenzeitung Das Parlament* 7 (12 February 1993).

Rupnik, Jacques. "Europe's New Frontiers: Remapping Europe." *Daedalus* 123, no. 3 (1994), pp. 91–123.

Russell, Sharon Stanton. "Migrant Remittances and Development." *International Migration Review* 30, nos. 3–4 (1992).

———. "Politics and Ideology in Migration Policy Formulation: The Case of Kuwait." *International Migration Review* 23, no. 1 (1988), pp. 24–47.

Seccombe, Wally. "Marxism and Demography." *New Left Review*, no. 137 (1983), pp. 22–47.

Simon, Rita J. "Immigration and American Attitudes." *Public Opinion* (July–August 1987).

Szporluk, R. "Dilemmas of Russian Nationalism." *Problems of Communism* (July–August 1989).

Teitelbaum, Michael S. "Advocacy, Ambivalence, Ambiguity: Immigration Policies and Prospects in the United States." *Proceedings of the American Philosophical Society* 136 (June 1992).

_____. "The De-legalization of Abortion in Romania." *Family Planning* (July 1974), pp. 38–41.

_____. "Fertility Effects of the Abolition of Legal Abortion in Romania." *Population Studies* 26 (November 1972), pp. 405–16.

_____. "Right versus Right: Immigration and Refugee Policy in the United States." *Foreign Affairs* 59, no. 1 (Fall 1980), p. 21.

_____. "Demographic Change Through the Lenses of Science and Politics." *Proceedings of the American Philosophical Society* 132 (1988), pp. 173–84.

_____. "The Population Threat." *Foreign Affairs* (Fall–Winter 1992).

_____. "Political Asylum in Theory and Practice." *The Public Interest* 76 (1984), pp. 74–86.

Trebici, Vladimir. "Romania's Ethnic Demography." *Romanian Journal of Sociology* 2, nos. 1–2 (1991), pp. 73–81.

Veltman, Calvin. "Impact of International Immigration on the Linguistic Balance in Montreal." *The Review of Demography and Its Implications for Economic and Social Policy,* Update Number Five (Winter 1988), pp. 50–51.

Weaver, Mary Anne. "The Trail of the Sheikh." *The New Yorker,* 12 April 1993, pp. 71–89.

Weber, C., and A. Goodman. "The Demographic Policy Debate in the USSR." *Population and Development Review* 7 (June 1981), pp. 279–95.

Wilkinson, Richard G. "Income Distribution and Life Expectancy." *British Medical Journal* 304 (1992), pp. 165–68.

II. BOOKS

Alexander, Stella. *The Triple Myth: A Life of Archbishop Alojzije Stepinac.* Boulder, Colo.: East European Monographs, 1987.

Ali, Rabia, and Lawrence Lifschultz, eds. *Why Bosnia? Writings on the Balkan War.* Stony Creek, Conn.: Pamphleteer's Press, [1993?].

Allcock, John B., et al., eds. *Yugoslavia in Transition: Choices and Constraints.* Oxford and New York: Oxford University Press, 1992.

Alonso, William, and Paul Starr, eds. *The Politics of Numbers.* New York: Russell Sage, 1987.

Anderson, Benedict. *Imagined Communities.* London and New York: Verso, 1984.

Andric, Ivo. *The Bridge on the Drina.* Trans. Lovett F. Edward. London: Allen & Unwin, 1978.

Banks, Joseph Ambrose, and Olive Banks. *Feminism and Family Planning in Victorian England.* New York: Schocken Books, 1972.

Beaujot, Roderic, ed. *Facing the Demographic Future.* Ottawa: The Royal Society of Canada, 1990.

256

Bissoondath, Neil. *Selling Illusions: The Cult of Multiculturalism in Canada*. Toronto: Penguin Books, 1994.

Böhning, W. R., P. V. Schaeffer, and T. Straubhaar. *Migration Pressure: What Is It? What Can One Do about It?* Geneva: ILO, 1991.

Bourke, Joanna. *Working Class Cultures in Britain*. London and New York: Routledge, 1994.

Briggs, Asa, and Julian H. Shelley, eds. *Science, Medicine, and the Community: The Last 100 Years*. 5th Boehringer Ingelheim Symposium. Amsterdam: Excerpta Medica, 1986.

Brown, Colin. *Black and White Britain: The Third PSI Survey*. London: Heinemann, 1984.

Brubaker, Rogers. *Citizenship and Nationhood in France and Germany*. Cambridge, Mass.: Harvard University Press, 1992.

Brumberg, Abraham, ed. *Chronicle of a Revolution: A Western-Soviet Inquiry into Perestroika*. New York: Pantheon Books, 1990.

Bruni, M., A. Venturini, and O. Stark. *Two Essays on Migration*. Geneva: ILO, 1991.

Canada. Immigration and Refugee Board. *Annual Report for the Year Ending December 31, 1994*. Ottawa, 1995.

———. Ministry of Citizenship and Immigration. *Backgrounder: A New Approach to Consultation for a New Vision of Immigration*. 2 February 1994.

———. Ministry of Immigration and Labor. *Demographic Aspects of Immigration*. Report of a meeting. Montreal, 14 December 1984.

———. Ministry of National Health and Welfare. *Review of Demography and Its Implications for Economic and Social Policy*. Ottawa, 29 April 1994.

Carrère d'Encausse, Hélène. *The End of the Soviet Empire: The Triumph of the Nations*. Trans. Franklin Philip. New York: Basic Books, 1992.

Cassen, Robert, et al. *Population and Development: Old Debates, New Conclusions*. New Brunswick, N.J.: Transaction Publishers, 1994.

Castles, Stephen, and Godula Kosack. *Immigrant Workers and Class Structure in Western Europe*. London: Oxford University Press, 1973.

Coale, Ansley, and Edgar M. Hoover. *Population Growth and Economic Development*. New York: Harper, 1958.

Cohen, Lenard J. *Broken Bonds: The Disintegration of Yugoslavia*. Boulder, Colo.: Westview Press, 1993.

Condorcet, Marquis de. *Esquisse d'un tableau historique des progrès de l'esprit humain* (1795). Trans. June Barraclough as *Sketch for a Historical Picture of the Progress of the Human Mind*. London: Weidenfeld and Nicolson, 1955.

Conquest, Robert, ed. *The Last Empire: Nationality and the Soviet Future*. Stanford, Calif.: Stanford University Press, 1986.

David, Henry P. *Family Planning and Abortion in the Socialist Countries of Central and Eastern Europe*. New York: The Population Council, 1970.

Dawidowicz, Lucy. *The War Against the Jews, 1933–1945*. New York: Holt, Rinehart and Winston, 1975.

Dawisha, Karen, and Bruce Parrott. *Russia and the New States of Eurasia: The Politics of Upheaval*. Cambridge: Cambridge University Press, 1994.

Day, Jennifer Cheeseman. *Population Projections of the United States, by Age, Sex, Race, and Hispanic Origin: 1993 to 2050*. U.S. Bureau of the Census, Current Population Reports, P25-1104. Washington, D.C.: U.S. Government Printing Office, 1993.

Dekmejian, R. Hrair. *Islam in Revolution*. Syracuse, N.Y.: Syracuse University Press, 1985.

Denber, Rachel, ed. *The Soviet Nationality Reader: The Disintegration in Context*. Boulder, Colo.: Westview Press, 1992.

Denitch, Bogdan. *Ethnic Nationalism: The Tragic Death of Yugoslavia*. Minneapolis: University of Minnesota Press, 1994.

Djilas, Aleksa. *The Contested Country: Yugoslav Unity and Communist Revolution, 1919–1953*. Cambridge, Mass.: Harvard University Press, 1991.

Donohue, William A. *The Politics of the American Civil Liberties Union*. New Brunswick, N.J., and Oxford: Transaction Books, 1986.

Duchène, François. *Jean Monnet: The First Statesman of Interdependence*. New York: Norton, 1994.

Easterman, Daniel. *Reflections on Islam: Fundamentalism and the Rushdie Affair*. London: Verso, 1993.

Ehrlich, Paul R. *The Population Bomb*. New York: Ballantine Books, 1968.

Eisenberg, Theodore. *Civil Rights Legislation: Cases and Materials*. Indianapolis: Michio Co., 1981.

Elkins, Stanley M., and Eric McKitrick. *The Age of Federalism*. New York: Oxford University Press, 1993.

el Sa'darwi, Nawal, et al. *Islamic Fundamentalism*. London: Institute for African Alternatives, 1989.

Enzensberger, Hans Magnus. *Civil Wars: From L.A. to Bosnia*. New York: The New Press, 1993.

Eurostat. *Statistics in Focus: Population and Social Conditions*. Luxembourg: Eurostat, 1996.

Feldman, David. *Englishmen and Jews*. New Haven, Conn.: Yale University Press, 1993.

Garza, Rodolfo de la, et al. *Latino Voices*. Boulder, Colo.: Westview Press, 1992.

Gay, Ruth. *The Jews of Germany*. New Haven, Conn.: Yale University Press, 1992.

Georgescu, Vlad. *The Romanians: A History*. Columbus: Ohio State University Press, 1991.

The Gerry-mander: A New Species of Monster, Which Appeared in Essex South District in Jan. 1812. Salem, Mass.: n.p., 1812.

258

Glazer, Nathan. *Affirmative Discrimination: Ethnic Inequality and Public Policy*. New York: Basic Books, 1975.

——, ed. *Clamor at the Gates: The New Migration*. San Francisco: ICS Press, 1985.

Glenny, Misha. *The Fall of Yugoslavia: The Third Balkan War*. Harmondsworth, U.K.: Penguin, 1992.

Gore, Al. *Earth in the Balance: Ecology and the Human Spirit*. Boston: Houghton Mifflin, 1992.

Graubard, Stephen, ed. *A New Europe?* Cambridge, Mass.: Houghton Mifflin, 1964.

Hajda, Lubomyr, and Mark Bussinger, eds. *The Nationalities Factor in Soviet Politics and Society*. Boulder, Colo.: Westview Press, 1990.

Heckscher, Eli. *Mercantilism*. Oxford: Oxford University Press, 1965.

Herf, Jeffrey. *Reactionary Modernism*. Cambridge: Cambridge University Press, 1989.

Hiro, Dilip. *Holy Wars: The Rise of Islamic Fundamentalism*. New York: Routledge, 1989.

Hobsbawm, E. J., and T. Ranger, eds. *The Invention of Tradition*. Cambridge: Cambridge University Press, 1980.

Howard, Sir Michael. *Clausewitz*. London: Fontana, 1980.

Huttenbach, Henry R. *Soviet Nationality Policies: Ruling Ethnic Groups in the USSR*. London: Mansell, 1990.

Inter-Governmental Consultations. "Asylum Applications in Participating States, 1983–1995." Geneva: Inter-Governmental Consultations, Mimeo, 21 March 1996.

Israeli, Raphael. *Fundamentalist Islam and Israel*. Lanham, Md.: University Press of America, 1993.

Izetbegovic, Alija. *The Islamic Declaration*. Belgrade: n.p., [1991?].

Jensen, Merrill, ed. *The Documentary History of the Ratification of the Constitution*. Madison: State Historical Society of Wisconsin, 1976.

Jones, Gareth Stedman. *Outcast London*. Harmondsworth, U.K.: Penguin, 1986.

Keely, Charles B. *U.S. Immigration: A Policy Analysis*. New York: The Population Council, 1979.

Keynes, Milo, David A. Coleman, and Nicholas H. Dimsdale, eds. *The Political Economy of Health and Welfare*. London: Macmillan, 1988.

King, Richard. *Civil Rights and the Idea of Freedom*. New York: Oxford University Press, 1992.

Kulischer, Eugene. *Europe on the Move: War and Population Changes, 1917–47*. New York: Columbia University Press, 1948.

Kundera, Milan. *Testaments Betrayed*. London: Faber and Faber, 1995.

Lapidus, Gail, Victor Zaslavsky, and Philip Goldman, eds. *From Union to Commonwealth: Nationalism and Separatism in the Soviet Republics*. Cambridge: Cambridge University Press, 1992.

Le Bras, Hervé. *L'Invention de la France*. Paris: Hachette, 1981.

———. *Marianne et les lapins: L'Obsession démographique*. Paris: Olivier Orban, 1991.

———. *Population*. Paris: Hachette, 1986.

———. *Les Trois Frances*. Paris: Odile Jacob, 1987.

Levesque, René. *An Option for Quebec*. Toronto: McClelland and Stewart, 1968.

Levine, David, Louise Tilly, and John Gillis, eds. *The Historical Experience of Fertility Decline*. London: Basil Blackwell, 1990.

Lewy, Guenter. *The Catholic Church and Nazi Germany*. London: Weidenfeld and Nicolson, 1964.

Linz, Susan, ed. *The Impact of World War II on the Soviet Union*. Totowa, N.J.: Rowman & Allenfeld, 1985.

Lynd, Staughton. *Class Conflict, Slavery, and the United States Constitution: Ten Essays*. Indianapolis: Bobbs-Merrill, 1967.

Marrus, Michael. *The Unwanted: European Refugees in the Twentieth Century*. New York: Oxford University Press, 1985.

Massell, Gregory. *The Surrogate Proletariat: Moslem Women and Revolutionary Strategies in Soviet Central Asia, 1919–1929*. Princeton, N.J.: Princeton University Press, 1974.

Meier-Braun, Karl-Heinz. *"Gastarbeiter" oder Einwanderer? Anmerkungen zur Ausländerpolitik in d. Bundesrepublik Deutschland*. Frankfurt/M.: Ullstein, 1980.

Menken, Jane, ed. *World Population & U.S. Policy: The Choices Ahead*. New York: W. W. Norton, 1986.

Mersky, Roy M., and Gary R. Hartman. *A Documentary History of the Legal Aspects of Abortion in the United States: Roe v. Wade*. Littleton, Colo.: F. B. Rothman, 1993.

Milward, Alan S. *The Reconstruction of Western Europe, 1945–51*. London: Methuen, 1984.

Moeller, Robert G. *Protecting Motherhood: Women and the Family in the Politics of Postwar West Germany*. Berkeley: University of California Press, 1993.

Morris, Benny. *The Palestinian Migration*. Cambridge: Cambridge University Press, 1984.

Moussalli, Ahmad S. *Radical Islamic Fundamentalism: The Ideological and Political Discourse of Sayyed Qut'b*. Beirut: American University of Beirut, 1992.

The Muslim Manifesto: A Strategy for Survival. London: The Muslim Institute, 1990.

Nab'il, Jabb'ur. *The Rumbling Volcano: Islamic Fundamentalism in Egypt*. Pasadena, Calif.: Mandate Press, 1993.

Nettl, J. P. *Rosa Luxemburg*. Oxford: Oxford University Press, 1966.

Olcott, Martha B., ed. *The Soviet Multinational State: Readings and Documents*. Armonk, N.Y.: M. E. Sharpe, Inc., 1990.

Organization for Economic Cooperation and Development, SOPEMI: Continuous Reporting System on Migration. *Trends in International Migration, 1994.* Paris: OECD, 1995.

Orwell, George. *Collected Letters and Essays.* Vol. 3. Harmondsworth, U.K.: Penguin, 1984.

Paddock, William, and Paul Paddock. *Famine, 1975! America's Decision: Who Will Survive?* Boston: Little, Brown, 1967.

Papademetriou, Demetrios G., and Philip L. Martin, eds. *The Unsettled Relationship: Labor Migration and Economic Development.* New York: Greenwood Press, 1991.

Pick, Daniel. *Faces of Degeneration.* Cambridge: Cambridge University Press, 1991.

Pole, J. R., ed. *The American Constitution—For and Against.* New York: Hill and Wang, 1987.

Postan, Michael Moissey. *An Economic History of Western Europe, 1945–1964.* London: Methuen, 1967.

Rady, Martyn C. *Romania in Turmoil: A Contemporary History.* New York: IB Tauris, 1992.

Ramet, Sabrina P. *Nationalism and Federalism in Yugoslavia, 1962–1991.* Bloomington: Indiana University Press, 1992.

Raspail, Jean. *Le Camp des saints: Roman.* Paris: Robert Laffont, 1978.

Reimann, Helga, and Horst Reimann, eds. *Gastarbeiter: Analyse und Perspektiven eines sozialen Problems.* Opladen: Westdeutscher, [1987?].

Riesebrodt, Martin. *Pious Passion.* Trans. D. Reneau. Berkeley: University of California Press, 1993.

Roberts, Walter R. *Tito, Mihailovic, and the Allies, 1941–1945.* New Brunswick, N.J.: Rutgers University Press, 1973.

Ronsin, Pierre. *La Grève des ventres.* Paris: Albin, 1980.

Rowbotham, Sheila. *The Past Is before Us: Feminism in Action since the 1960s.* London and Boston: Pandora, 1989.

Rubin, Barry M. *Islamic Fundamentalism in Egyptian Politics.* New York: St. Martin's Press, 1990.

Rupnik, Jacques, ed. *De Sarajévo à Sarajévo: L'Échec yougoslave.* Paris: Editions Complexe, 1992.

Rushdie, Salman. *Midnight's Children.* New York: Alfred A. Knopf, 1981.

———. *The Satanic Verses.* New York: Viking, 1988.

———. *Shame.* New York: Alfred A. Knopf, 1983.

Russell, Sharon Stanton, and Michael S. Teitelbaum. *International Migration and International Trade.* World Bank Discussion Paper, no. 160. Washington, D.C.: World Bank, 1992.

Ruthven, Malise. *A Satanic Affair: Salman Rushdie and the Rage of Islam.* London: Chatto & Windus, 1990.

Sadkovich, James J. *Italian Support for Croatian Separatism, 1927–1937.* New York: Garland, 1987.

Sauvy, Alfred. *Richesse et population.* Paris: Payot, 1943.

Sauvy, Alfred, and Robert Debré. *Des français pour la France.* Paris: Gallimard, 1946.

Simon, Julian L. *The Ultimate Resource.* Princeton, N.J.: Princeton University Press, 1981.

Sish, Timothy D. *Islam and Democracy: Religion, Politics and Power in the Middle East.* Washington, D.C.: United States Institute of Peace, 1992.

Sivan, Emmanuel. *Radical Islam.* New Haven, Conn.: Yale University Press, 1984.

Skerry, Peter. *Mexican Americans: The Ambivalent Minority.* New York: Free Press, 1993.

Skidelsky, Robert. *Oswald Mosley.* London: Weidenfeld and Nicolson, 1980.

Steinberg, Jonathan. *All or Nothing: The Axis and the Holocaust.* London: Routledge, 1990.

Stern, Fritz. *The Failure of Illiberalism: Essays on the Political Culture of Modern Germany.* New York: Alfred A. Knopf, 1971.

———. *Germany 1933: Fifty Years Later.* New York: Leo Baeck Institute, 1983.

Suny, Ronald. *The Revenge of the Past: Nationalism, Revolution, and the Collapse of the Soviet Union.* Stanford, Calif.: Stanford University Press, 1993.

Supple, Barry, and Mary Furnall, eds. *Economic Knowledge and the State.* New York: Cambridge University Press, 1990.

Teitelbaum, Michael S., and Jay M. Winter. *The Fear of Population Decline.* Orlando, Florida: Academic Press, 1985.

———, eds. *Population and Resources in Western Intellectual Traditions.* Cambridge: Cambridge University Press, 1988.

Thomas, Brinley. *Migration and Economic Growth: A Study of Great Britain and the Atlantic Economy.* Cambridge: Cambridge University Press, 1954.

Tomasevich, Jozo. *The Chetniks.* Stanford, Calif.: Stanford University Press, 1975.

Trachtenberg, Marvin. *The Statue of Liberty, Centenary Edition.* New York: Elisabeth Sifton Books, 1986.

Tudjman, Franco. *Croatia on Trial: The Case of the Croatian Historian F. Tudjman.* London: United Publishers, 1981.

United Nations High Commissioner for Refugees. *The State of the World's Refugees: The Challenge of Protection.* New York: Penguin Books, 1993.

United States. *Policy Statement.* International Conference on Population and Development, Mexico City, 1984.

U.S. Commission for the Study of International Migration and Cooperative Economic Development. *Unauthorized Migration: An Economic Development Response.* Washington, D.C.: U.S. Government Printing Office, 1990.

Van de Walle, Étienne. *The Female Population of France.* Princeton, N.J.: Princeton University Press, 1975.

Walter, Nicholas. *Blasphemy in Britain.* London: Macmillan, 1977.

262

Wattenberg, Ben J. *The Birth Dearth: What Happens When People in Free Countries Don't Have Enough Babies?* New York: Pharos Books, 1987.

Weindling, Paul. *Health, Race, and German Politics between National Unification and Nazism, 1870–1945.* Cambridge: Cambridge University Press, 1989.

Weiner, Myron, and Mary F. Katzenstein. *India's Preferential Policies: Migrants, the Middle Classes, and Ethnic Equality.* Chicago: University of Chicago Press, 1981.

West, Richard. *Tito and the Rise and Fall of Yugoslavia.* London: Sinclair-Stevenson, 1994.

Widgren, Jonas. "The Informal Consultations, 1985–1992." Geneva, Inter-Governmental Consultations on Asylum, Refugee and Migration Policies in Europe, North America and Australia, 4 February 1993.

Winter, Jay M. *The Great War and the British People.* London: Macmillan, 1985.

———, ed. *The Working Class in Modern British History.* Cambridge: Cambridge University Press, 1983.

Winter, Jay M., and Blaine Baggett. *The Great War and the Shaping of the Twentieth Century.* London: BBC Books, 1996.

Wrigley, E. A. *Population and History.* London: Edward Arnold, 1967.

NOTES

Notes to Chapter 1

1. See Ingo Hasselbach with Tom Reiss, "How Nazis Are Made," *The New Yorker*, 8 January 1996, p. 53.
2. Gerhard Hirschfeld, remarks to Bellagio Conference on Migration, Fertility, and National Identity, June 1993.
3. See Brubaker, *Citizenship and Nationhood in France and Germany*, p. 23.
4. Weindling, *Health, Race, and German Politics*.
5. Weindling, "Fascism and Population in Comparative European Perspective," in *Population and Resources in Western Intellectual Traditions*, ed. Teitelbaum and Winter, p. 108.
6. See Dawidowicz, *The War Against the Jews, 1933–1945*, conclusion.
7. See Moeller, "Women and the State."
8. Ibid., p. 114. For further details, see Moeller, *Protecting Motherhood*.
9. Meier-Braun, *"Gastarbeiter" oder Einwanderer?*; Reimann and Reimann, eds., *Gastarbeiter*.
10. See Stern's remarks in his *Germany 1933: Fifty Years Later* and in *The Failure of Illiberalism*.
11. Hirschfeld, remarks to Bellagio Conference on Migration, Fertility, and National Identity, June 1993.
12. See Ronge, "Öst-West-Wanderung nach Deutschland," table 3.
13. "Police Battle Rightist Youths in German City," *The New York Times*, 27 August 1992.
14. S. Kinzer, "In Germany the Raw Material of Violence, Too, Is Bountiful," *The New York Times*, 13 September 1992. See also letter of Holly Cartner of Helsinki Watch to *The New York Times*, 8 September 1992.
15. "Hostel for Refugees Attacked in Germany," *The New York Times*, 7 September 1992; "German Mayor Takes Steps to Stem Attacks on Foreigners in Eastern City," *The New York Times*, 4 September 1992; "Refugee Dwellings Hit in 10 German Cities," *The New York Times*, 5 September 1993; "Light Sentences Against Germans Who Killed Foreigner Stir Debate," *The New York Times*, 15 September 1992; "Foreigner Problem Wrenches German Psyche," *The New York Times*, 25 September 1992; and "Germans Emphasize the Non-Rioters at Rally," *The New York Times*, 9 November 1992.
16. Cited in "Gypsies: Refugee Issue Leaves Germans Confused," *The New York Times*, 25 September 1992.

17. Cited in "New Clashes in Germany as Politicians Voice Alarm," *The New York Times*, 3 October 1992.

18. "Germany and Romania in Deportation Pact," *The New York Times*, 24 September 1992; "Three Turks Killed; Germans Blame a Neo-Nazi Plot," *The New York Times*, 23 November 1992; and "Turkish Woman and 2 Girls Die in Neo-Nazi Attack in Germany," *The New York Times*, 23 November 1992.

19. "100,000 in Bonn Protest Plan to Limit Asylum," *The New York Times*, 14 November 1992; and "Germany Agrees on Law to Curb Refugees and Seekers of Asylum," *The New York Times*, 7 December 1992.

20. Cited in "Germany Agrees on Law to Curb Refugees and Seekers of Asylum."

21. Marjorie Miller, "German Sweep Seeks to Nab Illegal Immigrants before Borders Open," *The Los Angeles Times*, 25 February 1995, p. 6. And, from a different point of view, Jennifer Monahan, "Fortress Europe," *New Statesman & Society*, 26 May 1995.

Notes to Chapter 2

1. We are grateful for discussions with Gérard Calot, Jacqueline Hecht, and Hervé Le Bras on this matter. Martine Segalen's advice and reflections were, as always, acute and indispensable.

2. Calot, "Fécondité du moment."

3. The word Calot used was *trompeur*. Calot, "Fécondité du moment," p. 2.

4. Le Bras, *Marianne et les lapins*, pp. 24–26.

5. See Calot in an interview with *France Soir*, 5 May 1990; Gérard-François Dumont in an interview in *Le Quotidien de Paris*, 22 May 1990; Jacques Dupâquier and Dumont in an interview in *Figaro*, 6 May 1990; communiqués of "Les Syndicats CFDT et CGT de l'INED répondent à Elisabeth Badinter," 17 May 1990; communiqué from the department heads of INED to l'Agence France Presse, 11 May 1990; and, lastly, a communiqué signed by Patrick Festy, Henri Leriod, Thérèse Locoh, France Meslé, Francisco Muñoz-Perez, and Benôit Riandey, 10 May 1990.

6. See Elisabeth Badinter, "Les Ambiguités de l'INED," *Le Nouvel Observateur*, 17 May 1990; André Langaney, "Réponse aux offusques de l'INED," *L'Express*, 7–13 June 1990; and Sophie Coignard and Marie-Thérèse Guichard, "INED: Récit d'une mauvaise fièvre," *Le Point*, 28 May 1990.

7. Gérard Badou and Jacqueline Rémy, "Chrétiens-démographes contre sociaux-démographes," *L'Express*, 11 May 1990; and "Baby babadoum," *Le Canard Enchaîné*, 9 May 1990.

8. "Avis du conseil scientifique de l'INED," 21 June 1990. The three were Massimo Livi-Bacci, professor of demography at the University of Florence; Jean-Claude Chasteland, former director of the Population Division of the United Nations; and Henri Caussinus, professor of statistics at the University of Toulouse.

9. Transcript of Radio Europe 1, 4 May 1990 edition of *8 O'Clock*, from INED dossier "Turbulences sur la démographie," given to the authors by Gérard Calot, July 1990.

10. Le Bras, *Marianne*, p. 60.

11. "INED: Récit d'une mauvaise fièvre," p. 109. See also the open letter to Le Bras of 15 November 1991, signed by nine INED researchers, accusing him of ignoring attempts at cooling down the debate and of "deliberate aggression and provocation."

12. See Le Bras, *Marianne*, pp. 41–55, 237, 238, 240, 247, 268.

13. We are grateful to Tony Wrigley for comments on this point.

14. We are grateful to Antoine Prost for comments on this point.

15. Sauvy's life and work are ripe for a biography. See his *Richesse et population* and, with R. Debré, *Des français pour la France.*

16. See Eckart, "Effets et limites."

17. Le Bras, *Marianne*, pp. 79, 106, 170–83, 187, 190, 194.

18. Jean Raspail and Gérard-François Dumont, "Serons-nous encore Français dans 30 ans?" *Figaro-Magazine*, 26 October 1985, pp. 125–129 passim. See also Raspail, *Le Camp des saints.*

19. See Arlette Laguiller, "Le Racisme, un virus plus dangereux que le SIDA," *Lutte Ouvrière*, 2 November 1985; "France doit refuser la segrégation," *Le Monde*, 28 October 1985; and "Births," *International Herald Tribune*, 31 August 1987.

20. Michèle Tribalat, " 'On a fait menti les statistiques,' " *Quotidien de Paris*, 29 October 1985; Le Bras, "Immigration: Les Chiffres fous de *Figaro-Mag*," *Le Nouvel Observateur*, 7 November 1985; Raspail, "Le *Figaro-Magazine* et la controverse sur l'immigration," *Figaro-Magazine*, 2 November 1985; Dumont, "Contester nos chiffres, c'est refuser de prévoir," *Figaro-Magazine*, 2 November 1985; and Raspail and Dumont, "Notre réponse au gouvernement," *Figaro-Magazine*, 9 November 1985.

Notes to Chapter 3

1. Organization for Economic Cooperation and Development, SOPEMI: Continuous Reporting System on Migration, *Trends in International Migration*, p. 195, table A2.

2. Ian Diamond and Sue Clarke, "Demographic Patterns among Britain's Ethnic Groups," in *The Changing Population of Britain*, ed. Heather Joshi (London: Basil Blackwell, 1989), pp. 179, 181.

3. See John Hobcraft and Heather Joshi, "Population Matters," in *Changing Population*, ed. Joshi, p. 9.

4. Paul Valleley and Andrew Brown, "Pride and Prejudice," *The Independent*, 6 December 1995, p. 2.

266

5. See Jay Winter, "Population, Economists, and the State: The Royal Commission on Population," in *Economic Knowledge and the State*, ed. Supple and Furnall.

6. See "The Rushdie Affair," *Glasgow Herald*, 26 August 1995.

7. *Shame*, p. 134; *Midnight's Children*, pp. 357–75.

8. Rushdie himself made the point about the treatment of nonwhite immigrants in Britain after the furor over his book erupted. See Hamilton, "Salman Rushdie's First Life," p. 89. See also *Satanic Verses*, p. 439.

9. Kundera, *Testaments Betrayed*, p. 27.

10. Walter, *Blasphemy in Britain*.

11. "Rushdie Says His Barring from India Hurts the Most," Reuters, 10 September 1993.

12. "The Itch of Guilt Won't Go Away," *The Independent*, 23 July 1995.

13. "Rushdie to Make First Public Appearance on Thursday," Agence France Press, 7 September 1995.

14. Yasmine Bahrani, "The Rushdie Specter," *The Washington Post*, 14 August 1994.

15. Paper presented by David Coleman to Bellagio Conference on Migration, Fertility, and National Identity, June 1993.

16. See Ruthven, *A Satanic Affair*, ch. 3.

17. On this group, see Kathy Evans, "Radical Time-Bomb under British Islam," *The Guardian*, 7 February 1994, p. 6. See also Bodansky, "Islamist Leaders 'Legalize' War," p. 17.

18. See the recollection of the speech by the Labour M.P. Roy Hattersley, "Heroes and Villains," *The Independent*, 14 January 1995.

19. Ibid.

20. "Intolerable Strain," *Daily Mail*, 6 February 1995.

21. "I Think the European Union Is Destined to Break Down," *Scotsman*, 9 June 1994.

22. Ibid.

23. See Diamond and Clarke, "Britain's Ethnic Groups," p. 180; and Andrew Marshall, "Rush to Leave Britain Explodes Migrant Myths," *The Independent*, 19 February 1995.

24. Alan Raybould, "Race Resurfaces as Political Issue in Britain," *Reuter European Community Report*, 17 July 1995.

25. "Immigration: Rivers of Bluster," *The Economist*, 1 April 1995.

26. Robin Harris, "Why Immigration Is Now the Question," *Sunday Telegraph*, 19 February 1995.

27. "Wardle Resigns," *Daily Mail*, 13 February 1995.

28. "Numbers Seeking Asylum Soar in Britain and Fall in Europe," *Daily Mail*, 26 September 1995.

29. See Alan Raybould, "British Law on Asylum Seekers Comes under Attack," *Reuter European Community Report*, 29 December 1995; and Nick Cohen, "Fortress Britain," *The Independent*, 29 October 1995.

30. Michael Binyon, "Britain Shuts Door on Fundamentalists," *The Times* (London), 5 January 1996.

Notes to Chapter 4

1. See Ljubica Gaćeša, *Tranzverzalni i Kohortni Pristup Analizi Fertaliteta Ženskog Stanovništva SFR Jugoslavije U Periodu 1950–1987, Studije, Analize I Prikazi 128* (Belgrade, 1991), pp. 131–36. Total fertility data are from Council of Europe, *Recent Demographic Developments in Europe and North America, 1992* (Strasbourg: Council of Europe Press, 1993), pp. 352–78.

2. We are grateful to Dr. Sylva Mežnarić for comment on this point, derived from her paper delivered to Bellagio Conference on Migration, Fertility, and National Identity, June 1993.

3. For some aggregate statistics, see Council of Europe, *Recent Demographic Developments*, tables T4.1 and T4.2.

4. Winter, *The Great War and the British People*, table 3.4.

5. On the history of Croatia and the Roman Catholic Church in the Ustashe period, see Sadkovich, *Italian Support for Croatian Separatism;* and Alexander, *The Triple Myth.*

6. Steinberg, *All or Nothing;* and, on the massacres in Yugoslavia, Boban, "Jasenovac and the Manipulation of History." See also Djilas, *Contested Country*, pp. 21 ff. and 125.

7. See Roberts, *Tito, Mihailovic, and the Allies;* and Tomasevich, *Chetniks.*

8. Banac, "Fearful Asymmetry of War," p. 168.

9. See Glenny, *Fall of Yugoslavia*, p. 134.

10. See Djilas, *Contested Country*, pp. 176–83; and West, *Tito and the Rise and Fall of Yugoslavia.*

11. See Ramet, *Nationalism and Federalism in Yugoslavia*, p. 239.

12. See Rupnik, ed., *De Sarajévo à Sarajévo*; and Denitch, *Ethnic Nationalism*, p. 62. On Milošević, see John B. Allcock, "Rhetorics of Nationalism in Yugoslav Politics," in *Yugoslavia in Transition*, ed. Allcock et al., pp. 276–96, esp. pp. 291–94; and Ramet, *Nationalism and Federalism*, pp. 225–38. On Tudjman, see Tudjman, *Croatia on Trial.* Karadžić worked as a psychiatrist for Sarajevo's soccer team. See Glenny, *Fall of Yugoslavia*, p. 154.

13. Cited in Ramet, *Nationalism and Federalism*, p. 240.

14. On this sequence, see Glenny, *Fall of Yugoslavia*, pp. 188–93.

15. See Ramet, *Nationalism and Federalism*, p. 259. On torture and rape, see Crane-Engel, "Germany vs. Genocide"; Cohen, *Broken Bonds*, pp. 257–58; and Laber, "Bosnia: Questions about Rape." See also Rupnik, "Europe's New Frontiers," and Enzensberger, *Civil War*, pp. 20 ff.

16. William Safire, "On Language," *The New York Times Sunday Magazine*, 14 March 1993, p. 24. See also Banac, "Bosnian Muslims," p. 143.

268

17. See Albert Wohlstetter, "Creating a Greater Serbia," *The New Republic*, 1 August 1994, p. 22; and Bell-Fialkoff, "A Brief History of Ethnic Cleansing."

18. See Jay M. Winter, "Le Massacre des Arméniens," *Le Monde*, 3 August 1994.

19. See Benny Morris, *The Birth of the Palestinian Refugee Problem, 1947–1949* (Cambridge: Cambridge University Press, 1987).

20. Blaine Harden, "Serbs Accused of '91 Croatia Massacre," *The Washington Post*, 26 January 1993, p. A13.

21. Robert Fisk, "Waging War on History," *The Independent*, 20 June 1994, p. 18; and Rabia Ali and Lawrence Lifschultz, "Why Bosnia?" *Monthly Review* 45, no. 10 (1994), p. 1.

22. Fisk, "Waging War," p. 18.

23. See "The Balkan Conflict: Croatia Background Paper," Defense and Foreign Affairs Strategic Policy, 31 January 1993, pp. 1–6; Davor Huic, "Mothers Band Together to Trace Croatian Town's Missing," Reuters, 23 September 1993; "U.N. Investigating Croats' Grave Site," *The New York Times*, 29 November 1992, p. 1; "Mass Grave May Spark War Crimes Hearings," *Toronto Star*, 1 December 1992; and "U.S. Wants Mass Grave Investigated in Croatia," Reuters, 6 January 1994.

24. See Nicolas Miletitch, "Zhirinovsky Calls for Slav State from 'Vladivostok to Knin,'" Agence France Presse, 31 January 1994; and "Zhirinovsky in Vukovar," BBC, 2 February 1994.

25. See John F. Burns, "Vicious Ethnic Cleansing Infects Croat-Muslim Villages in Bosnia," *The New York Times*, 20 April 1993, p. 1.

26. See Robert Fisk, "Following the Devil's Tracks," *The Independent on Sunday*, 19 June 1994.

27. See Acheson, "Health, Humanitarian Relief, and Survival in Former Yugoslavia"; "U.N. Panel Finds Evidence of Serb War Crimes," *The Los Angeles Times*, 2 June 1994, p. 4; "Report Says Ethnic Cleansing in Yugoslavia Is Systematic," Reuters, 3 December 1992; and Meron, "The Case for War Crimes Trials in Yugoslavia," p. 122.

28. Gottlieb, "Nations Without States," p. 100; Gedmin, "Comrade Slobo"; Glenny, *Fall of Yugoslavia*, pp. 66–70.

29. "Police 'Raids, Brutality and Arrests' Against Albanians," BBC World Service, 18 October 1994; Helena Smith, "Will Blood Again Drench Kosovo?" *World Press Review* 41 (May 1994).

30. See Colin McIntyre, "Ethnic Minorities Say Serbia Wants to Expel Them," Reuters, 15 June 1994; and Milan Vojnović, "Glavni problemi srpskog naroda," *Otadžbina* (Nova Pazova), 8 August 1991, p. 9, cited in Banac, "Fearful Asymmetry of War," p. 151n. Banac's brilliant article is an important source for us in this entire discussion.

31. Iain Guest, "Getting the Refugees Home Is Going to Take Time and Care," *Inter-*

national Herald Tribune, 3 January 1996; "Return of 320,000 Bosnian Refugees in Germany to Begin in July," Deutsche Presse-Agentur, 11 January 1996.

Notes to Chapter 5

1. See Scott Shane, " 'Demographic Collapse' in Former Soviet Union," *The Baltimore Sun*, 10 January 1995, p. 32.
2. Witold Laskowski, "Russia," *The Warsaw Voice*, 10 December 1995.
3. O. Zakharova, V. Mindogulov, and L. Rybakovsky, "Illegal Immigration in Border Regions of Russia's Far East," *Russica*, 30 December 1994.
4. See Suny, *Revenge of the Past,* pp. 3–4.
5. On this point, see Hobsbawm and Ranger, eds., *Invention of Tradition.*
6. Anderson, *Imagined Communities*, ch. 1.
7. Suny, *Revenge*, p. 25.
8. Ibid., p. 31.
9. Nettl, *Rosa Luxemburg*, vol. 2.
10. On this subject in general, see Olcott, ed., *The Soviet Multinational State*; Huttenbach, *Soviet Nationality Policies*; and Denber, ed., *The Soviet Nationality Reader.*
11. Suny, *Revenge*, p. 102.
12. See Barbara Anderson and Brian Silver, "Demographic Consequences of World War II on the Non-Russian Nationalities of the USSR," in *The Impact of World War II on the Soviet Union*, ed. Susan Linz, pp. 207–42.
13. See Suny, *Revenge*, p. 111, for these and other Soviet demographic statistics.
14. See Massell, *Surrogate Proletariat*, p. 83.
15. The literature on this subject is vast. For a taste of it, the reader might try Carrère d'Encausse, *End of the Soviet Empire*; Brumberg, ed., *Chronicle of a Revolution*; Lapidus, Zaslavsky, and Goldman, eds., *From Union to Commonwealth*; and Dawisha and Parrott, *Russia and the New States of Eurasia.*
16. Suny, *Revenge*, p. 154.
17. See Wolfgang Lutz, Sergei Scherbov, and Andrei Volkov, eds., *Demographic Trends and Patterns in the Soviet Union before 1991* (London: Routledge, 1994), p. xxxiii, and, for literature on this subject, chapters 1–8; also Ansley J. Coale, Barbara Anderson, and Erna Härm, *Human Fertility in Russia since the Nineteenth Century* (Princeton, N.J.: Princeton University Press, 1986); A. Blum, "La Transition démographique dans les républiques orientales d'URSS," *Population* 42 (1987), pp. 337–58; and Anatoly Vishnevsky, "Révolution démographique et fécondité en URSS du xix⁰ siècle à la période contemporaine," *Population* 43 (1988), pp. 799–814.
18. See Evgeny M. Andreev, Leonid E. Darsky, and Tatiana L. Kharkova, "Population Dynamics: Consequences of Regular and Irregular Changes," in *Demographic Trends and Patterns in the Soviet Union before 1991*, ed. W. Lutz et al., p. 429.

270

19. See Lutz, *Demographic Trends*, p. xxxiii.

20. See Ansley J. Coale, "Changes in Nuptiality and Fertility Since 1900 in the Republics of the Soviet Union and Neighboring Foreign Populations," paper presented to Bellagio Conference on Fertility, Migration and National Identity, June 1993, p. 15.

21. See Ellen Jones and Fred W. Grupp, *Modernization, Value Change, and Fertility in the Soviet Union* (Cambridge: Cambridge University Press, 1987), pp. 120–21 and table 2.11.

22. Carl Haub, "Population Change in the Former Soviet Republics," *Population Bulletin* 49 (December 1994), p. 13 and table A-3.

23. See Barbara A. Anderson and Brian D. Silver, "Assessing Trends and Levels in Working Age Mortality in the Newly Independent States" (paper presented at the Workshop on Mortality and Disability in the Newly Independent States, National Research Council and National Academy of Sciences, Washington, D.C., 8–9 September 1994), pp. 1–34, esp. pp. 2–12 and pp. 10–11, n. 10; and Vladimir Shkolnikov, France Meslé, and Jacques Vallin, "Recent Trends in Life Expectancy and Causes of Death in Russia (1970–1993)" (paper presented at the same workshop), pp. 4–5, 7.

24. Evgeny M. Andreev, "Life Expectancy and Causes of Death in the USSR," in *Demographic Trends*, ed. Lutz et al., p. 286; and Andreev, Darsky, and Kharkova, "Population Dynamics," p. 429.

25. Boris Urlanis, *Wars and Population* (Moscow: Century Publishers, 1960), p. 115.

26. On Soviet mortality trends in the 1960s and 1970s, see Jacques Vallin and Jean-Claude Chesnais, "Évolution récente de la mortalité en Europe, dans les pays Anglo-Saxons et en union soviétique, 1960–1970," *Population* 29 (1974), pp. 861–98. For the early 1980s, see Alain Blum and Alain Monner, "Recent Mortality Trends in the USSR: New Evidence," *Population Studies* 43 (1989), pp. 843–62; and Barbara Anderson and Brian Silver, "Patterns of Cohort Mortality in the Soviet Population," *Population and Development Review* 15 (1989), pp. 471–501.

27. Shkolnikov et al., "Recent Trends," pp. 8–9, table 1, and fig. 3.

28. Ibid., fig. 1.

29. Care must be taken in interpreting Russian cause-of-death codings involving alcohol. Russian deaths due to acute alcoholism are coded as "accidental poisoning by alcohol," whereas in the West this code is reserved for rare cases of accidental poisoning from industrial alcohol. Few Russian deaths due to drinking alcoholic beverages are coded under the conventional Western categories "alcoholic cirrhosis of the liver" and "alcohol dependence syndrome." For a discussion of these differences, see ibid., pp. 36–37, and, in general, pp. 32–36.

30. On Chernobyl, see Gregori Medvedev, *The Truth about Chernobyl*, trans. Evelyn

Rossiter (New York: Basic Books, 1991); Iurii Shcherbak, *Chernobyl: A Documentary Story*, trans. Ian Press (Basingstoke, U.K.: Macmillan, 1989); Nigel Hawkes et al., *Chernobyl: The End of the Nuclear Dream* (New York: Vintage Books, 1987); and David R. Marples, *The Social Impact of the Chernobyl Disaster* (New York: St. Martin's Press, 1988).

31. Jones and Grupp, *Modernization*, pp. 364–65 and p. 366, table 6.9.

32. See Murray Feshbach, "Prospects for Outmigration from Central Asia and Kazakhstan in the Next Decade," in *Soviet Economy in a Time of Change* (Washington, D.C.: GPO, 1979), pp. 656–709; Herbert E. Meyer, "The Coming Soviet Ethnic Crisis," *Fortune,* 14 August 1978; and James N. Wallace, "In USSR, Minority Problems Just Won't Wither Away," *US News and World Report,* 14 February 1977.

33. See Mikhail Guboglo, "Demography and Language in the Capitals of the Union Republics," *Journal of Soviet Nationalities* 1 (Winter 1990–91), pp. 1–42; and Juris Dreifelds, "Immigration and Ethnicity in Latvia," *Journal of Soviet Nationalities* 1 (Winter 1990–91), pp. 43–81.

34. See Hollander, "Marx and Malthusianism"; and Seccombe, "Marxism and Demography."

35. See Teitelbaum, "Demographic Change through the Lenses of Science and Politics." See also William Petersen, "Marxism and the Population Question: Theory and Practice," in *Population and Resources in Western Intellectual Traditions*, ed. Teitelbaum and Winter.

36. See Lapidus, "Ethnonationalism and Political Stability" and "Gorbachev and the 'National Question.' "

37. The following paragraphs rely on Lutz et al., *Demographic Trends*, pp. xxxii–xxxvi.

38. See Catherine Merridale, "The 1937 Census and the Limits of Stalinist Rule" (paper presented at the Bellagio Conference on Fertility, Migration, and National Identity, June 1993).

39. Shkolnikov et al., "Recent Trends," pp. 8–9.

40. Ibid., pp. 4–5; and Anderson and Silver, "Assessing Trends," pp. 10–11, citing Barbara A. Anderson and Brian D. Silver, "The Geodemography of Infant Mortality in the Soviet Union, 1950–1990" (paper presented at the Seminar on the Geodemography of the Former Soviet Union, Radford University, Radford, Virginia, 5–7 August 1994), pp. 1–22; and N. Iu. Ksenofontova, "Nekotorye tendentsii mladencheskoi smertnosti v poslednee desiatiletie" (Some trends in infant mortality in the last decade), in *Demograficheskie protsessy v SSSR* (Demographic processes in the USSR), ed. A. G. Volkov (Moscow: Nauka, 1990), pp. 116–34.

41. Cited by A. Vishnevsky, "Ideologized Demography" (paper presented at the Bellagio Conference on Migration, Fertility, and National Identity, June 1993), p. 2;

originally published in Russian in *Herald of the USSR Academy of Sciences* 10 (1991), pp. 3–18.

42. Ibid., p. 2.

43. See ibid., p. 3.

44. Jones and Grupp, *Modernization*, pp. 268–70.

45. For example, M. B. Tatimov, *Razvitiye narodonaseleniya I demografisheskaya politika* (Alma Ata: Izdatel'stvo Nauka Kazakhskoy SSSR, 1978), p. 86, cited in Jones and Grupp, *Modernization*, pp. 271–72.

46. See McIntyre, "On Demographic Policy Debates in the USSR," pp. 363–64; and Weber and Goodman, "Demographic Policy Debate in the USSR."

47. See Jones and Grupp, *Modernization*, pp. 273–74.

48. See Szporluk, "Dilemmas of Russian Nationalism"; Hajda and Bussinger, eds., *Nationalities Factor in Soviet Politics and Society*; and Teitelbaum and Winter, *Fear of Population Decline*. Bernstam's essay, the original title of which was "The Demography of Soviet Ethnic Groups in World Perspective," is in *The Last Empire: Nationality and the Soviet Future*, ed. Conquest.

49. Translated by Vishnevsky in "Ideologized Demography," p. 4; we have made minor grammatical corrections to the translation.

50. See Andrei Baiduzhy, "It Is Now a Fact That There Is a Demographic Catastrophe in the Country," *Nexavisimaya Gazeta*, 16 July 1994, pp. 1, 4; translated as "Demographic Disaster: Birth Gap Widens," in *Current Digest of the Post-Soviet Press* 46, no. 28 (1994), p. 8.

51. For a discussion of the often misleading use of such period measures of fertility for longer-term scenarios, see Teitelbaum and Winter, *Fear of Population Decline*, pp. 10 and 142–43.

52. Jan Cienski, "Russia Faces a Population Crisis," Deutsche Press-Agentur, 13 August 1994.

53. "Zhirinovsky's Population Plan: To Father a Child per Region," *The Washington Post*, 10 September 1994, p. A16.

54. *The Wall Street Journal*, 3 July 1986, and repeated on 3 July 1990.

Notes to Chapter 6

1. See Teitelbaum, "De-legalization of Abortion in Romania"; and David and Wright, "Abortion Legislation."

2. See David, *Family Planning and Abortion*, pp. 129–36.

3. See ibid., p. 46; and Field, "Re-legalization of Abortion in Soviet Russia."

4. Trebici, "Romania's Ethnic Demography," esp. table 2.

5. See Georgescu, *Romanians*, pp. 1–18.

6. Rady, *Romania in Turmoil*, p. 28. This entire section relies on ibid., pp. 28–93, and Georgescu, *Romanians*, pp. 232–56.

7. See Eugen Weber and Hans Rogger, *The European Right* (Berkeley and Los Angeles: University of California Press, 1966), p. 567.
8. Rady, *Romania in Turmoil*, p. 32. There is some dispute about the actual numbers, but this does not affect the main point that membership growth was rapid after the Communists took effective power in March 1945.
9. Fertility trends in Romania prior to 1970 were considered previously in Teitelbaum, "Fertility Effects of the Abolition of Legal Abortion in Romania."
10. See Council of Europe, *Recent Trends,* tables R-3 and R-4.
11. See Rady, *Romania in Turmoil*, pp. 73–75.
12. Broadcast on RFE/REE, 2 February 1990, and quoted in Rady, *Romania in Turmoil,* p. 89.
13. *Romania Libera,* 9 January 1990; and *Lumea,* 19 January 1990, quoted in Rady, *Romania in Turmoil,* pp. 94 and 93.
14. See Jane Perlez, "Romania's Communist Legacy: 'Abortion Culture,'" *The New York Times*, 21 November 1996, p. A3, and data in *WIIW Databook*, table V/1.6.
15. See "Palestinians Lose Israeli Jobs," *Migration News* 3 (August 1996); "Foreign Workers in the Middle East," *Migration News* 2 (December 1996); "Israel Is Preparing to Deport 2,000 Illegal Aliens Monthly," Associated Press, 7 November 1996; and "Israel to Open Detention Camp for Illegal Immigrants," Agence France Presse, 6 November 1996.
16. "Germany: Asylum, Illegals, and Ethics," *Migration News* 2 (September 1995); and "Poland/Romania Emigration," *Migration News* 3 (May 1996).

Notes to Chapter 7

1. Some portions of this chapter draw on previously published work in Teitelbaum, "Population Threat."
2. Ansley J. Coale reports that during his tenure then as U.S. representative to the United Nations Population Commission, the Soviet delegates objected to use of the word "fertility" in commission reports on grounds that it reflected "Malthusianism." Compliance with their request to avoid it required considerable linguistic effort. Personal communication, 30 June 1993.
3. See Cassen et al., *Population and Development.*
4. See Mersky and Hartman, *A Documentary History of the Legal Aspects of Abortion.*
5. Wattenberg later summarized his concerns in *The Birth Dearth.*
6. One notable example is Simon, *The Ultimate Resource.*
7. See "Policy Statement at the United Nations International Conference on Population," Mexico City, August 1984.
8. Rowbotham, *The Past Is before Us.*
9. See Gore, *Earth in the Balance.*
10. Quotations cited in Reimers, "An Unintended Reform."

11. See ibid., pp. 23–24.

12. *Immigration and Nationality Act*, sect. 274(a). See Teitelbaum, "Right versus Right."

13. See Skerry, *Mexican Americans*, p. 101.

14. Simon, "Immigration and American Attitudes," p. 50.

15. The phrase is ours, but see Keely, *U.S. Immigration.*

16. See Trachtenberg, *Statue of Liberty*, esp. pp. 25–33.

17. American civil libertarian groups, the American Civil Liberties Union (ACLU) their archetype, used to include conservative opponents of governmental intrusion on individual rights. During the 1970s and 1980s, a parting of the ways developed, as supporters of the civil-rights movement came increasingly to dominate. Conservative libertarians of the New Right (in the Libertarian Party and the Cato Institute) continue to share some views with the liberal civil libertarians of the ACLU, but by 1988 George Bush could pillory Michael Dukakis as "a card-carrying member of the American Civil Liberties Union." For a contentious political history of the ACLU, see Donohue, *Politics of the American Civil Liberties Union.*

18. See *Migration News* 3 (July 1996), p. 6.

19. Karen Brandon, "Wilson Holds Fast to Immigration Issue: California Governor Seeks More U.S. Help," *Chicago Tribune*, 7 January 1996.

20. *Migration News* 3 (July 1996), p. 6.

Notes to Chapter 8

1. For differing interpretations, see Elkins and McKitrick, *The Age of Federalism*; Jensen, ed., *Documentary History*; and Lynd, *Class Conflict, Slavery, and the United States Constitution.*

2. See Pole, ed., *American Constitution.*

3. *The Gerry-mander: A New Species of Monster* (1812).

4. See King, *Civil Rights and the Idea of Freedom*; and Eisenberg, *Civil Rights Legislation.*

5. On the complexities and ambiguities of the redistricting efforts under the Voting Rights Act, see Morrison, "Demographic Perspectives on the Voting Rights Act."

6. See Steven A. Holmes, "Majority Rules: But Will Whites Vote for a Black?" *The New York Times*, 16 June 1996, Week in Review, pp. 1, 4.

7. See William Petersen, "Politics and the Measurement of Ethnicity," in *The Politics of Numbers*, ed. Alonso and Starr, pp. 208–9.

8. Jeffrey S. Passel, comments and documents submitted to Bellagio Conference on Migration, Fertility, and National Identity, June 1993. We have relied on Passel's material throughout this section.

9. On this subject, see Petersen, "Politics and the Measurement of Ethnicity,"

pp. 199–201. For an instructive analysis of a very different setting, post-British India, see Weiner and Katzenstein, *India's Preferential Policies.*

10. Cited in Petersen, p. 200.

11. See Glazer, *Affirmative Discrimination.*

12. See Penalosa, "Toward an Operational Definition of the Mexican American."

13. Margo A. Conk, "The 1980 Census in Historical Perspective," in *The Politics of Numbers,* ed. Alonso and Starr, p. 176. The following discussion is based in part on her article, notably pp. 171–81.

14. For a useful bibliography on the undercount issue, see ibid., p. 181, n. 62.

15. As cited in ibid., p. 183.

16. As cited in "Court: 1990 Census Can Stand," Associated Press, 20 March, 1996.

Notes to Chapter 9

1. Bouchard cited by Craig Turner, "Quebec Separatism Brings Fear of Intolerance," *The Los Angeles Times,* 10 November 1995, p. A10. Parizeau quoted in Sylvia Adcock, "Nothing Settled: Quebec Anxiety Follows Election," *Newsday,* 1 November 1995, p. A3; also in "The 'Ethnic' Shock," *Maclean's,* 13 November 1995, p. 20. Statistics in "Bitter Victory: Canada Holds It Together . . . but Quebec Separatists Vow to Try Again," *Time,* 13 November 1995, p. 32; and Mark Clayton, "Quebec Minorities Get Caught by 'Us' vs. 'Them,' " *Christian Science Monitor,* 7 November 1995, p. 6.

2. Adcock, "Nothing Settled," p. A3.

3. See Minister of National Health and Welfare, *Charting Canada's Future: A Report of the Demographic Review* (Ottawa: Minister of Supply and Services Canada, 1989).

4. See M2 Presswire, 16 January 1997.

5. Henry, "Some Data on Natural Fertility."

6. See *Charting Canada's Future,* p. 28.

7. Jean-Pierre Garson and Agnes Puymoyen, "New Patterns of Immigration," *OECD Reporter* 192 (February 1995), p. 1.

8. Organization for Economic Cooperation and Development (OECD), SOPEMI: Continuous Reporting System on Migration, *Trends in International Migration* (Paris: OECD, 1990).

9. *Charting Canada's Future,* p. 32.

10. M2 Presswire, 19 January 1996.

11. See Richard Gwin, "The First Borderless State" (D. G. Willmot Distinguished Lecture, Brock University, St. Catharines, Ontario, 23 November 1994); excerpted in *Toronto Star,* 26 November 1994, p. B1.

12. Gwin, "The First Borderless State."

13. Mark Clayton, "Canadians Tire of Multiculturalism," *Christian Science Monitor,* 25 April 1995, p. 1.

14. Out of 21,666 claims in 1994, 15,224 were approved, after 3,403 were withdrawn or abandoned. See Immigration and Refugee Board, *Annual Report for the Year Ending December 31, 1994*, pp. 9–10. See also Allan Thompson, "70% Acceptance Rate for Refugee Claims, but Number of Applications Down by 38%," *Toronto Star*, 14 March 1995, p. A14.

15. OECD, *Trends in International Migration, 1994*, table II.8, n 1, and table C2.

16. Canada, Ministry of Immigration and Labor, *Demographic Aspects of Immigration*, Report of a meeting, Montreal, 14 December 1984, pp. 5, 8. For a discussion of the intellectual and political tradition of this perspective, see Teitelbaum and Winter, *Fear of Population Decline*.

17. Georges Mathews, "European Pro-Natalist Policies and Family Policy in Canada," in *The Review of Demography, Update Five*, pp. 72–73.

18. See Mary Gooderham, "Canada Pulling in the Welcome Mat," *The San Francisco Chronicle*, 22 March 1995, p. A1.

19. Canada, Ministry of National Health and Welfare, *Review of Demography and Its Implications for Economic and Social Policy*. For a summary, see Beaujot, ed., *Facing the Demographic Future*.

20. Reported in *The Vancouver Sun*, 10 April 1993.

21. OECD, *Trends in International Migration, 1994*, p. 73, table II.7.

22. Eric Beauchesne, "Immigration Keeps Canada Growing," *Calgary Herald*, 17 November 1994, p. A3.

23. Canada, Ministry of Citizenship and Immigration, *Backgrounder*.

24. "Quebec Closes Birth Gap as National Rate Hits Low," *The Financial Post*, 17 November 1994, p. 13; M2 Presswire, 28 May 1996.

25. Levesque, *An Option for Quebec*, p. 7, appendix 4, pp. 92–93, and p. 23, n.; also Parizeau, "Quebec-Canada: A Blind Alley," p. 81.

26. See Teitelbaum, "Right versus Right."

27. See Veltman, "Impact of International Immigration on the Linguistic Balance in Montreal."

28. See Gwin, "The First Borderless State."

29. Bissoondath, *Selling Illusions*; and Gwin, "The First Borderless State."

30. E. J. Dionne, Jr., "Looking North," *The Washington Post*, 2 November 1993, p. A19.

31. Jordan Bishop, "The Tories Say Goodbye; 1993 Canada Election Results," *Commonweal*, 19 November 1993, p. 4.

32. Dionne, "Looking North."

33. See Bob Cox, "Poll Finds Canadians Favor Five-Year Immigration Ban," *The Ottawa Citizen*, 18 May 1995, p. A3.

34. *Calgary Herald*, 6 March 1995.

35. Lynn Moore, "Head Tax Unfair to Newcomers, Refugee Support Groups Charge," *The Gazette* (Montreal), 1 March 1995, p. A1.

36. David Matas and Nancy Worsfold, "Anti-Refugee Policy Shifts Made under Smokescreen," *Toronto Star*, 8 March 1995, p. A21.

37. "Canadian Immigration Falls," *Migration News* 3 (November 1996); and "Canada: Immigration Goals–Reality Gap," *Migration News* 4 (January 1997).

38. Kenneth Whyte, "Of Mousse and Men: You Can Dress Him Up, but Will the Reform Leader Go Anywhere?" *Saturday Night*, November 1996. See also Bernard Simon, "Canada's Opposition Fights for Life," *Financial Times* (London), 10 December 1996, p. 3.

39. Gwin, "The First Borderless State."

40. "Quebec Leader Fields Death Threats," Agence France Presse, 10 January 1996.

41. Barry Brown, "Force May Be Used to Keep Parts of Quebec in Canada," *The Times Union* (Albany, N.Y.), 24 December 1995, p. E2.

42. Charles Trueheart, "Bitter Discord Pervades Canadian Politics since Quebec Referendum," *The Washington Post*, 19 December 1995, p. A26.

43. Clyde H. Farnsworth, "Haitians at Center of Montreal Election," *The New York Times*, 25 March 1996, p. 8. See also Stephen Dale, "Haiti-Canada: Ottowa Pledges to Stand behind Haiti," Inter Press Service, 23 March 1996.

44. Quoted by Farnsworth, "Haitians at Center."

45. "Counting Canadians Correctly," *The Economist*, 11 May 1996, p. 41.

46. See Douglas Fisher, "Segal's 'No Surrender' a Rallying Cry for Tories; Such a Loyalist Would Never Approve of a Merger with Reform," *The Toronto Sun*, 7 April 1996, p. C3; see also Whyte, "Of Mousse and Men"; and Simon, "Canada's Opposition Fights for Life."

Notes to Chapter 10

1. The literature in this field is extensive. For some preliminary references, see Georges Tapinos, "Migration and International Cooperation: Challenges for OECD Countries," Bellagio Conference on Migration, Fertility, and National Identity, June 1993.

2. See Marquis de Condorcet, *Esquisse d'un tableau historique,* pp. 187–92. See also Sylvana Tomaselli, "Moral Philosophy and Population Questions in Eighteenth Century Europe," in *Population and Resources in Western Intellectual Traditions*, ed. Teitelbaum and Winter, pp. 7–29.

3. See Teitelbaum, "Demographic Change Through the Lenses of Science and Politics."

4. See Frank Notestein, *Proceedings of the Eighth International Conference on Agricultural Economics* (London: Oxford University Press, 1953), pp. 15–31.

5. See Levine, Tilly, and Gillis, eds., *Historical Experience of Fertility Decline.*

6. See Ansley J. Coale and Susan Cotts Watkins, eds., *The Decline of Fertility in Europe: The Revised Proceedings of a Conference on the Princeton European Fertility Project* (Princeton, N.J.: Princeton University Press, 1986); and the

classic study by Coale and Hoover, *Population Growth and Economic Development.*

7. See Thomas, *Migration and Economic Growth.*
8. See Marrus, *The Unwanted.*
9. Castles and Kosack, *Immigrant Workers and Class Structure in Western Europe.*
10. See U.S. Commission for the Study of International Migration and Cooperative Economic Development, *Unauthorized Migration.*
11. See Böhning, Schaeffer, and Straubhaar, *Migration Pressure;* and Bruni, Venturini, and Stark, *Two Essays on Migration.*
12. See Ansley J. Coale, "Population Trends and Economic Development," in *World Population & U.S. Policy,* ed. Menken.
13. A "neutral" vote was cast, as we have seen, in the United States' policy statement at the International Conference on Population and Development in Mexico City, 1984. For a "positive" vote, see, for example, Simon, *Ultimate Resource.*
14. For more complete discussions, see Russell and Teitelbaum, *International Migration and International Trade;* Russell, "Migrant Remittances and Development"; Papademetriou and Martin, eds., *Unsettled Relationship;* and U.S. Commission for the Study of International Migration and Cooperative Economic Development, *Unauthorized Migration.*
15. See Russell, "Migrant Remittances and Development," p. 269; Russell and Teitelbaum, *International Migration and International Trade,* p. 1 and tables 4–6.
16. *Proceedings of the World Population Conference* (Bucharest, 1974), vol. 3, p. 223.
17. United Nations High Commissioner for Refugees, *The State of the World's Refugees,* p. 153.
18. ICPD Secretariat, *Analytical Tools for the Study of the Draft Programme of Action of the International Conference on Population and Development* (New York: United Nations, July 1994).
19. See Glazer, ed., *Clamor at the Gates.*
20. Raspail, *Le Camp des saints.*

Notes to Chapter 11

1. See Marrus, *The Unwanted.*
2. See Eugene Kulischer, *Europe on the Move.*
3. Cited in Michael S. Teitelbaum and Sharon Stanton Russell, "International Migration, Fertility, and Development," in Robert Cassen et al., *Population and Development,* pp. 229–52.
4. See Teitelbaum, "Advocacy, Ambivalence, Ambiguity," pp. 214–15.
5. Teitelbaum, "Political Asylum in Theory and Practice."
6. Eurostat, "Asylum-Seekers in Europe, 1985–1995," in *Statistics in Focus;* also, Inter-Governmental Consultations, "Asylum Applications in Participating States, 1983–1995."

7. Ronge, "Öst-West-Wanderung nach Deutschland."

8. Calculated by authors from Organization for Economic Cooperation and Development, Continuous Reporting System on Migration, *Trends in International Migration, 1990* (Paris: OECD, 1991), table 3.

9. *The New York Times,* 19 October 1991, p. 3.

10. See Eurostat, "Asylum Seekers in Europe"; and "Asylum and Immigration Controls in EU," *Migration News* 3 (July 1996).

11. Quoted in "Germany Agrees on Law to Curb Refugees and Seekers of Asylum," *The New York Times,* 8 December 1992, p. A1.

12. Data on asylum claims from OECD and UNHCR, cited, among other places, in John Pomfret, "New Global Challenge: Millions of Refugees Seeking a Better Life," *International Herald Tribune,* 12 July 1993.

13. See Widgren, "The Informal Consultations."

14. Organization for Economic Cooperation and Development, *Financial Resources for Developing Countries: 1992 and Recent Trends* (Paris: OECD, 1993), table 1.

Notes to Chapter 12

1. See Benny Morris, *The Birth of the Palestinian Refugee Problem, 1947–1949* (Cambridge: Cambridge University Press, 1987).

2. See Hiro, *Holy Wars.*

3. See Sivan, *Radical Islam*; and Riesebrodt, *Pious Passion.*

4. Sivan, remarks to Bellagio Conference on Migration, Fertility, and National Identity, June 1993.

5. Sivan, paper on Iranian fertility, Bellagio Conference, June 1993.

6. Martine Segalen, remarks on immigrants and residents of Nanterre to Bellagio Conference, June 1993; see also Easterman, *Reflections on Islam.*

7. Jacob M. Landau, *The Arab Minority in Israel, 1967–1991: Political Aspects* (Oxford: Clarendon Press, 1993).

8. See Dov Friedlander and Calvin Goldscheider, *The Population of Israel* (New York: Columbia University Press, 1979).

9. The work of the human rights organization, Al Haq, based in Ramallah, illustrates this point. Their surveillance of women's rights issues has been restricted, given the controversial nature of the issue.

10. Judith Miller, "Faces of Fundamentalism," *Foreign Affairs* 74, no. 6 (November–December 1994).

11. The literature on this subject is vast. For an opener, the reader should consult: Hala Kaleh and Simonetta Calderini, *The Intifada: The Palestinian Uprising in the West Bank and Gaza Strip: A Bibliography of Books and Articles, 1987–1992* (Oxford: Middle East Libraries Committee, 1993).

12. See Sish, *Islam and Democracy*; and Israeli, *Fundamentalist Islam and Israel.*

13. See Dekmejian, *Islam in Revolution*; and Riesebrodt, *Pious Passion.*

280

14. Martin S. Kramer, *Hezbollah's Vision of the West* (Washington, D.C.: Washington Institute for Near East Policy, [1989?]).

15. See Sivan, *Radical Islam*, p. 130, the finest exposition of the subject. See also pp. 151 and 183.

16. See el Sa'darwi et al., *Islamic Fundamentalism*; Nab'il, *Rumbling Volcano*; and Rubin, *Islamic Fundamentalism in Egyptian Politics*.

17. See Sivan, *Radical Islam*, pp. 132 ff. and 145; and Moussalli, *Radical Islamic Fundamentalism*.

18. Cited in Sivan, *Radical Islam*, p. 31.

19. Transcripts and translations provided by Emmanuel Sivan at Bellagio Conference on Migration, Fertility, and National Identity, June 1993.

20. Data provided by Sivan at Bellagio Conference on Migration, Fertility, and National Identity, June 1993.

21. We are grateful to Sivan for comments on this and related points.

22. Herf, *Reactionary Modernism*.

23. Russell, "Politics and Ideology in Migration Policy Formulation."

24. Izetbegovic, *The Islamic Declaration*, pp. 47–48, 56. See also Banac, "Bosnian Muslims," pp. 147–148.

25. See Weaver, "The Trail of the Sheikh."

Notes to Conclusion

1. See Carl Ipsen, *Dictating Demography: The Problem of Population in Fascist Italy* (Cambridge: Cambridge University Press, 1996).

2. See, for example, U.S. Commission on International Migration and Cooperative Economic Development, *Unauthorized Migration*.

INDEX

Abdel-Rahman, Sheikh Omar, 238–39
Academy of Sciences, Soviet, 101
Adenauer, Konrad, 20
Afghanistan, 28, 90, 238, 242
Agency for International Development, 129, 133; Population Office, 130
Albania, 68, 120
Albanians, ethnic, in Kosovo, 65, 67, 71, 72, 78–80
Alexander, King of Yugoslavia, 68
Algeria, 222, 223, 230, 234, 236
Alia, Josette, 34
American Civil Liberties Union, 144
American Enterprise Institute, 133
American Indians, 74, 156–57
Anabaptists, 175
Anderson, Benedict, 87
Anglophone Assault Group, 188
Angola, 27
Anti-Terrorism and Effective Death Penalty Act (1996), U.S., 151
Antonescu, Marshal Ion, 112–13
Arab-Israeli conflict, 23, 221, 224–29
Armenia, 86n, 87, 89, 91–93
Armenians, ethnic, 107; in Azerbaijan, 89; Turkish genocide of, 69, 75
Association of Conservative Graduates, 57
Association of Serbian Writers, 80
Australia, 50, 58, 145; multiculturalism in, 176; population growth in, 179; postwar baby boom in, 21, 174
Austria, 14, 214
Austria-Hungary, 67
Axworthy, Lloyd, 189–90

Azerbaijan, 86n, 87, 89, 92, 93; war in, 74, 242

Badinter, Elisabeth, 35
Banac, Ivo, 70, 74, 79, 238
Bangladesh, 54, 202
Barbados, 202
Barr, Bob, 171
Belgium, 176
Belorussia, 86n, 87, 100, 105
Benedick, Richard, 134
Berlin Wall, 24, 120, 212, 217
Bernstam, Mikhail, 105
Bhutto, Benazir, 52
Bildungsbürgertum, 14
Bloc Québecois, 185, 186, 191
Booker Prize, 53
Border Patrol, U.S., 142, 151
Bosnia, 65–69, 71, 237–38; refugees from, 26, 60; war in, 65, 73–75, 77, 207, 242
Bouchard, Lucien, 173, 174, 188, 191
Brandenburg, 14, 18
Brecht, Bertolt, 54
Bretons, 14
Brezhnev, Leonid, 91
Britain, 6, 41, 47, 49–62, 147, 178, 180, 244; eugenics in, 16, 39–40; fertility rate in, 31, 32, 44, 49, 198; immigration to, 49–51, 57–59, 61–62, 182; Islamic fundamentalism in, 51–57, 60–61; Middle East colonies of, 221; mortality rate in, 102; Poor Laws in, 196; refugee policy of, 59–60, 217

British Commonwealth Immigration Act (1971), 51

Brown, Kathleen, 149, 150

Brown University, 244

Buckley, James, 131, 133, 135

Bulgaria, 27, 29, 69; fall of Communism in, 120

Burgeon, T. G., 37

Burguière, Andre, 34

Bush, George, 136, 137, 205, 208, 216, 219

California, anti-immigrant legislation in, 149–50

California, University of, at Berkeley, 244

Calot, Gérard, 33, 34, 37, 40, 43–44, 45n

Cambodians, 141

Cambridge University, 52, 244

Campbell, Kim, 184, 185

Camp des saints, Le (Raspail), 46, 208

Canada, 6, 7, 50, 58, 145, 173–92, 251; baby boom in, 21; fertility rates in, 173–75, 177–78, 180–82; immigration to, 175–80, 182–84, 241, 242; multiculturalist policies in, 176–77, 184; refugee policy of, 177, 219; shift in political dominance in, 57, 184–92

Canada-Quebec Accord, 183

Canadian Council on Refugees, 187

Canard Enchaîné, 36

Carnegie Foundation, 143

Carrel, Alexis, 43

Cartagena Declaration, 210

Carter, Jimmy, 130, 147, 167

Catholics, 55; American, 129, 131; Croatian, 72; French, 16, 41, 42; German, 20; Polish, 13, 14; Slav, 68, 79–80, 81

Cato Institute, 133

Ceausescu, Elena, 116, 121–22

Ceausescu, Ilia, 121

Ceausescu, Nicolae, 6, 109–12, 114–19, 121–22, 249

Celler, Emanuel, 140

Central Intelligence Agency (CIA), 238

Charest, Jean, 190

Chernobyl nuclear accident, 96

Chetniks, 69–70, 72, 74

Chicago, University of, 244

China, 85, 93, 116, 197; asylum seekers from, 216, 219; shift in population policy in, 204–6, 233

Chrétien, Jean, 187–90

Christian Democratic Party, German, 20, 212, 213

Christians, 53, 54, 224; Lebanese, 228; see also specific denominations

Churchill, Winston III, 57

Civil Rights Act (1964), 165

Clinton, Bill, 127, 137, 205, 206, 208, 219

Clinton, Hillary, 137

Coale, Ansley, 92

Coast Guard, U.S., 216

Code de la famille, 43

Cold War, 66, 207, 217, 218, 241, 243

Commission on Immigration Reform, 150–53

Commission on Safeguarding the Health of the Population, Russian, 106

Communists, 66, 129, 199; Chinese, 197, 205; East German, 19; French, 43; Nazi persecution of, 17; Romanian, 109, 111–17, 119, 123; Soviet, 88, 90, 91, 98, 100; Yugoslav, 69–72

Condorcet, Marquis de, 195–96, 200

Congress, U.S., 167; immigration legislation in, 128, 147–48, 150–51, 218; population programs opposed in, 131, 138, 206

Conk, Margo, 167–69

Conservative Party, British, 56–59

Constantinescu, Emil, 122

Constitution, U.S., 127, 147, 155–57, 161

Copps, Sheila, 189

Cornea, Doina, 119

Critique of Pure Reason (Kant), 13

Croatia, 65–77, 79

Cuban Missile Crisis, 242

Czechoslovakia, 27, 68; ethnic Germans in, 18, 75, 250; fall of Communism in, 120; Soviet invasion of, 116

Czech Republic, 214

Dalmatia, 69

Democratic Party, U.S., 129, 130, 142, 149, 150, 158

Denmark, 217

Deutsche Bank, 27

Dickens, Charles, 55, 57

Dole, Bob, 150

Draper, Gen. William, 203

Dreyfus affair, 42

Dumont, Gérard-François, 46, 47

East Germany, 19; fall of Communism in, 120; fertility rate in, 12, 32; guest workers in, 28; pro-natalist policy in, 178; and reunification, 22, 24, 212

Ecole des Hautes Etudes en Sciences Sociales, 35

Egypt, 222, 232, 238; fertility rate in, 233; Islamic fundamentalism in, 223, 229, 230, 234, 242

Employment Equity Act, Canadian, 190

Equal Employment Opportunity Commission, U.S., 165

Estonia, 86n, 87, 92–93, 97

Ettelaat (journal), 232

European Communities Act (1972), 58

European Community, 21, 22, 250; Britain and, 52, 58–59, 61; elimination of passport controls among members of, 29

Express, L', 36

Fabius, Laurent, 46

Fear of Population Decline, The (Teitelbaum and Winter), 45n

Federal Office for the Recognition of Foreign Refugees, 26

Figaro-Magazine, 45–47

Finland, 87

Fisher, Joschka, 27

Fondation Alexis Carrel, 35, 38, 39

Ford, Gerald, 130, 147

Ford Foundation, 143

France, 6, 31–47, 49, 128, 147, 237, 244, 248; definition of nationality in, 15, 250; in European Community, 22, 58, 61; fertility rate in, 31–32, 197, 198; immigration to, 45–47, 51, 145; Middle East and, 221, 236; mortality rate in, 102; pro-natalism in, 34, 36–45, 104, 178, 249; Québecois ties to, 180, 189; refugee policy of, 216–18

Francophone Canada, *see* Québecois nationalism

Franco-Prussian War, 14, 42, 145

Frankfurter, Felix, 169

Franklin, Benjamin, 161n

Free Democratic Party, German, 28

French Revolution, 41, 42

Gagnon, Alain, 190

Gama'a el-Islamiya (Islamic Group), 238

Gandhi, Indira, 53, 197

García Márquez, Gabriel, 53

Gastarbeiter system, 21, 23, 211

Geneva Convention (1951), 25

Genscher, Hans-Dieter, 73

Georgia, 86n, 87, 89; Jewish immigrants from, 225

Germany, 6, 11–30, 59, 178, 237, 241, 244; and Balkans, 68; citizenship in, 15–16; in European Community, 58, 61; fertility rate in, 12, 32, 108, 247, 248; France and, 40–43; immigration to, 21–24, 51, 145, 182; imperial, 14–15; Nazi, *see* Nazis; postwar repatriation of ethnic Germans to, 18–19, 75; refugee policy of, 25–29, 49, 211–14, 216–19; reunification of, 22, 24–25, 73; Romania and, 112, 123; *see also* East Germany; West Germany

Gerry, Elbridge, 157, 158

Gheorghiu-Dej, Gheorghe, 112–16

Glass, David, 40

Good Woman of Szechuan, The (Brecht), 54

Gorbachev, Mikhail, 91, 95

Gore, Albert, 137, 205

Göring, Hermann, 17

Goskomstat (U.S.S.R. State Statistical Committee), 95

Grass, Günter, 29–30

Great Depression, 106, 128, 138, 174, 198

Great Society, 129

Greece, 68, 140

Green Party, German, 27

Grossman, Vassily, 90

Group of 77, 204

Groza, Petru, 113

Grundgesetz (Basic Law of the Federal Republic of Germany), 16, 19–20, 25, 26, 29, 211–13

Gypsies, 17, 26, 69

Hague, International Court of Justice at, 65

Haiti, 189–90, 216, 218–19

Hamas, 226–27

Hanger, Art, 187

Hattersley, Roy, 56

Headbirths (Grass), 30

Heath, Edward, 57, 58

Helms, Jesse, 138

Henry, Louis, 175

Heritage Foundation, 133

Herzegovina, 69

Hezbollah, 228

Hill, Anita, 136

Hindus, 51, 52, 75

Hitler, Adolf, 16, 17, 249

Hizb al-Tahrir (Liberation Party), 56

Holocaust, 17, 25

Holy See, 129

Hong Kong, 108, 175, 247

House of Representatives, U.S., 156, 158; Immigration Subcommittee, 142

Humphrey, Hubert, 165–66

Hungarians, ethnic, in Romania, 112, 115, 120

Hungary, 18, 69, 93, 110; fall of Communism in, 120

Hutterites, 175

Iliescu, Ion, 121, 122

Immigration Act (1990), U.S., 148

Immigration Association of Canada, 187

Immigration Control and Financial Responsibility Act, U.S., 151

Immigration and Nationality Act, U.S., 142

Immigration and Refugee Board, Canadian, 187

India, 53, 54, 75, 197; immigrants from, in Britain, 49, 50, 52, 58

Industrial Revolution, 198

Institutes of Demography, Soviet, 101

Institut National d'Etudes Démographiques (INED), 6, 31–40, 43–45, 47, 244

Institut National de la Recherche Scientifique, 178

Inter-Governmental Consultations on Asylum, Refugee and Migration Policies (IGC), 217

International League for Human Rights, 78

International Red Cross, 76

Iran, 226, 231, 235, 242; family planning in, 224, 232–33; immigrants from, 243; Ministry of Islamic Guidance, 52; refugees from, 28; Rushdie and, 6, 49, 54–55; Shi'ite revolution in, 221–23, 227–29, 236

Iraq, 228, 235

Ireland, 51, 182

Islam, *see* Muslims

Israel, 13, 145, 224–29, 238; foreign workers in, 122–23; Law of Return, 224; Palestinian refugees from, 75, 221

Italy, 140, 244; fertility rate of, 49, 108, 175, 247, 248; refugee policy of, 216; in World War II, 68, 69

Izetbegovic, Alija, 237–38

Jackson-Vanik Amendment, 107

Japanese American Citizens League, 140

Jews, 14, 28, 53, 55; Bosnian, 73; desecration of gravestones of, 27, 237; Hassidic, 243; Israeli, 224–25; Nazi genocide of, 16, 17, 69, 74, 221; Polish, 13, 17; Romanian, 112, 113, 115; Russian, 87, 90, 107

Johnson, Daniel, 188

Johnson, Lyndon B., 129, 140

Jordan, 202

Justice Department, U.S., 158

Kadijević, Veljko, 73

Kahane, Meir, 239

Kaiserreich, 14

Kant, Immanuel, 13

Karadžić, Radovan, 71–72

Kasch, Kurt, 27

Kazakhstan, 86n, 92, 93, 97, 104

Kazantzakis, Nikos, 54

Kennedy, Edward M., 140

Kennedy, John F., 129, 139–40

Kennedy, Robert F., 140

Kenya, 97

Kerbala, Battle of, 228

Keyhan (journal), 232

Khomeini, Ayatollah, 49, 54, 227

Khrushchev, Nikita, 114

Kindergeld system, 20

King, Martin Luther Jr., 56

Kirkup, James, 54

Knijiževne novine (literary magazine), 79

Kohl, Helmut, 24

Komsomolskaya Pravda, 104

Koran, 53–55

Kuwait, 145, 201, 235, 236

Kyrgyzstan, 86n

Labor Party, Israeli, 226, 227

Laotians, 141

Last Temptation of Christ, The (Kazantzakis), 54

Latvia, 86n, 87, 92–93, 97

Laurier, Wilfrid, 178

Law in the Service of Man, 226

Lazarus, Emma, 146

League of Communists of Serbia, 71

Lebanon, 226–29

Lebensraum colonizers, 18

Le Bras, Hervé, 33–39, 43–45, 47

Lemeshev, Mikhail, 85

Lenin, V. I., 87, 88, 100

Leninism, 111

Le Pen, Jean-Marie, 46

Leuninger, Herbert, 214

Levesque, René, 181–82

Liberal Democratic Party of Russia (LDPR), 107

Liberal Party, Canadian, 179, 181, 186–91

Life of Brian (film), 54

Life and Fate (Grossman), 90

Likud Party, Israeli, 227

Literaturnaya Gazeta, 104

Lithuania, 86n, 87, 97

London *Daily Mail*, 60

London School of Economics, Population Investigation Committee, 39, 244

Lutherans, 13

Luxembourg, 175

Luxemburg, Rosa, 88

Macedonia, 66

McGill University, 190

Maclean's magazine, 191

Madison, James, 157

Major, John, 57

Malthus, Thomas, 98–99, 196–97, 200

Malthusianism, 109, 111, 197

Manning, Preston, 185, 188–89

Marianne et les lapins (Le Bras), 38

Marshall, Thurgood, 136

Marshall Plan, 20, 203

Marx, Karl, 98–99, 196

Marxism, 88, 98–100, 109, 123, 205–7

Masari, Muhammed al-, 60–61

Maurer, Ion Gheorghe, 114–16

Medicaid, 152

Mennonites, 243

Mexican American Legal Defense and Education Fund, 143, 167

Mexico, 141, 152, 202

Michael, King of Romania, 113

Michigan, University of, 244

Midnight's Children (Rushdie), 52, 53

Mihailović, Gen. Draža, 69–70

Mihajlović, Milenko, 79, 80

Mikoyan, Anastas I., 102

Milea, Vasile, 121

Milošević, Slobodan, 71–72, 78

Mincu, Iulian, 122

Moldova, 86n

Monde, Le, 43

Montenegro, 66, 70

Monty Python, 54

Morocco, 221, 223, 229, 236

Moskva magazine, 104, 105

Mosley, Oswald, 51

Mozambique, 27

Mulroney, Brian, 177, 179, 184, 186

Muslim Brotherhood, 222, 234

Muslims, 6, 23, 138, 242–43; Albanian, 78–79; Bosnian, 26, 65, 67–69, 72, 73, 77, 237–38; in France, 248; fundamentalist, 6, 49, 51–57, 60–61, 195, 221–40, 242–43; Pakistani, 75; in Soviet Union, 90, 97–98, 100, 103

Mussolini, Benito, 248

Nagorno-Karabakh, 74

National Abortion Rights League, 136

National Association for the Advancement of Colored People (NAACP), 143, 170

National Conference of Catholic Bishops, 131

National Front, 35, 39, 45, 46

National Health Service, British, 58

National Legionary State, Romanian, 112

National Organization for Women, 136

National Origins Quota System, U.S., 138–40

National Salvation Front, Romanian, 121

NATO, 65

Nazis, 20, 22, 23, 250; extermination policies of, 16–18, 29, 74, 213, 221; French Resistance to, 43; in Romania, 112; Soviet Union invaded by, 89, 94, 97; in Yugoslavia, 68–69, 76

Netanyahu, Benjamin, 227

Netherlands, 217

New Democratic Party, Canadian, 179, 185, 186, 191

New International Economic Order (NIEO), 204

New Party, British, 51

New Right, 132, 205, 208

New York Times, The, 74, 213

New Zealand, 21, 50, 58, 174

Nigeria, 58, 60

Nixon, Richard M., 129, 130, 135, 147

North American Free Trade Agreement (NAFTA), 248

Northern Ireland, 56–58

Notestein, Frank, 129

Nouvel Observateur, Le, 34

Office of Management and Budget, U.S., 171

Organization of African Unity (OAU), 210

Organization for Economic Cooperation and Development (OECD), 218

Orthodox Christians, 68, 78, 79, 100

Orwell, George, 55

Ostjüden, 14

Ottoman Empire, see Turkey

Pahlavi, Shah Reza, 222, 226–28

Pakistan, 52, 75; asylum seekers from, 60, 212; immigrants from, 49, 50, 54, 58, 243; Muslim fundamentalists in, 221, 223, 242

Palestine Liberation Organization (PLO), 226, 228

Palestinians, 75, 122, 221, 225–26, 228, 236

Paris Commune, 42

Parizeau, Jacques, 173, 181, 182

Parti Québecois, 181

Pavelić, Ante, 69

Paz, Octavio, 53

Pennsylvania, University of, 244

Peres, Shimon, 227

Personal Responsibility and Work Opportunity Reconciliation Act (1996), U.S., 151

Pétain, Philippe, 35

Pettigrew, Pierre S., 189

Philippines, 152, 229

Poland, 13, 17, 140, 214; expulsion of ethnic Germans from, 18, 75, 250; fall of Communism in, 119; in Russian Empire, 87; in World War II, 97

Poles, ethnic, 13–14; Nazis and, 18

Pomerania, 14, 18

Population (journal), 33

Population Studies (journal), 39–40

Powell, Enoch, 56–58, 61

Presidential Commission on Population Growth and the American Future, U.S., 129–30

Pressat, Roland, 36

Préval, René, 189

Princeton University, 129, 244

Pro Asyl, 214

Progressive Conservative Party, Canadian, 176, 184–87, 190–92

Promised Land, The (film), 13

Proposition 187, 149

Protestants, 16, 243; American, 131; German, 14

Provençals, 14

Prussia, 13, 14, 18, 42

Québecois nationalism, 173–74, 180–92, 242, 251

Qutb, Sayyid, 230, 231

Rabelais, François, 53

Rabin, Yitzhak, 226–27

Rady, Martyn, 117

Randall, Chris, 60

Raspail, Jean, 46, 47, 208

Reagan, Ronald, 127, 130, 131, 132n, 133–37, 205, 208, 228

Reformed Church, 120

Reform Party, Canadian, 180, 185–88, 190–92

Reichsdeutsche, 18

Renan, Joseph-Ernest, 46

Republican Party, U.S., 129, 130, 138, 149, 150, 158, 170, 206

Republikaners, German, 214

Ricardo, David, 196

Rockefeller, John D. 3rd, 129, 130

Rockefeller Foundation, 143

Rodino, Peter, 142, 143, 147

Roe v. Wade (1973), 130, 136

Romania, 6, 18, 109–23, 249; "Christmas Revolution" in, 120–22; pro-natalism in, 110–12, 118–19; refugees from, in Germany, 25–27, 29; during World War II, 112–13

Rome, Treaty of, 5

Royal Commission on Population, British, 51

Rushdie, Salman, 6, 49, 52–57

Russia, 6, 18, 59, 85, 86n, 98, 104–8; and Balkans, 68; fertility rate in, 94, 106, 247; former Prussian territory in, 13; Jewish immigrants from, 225; scientists in, 44; Serbia and, 77; State Archive of Economics, 95; tsarist, 87–88, 100–1; see also Soviet Union

Rwanda, 207

Sadat, Anwar al-, 222, 230, 238

Safire, William, 74

Satanic Verses, The (Rushdie), 49, 53–54

Saudi Arabia, 54, 60, 201, 235

Sauvy, Alfred, 43

Senate, U.S., 143, 156; Foreign Relations Committee, 120, 138; Judiciary Committee, 136

Serbia, 65–80, 237

Shame (Rushdie), 52

Shari'a (Islamic law), 223, 230, 232

Shengen agreements, 28

Shi'ite Muslims, 221–23, 226, 228–30, 235

Silesia, 14, 18

Singapore, 197

Sivan, Emmanuel, 229

Slovak Republic, 214

Slovenia, 66–69, 72–73

Social Democratic Party: German, 28, 88, 212, 213; Romanian, 113

Socialist Party, French, 216, 218

Solidarity, 119

Solms, Hermann-Otto, 28

Solzhenitsyn, Aleksandr, 104

Somalia, 212

South Africa, 54; Jewish immigrants from, 225

South Korea, 202

Sovereignty Association Movement, 181

Soviet Union, 17, 26, 74, 83, 85–108, 129; collapse of, 5, 6, 24, 66, 108, 206, 242, 250; Czechoslovakia invaded by, 116; emigration policy of, 107; fertility rate in, 92–94, 97–98, 106; Group of 77 and, 204; Middle East and, 222; mortality rate in, 94–96, 102; Romania and, 111, 113–15; in World War II, 68, 69, 70, 74, 89, 90, 92, 94–95, 97

Spain, 236, 247

Sri Lanka, 60, 212

Stalin, Joseph, 70, 88–91, 100, 102, 103, 113, 249

Stalinism, 111, 114

Stanovnik, Janez, 72

Stasi, 27

State Department, U.S., 133–35, 137

Statistics Canada, 179, 181

Statue of Liberty, 145–46

Stern, Fritz, 22

Stoica, Chivu, 114

Sudan, 230, 231

Sunni Muslims, 221–23, 226, 229–30, 238

Suny, Ronald, 88

Supplementary Security Income (SSI), 152

Supreme Court, U.S., 130, 136, 160, 168–70

Sweden: fertility rate in, 33, 37, 43, 248; refugee policy of, 214, 217, 218

Swift, Jonathan, 53

Switzerland, 145, 175, 217

Syria, 222, 230

Tadzhikistan, 86n, 93–94, 97

Taymiyya, Ibn, 230

Texas Proviso, 141–43

Thatcher, Margaret, 50, 55

Thomas, Clarence, 136

Tin Drum, The (Grass), 29–30

Tito, Josip Broz, 69–71, 79, 80

Toekes, Laszlo, 120–21

Tompkins, Peter, 59–60

Tribalat, Michèle, 47

Trotsky, Leon, 87

Trudeau, Pierre, 176–77

True Quebecois Sovereignty group, 188

Tudjman, Franco, 71–72

Turkey, 60; Armenian genocide in, 69, 75; and Balkans, 68; immigrants from,

in Germany, 11, 21, 28, 29, 211, 213, 237

Turkmenistan, 86n, 93–94

Ukraine, 86n, 87–89, 93, 94, 96–97, 100, 101, 105

Unemployment Benefit, British, 58

United Nations, 130; Commission on Balkan War Crimes, 76, 78; Convention and Protocol Relating to the Status of Refugees, 177, 209–11, 217; Fund for Population Activities, 129; High Commission for Refugees (UNHCR), 83, 217; Population Conferences, 132–35, 137, 203–6, 208, 245

United States, 41, 56, 127–60, 179, 208, 242, 244–45, 247; abortion rights in, 130–31, 135–36; census of, 6, 153, 155, 161–71, 247; eugenics in, 16, 17; fertility rate in, 128–30, 246, 248; forced relocation of Indians in, 74; Haiti and, 189–90; immigration to, 107, 127–28, 138–53, 175, 176, 182, 188, 198, 241, 242; international population policy of, 127, 129–35, 137–38, 204–6; Jewish immigrants from, 225; Middle East and, 222; mortality rate in, 102; Muslim fundamentalists in, 238–39; postwar baby boom in, 21, 128–29, 174; refugee policy of, 177, 211, 216, 218–19

Ustashe, 68, 69, 72, 76, 79, 80

Uzbekistan, 86n, 93–94, 97

Vatican, 138

Vichy France, 35, 38, 42–43, 45

Vietnamese, 28, 141

Vietnam War, 135, 242

Vishinsky, Andrei, 113

Vishnevsky, A., 102

Volksdeutsche, 18

Voting Rights Act (1965), U.S., 158

Wajda, Andrzej, 13

Wall Street Journal, The, 107, 133, 140, 146

Wardle, Charles, 59

Warsaw Pact, 105, 217

Wattenberg, Ben J., 105, 132

Weimar Republic, 16, 20

Weinberger, Caspar, 130

Weizäcker, Richard von, 27

West Germany, 12, 24, 31, 241; economic growth in, 19–22; fertility rate in, 32, 175; guest worker program of, 13; refugee policy of, 25, 211–12

Wilson, Pete, 149–50

Wirth, Timothy, 137

Wirtschaftswunder, 21

Wisconsin, University of, 244

Workers Party, Romanian, 113

World Health Organization (WHO), 94, 102

World Institute of Science, 44

World Trade Center bombing, 238

World War I, 16, 42, 67, 146, 175

World War II, 128, 198, 203, 209; France in, 42–43; Germany in, 12, 13, 18, 89; Romania in, 112–14; Soviet Union in, 89, 90, 92, 94–95, 97, 113; United States in, 139, 141; Yugoslavia in, 68–69, 74

Wuermeling, Franz-Josef, 20

Young Offenders Act, 185

Yugoslavia, 18, 65–83, 86, 111, 250; ethnic conflict in, 5, 6, 65–67, 71–81, 237; refugees from, 25, 60; in World War II, 68–70

Zaire, 60

Zhirinovsky, Vladimir, 77, 107

Zola, Émile, 104